Gothic America

Gothic America

Narrative, History, and Nation

Teresa A. Goddu

Columbia University Press
New York

Columbia University Press
Publishers Since 1893
New York   Chichester, West Sussex
Copyright © 1997 Columbia University Press
All rights reserved

Library of Congress Cataloging-in-Publication Data

Goddu, Teresa A.
  Gothic America: narrative, history, and nation / Teresa A. Goddu.
   p. cm.
  Includes bibliographical references (p. 193) and index.
  ISBN 978-0-231-10817-1 (pbk.)
  1. Gothic revival (Literature)—United States. 2. National characteristics,
American, in literature. 3. Horror tales, American—History and criticism.
4. Literature and history—United States. 5. Women and literature—United
States. 6. Southern States—In literature. 7. Afro-Americans in literature.
8. Psychology in literature. 9. Narration (Rhetoric).   I. Title.
PS374.G68G63   1997
813'.0872909—dc20   96-41038
                                                             CIP

Casebound editions of Columbia University Press books are printed on
permanent and durable acid-free paper.
Printed in the United States of America

The author and publisher wish to thank Vanderbilt University for contributing
to the cost of reproducing the jacket illustration.

In memory of my father

Roland Goddu

Contents

Acknowledgments	ix
Introduction	1
1. Haunted by History: Crèvecoeur's National Narrative and the Gothic	13
2. Diseased Discourse: Charles Brockden Brown's *Arthur Mervyn*	31
3. Literary Nationalism and the Gothic: John Neal's *Logan*	52
4. The Ghost of Race: Edgar Allan Poe and the Southern Gothic	73
5. (Un)Veiling the Marketplace: Nathaniel Hawthorne, Louisa May Alcott, and the Female Gothic	94
6. Haunting Back: Harriet Jacobs, African-American Narrative, and the Gothic	131
Epilogue: Remembering History	153
Notes	161
Works Cited	193
Index	219

Acknowledgments

This project has benefited from the advice, comments, and encouragement of numerous individuals. I am grateful to Joan Dayan, who first introduced me to the American gothic (and indeed to the study of literature) as an undergraduate at Yale University. Her intellectual rigor set a high standard for me to follow. Betsy Erkkila helped me to conceptualize this project at its earliest stages and believed in it from the start. Her friendship and advice continue to be invaluable. Houston Baker had the uncanny ability to know what this project was about before I did. His criticisms have been as necessary as his unwavering support.

I have been lucky to work and to write in a collegial community. My students have forced me to clarify and refine my ideas, and have re-energized me with their enthusiasm and interest. Many of my colleagues have read and reread my work, providing me with useful recommendations. In particular, I would like to thank Jay Clayton, Sam Girgus, Michael Kreyling, Cecelia Tichi, and Nancy Walker for their careful readings, and Paul Elledge, who always seems to have the right advice. Mark Schoenfield and Valerie Traub, who taught me the meaning of intellectual companionship, have both been ideal readers and, more importantly, friends. Their support at crucial junctures enabled the completion of this project. I am also deeply appreciative of other colleagues and friends who commented on or advised me on portions of the manuscript: Joyce Chaplin, Phyllis Frus, Vivien Fryd, Myra Jehlen, Amy Kirschke, Jane Landers, Elisa New, and Eric Sundquist. In addition, the reviewers of the manuscript offered important insights and understandings that shaped my final revisions.

This project has been generously funded by the Vanderbilt University Research Council and the Robert Penn Warren Center for the Humanities at Vanderbilt University, which provided me with not only financial support but also a wonderful space in which to think and write. Mona Frederick's professionalism and humor made the act of writing productive and less isolating. I am grateful to Maya Socolovsky and Rory Dicker for helping to prepare the manuscript for publication; Lisa Cullum for her administrative assistance; and Janis May for her unflagging interest and good will. At Columbia University Press, I have been fortunate to work with Leslie Kriesel and Jennifer Crewe, who have expertly guided this book through the publication process.

My friends and family supplied the support that sustained this project. Beverly Ballaro's humor and insight kept my perspective in balance. Jay Grossman, Andrea Henderson, Jeff Masten, and Craig Smith prove that graduate school can produce good friends as well as colleagues. My family provided love and encouragement. This book is dedicated to my father, who died as this project was nearing completion; his commitment to an intellectual and ethical life continues to serve as a map for my own. Finally, my thanks to Yoshikuni Igarashi, who makes everything possible.

Gothic America

Introduction

About halfway through his autobiography, *Black Boy*, Richard Wright describes his first job selling newspapers. The young Wright takes the job in order to make money and to read the newspaper's magazine supplement, which contains tales such as Zane Grey's *Riders of the Purple Sage* and "thrilling horror stories" of mad scientists who electrify their victims in the basement (144). Hungry not only for money to buy food but also for knowledge, Wright uses these stories of "outlandish men in faraway, outlandish cities" as his "gateway to the world" (142). Before long, Wright learns from one of his black customers that the newspaper he is selling endorses the doctrines of the Ku Klux Klan. When he reads the news sections of the paper for the first time, Wright breaks out in goose pimples at the uncanny images of racism and the "brutally anti-Negro" articles that the paper espouses; its stereotypical cartoons of black men and its call for the defense of white womanhood "all seemed so strange and yet familiar" (146, 145). Wright responds to the accusation that he is supporting white supremacist doctrine by arguing that he was unaware of the connection between the magazine and the content of the newspaper: "I read the magazine, but I never read the paper," he defensively repeats three times in the scene (145). Looking back on his mistake, the older Wright states: "The way I had erred was simple but utterly unbelievable. I had been so enthralled by reading the serial stories in the magazine supplement that I had not read a single issue of the newspaper" (146). Rather than completely own up to his unwitting dissemination of white supremacist doctrine, the young Wright stops selling the newspaper, claiming he no longer has time. His shame silences him. It is the older Wright who resurrects the episode and voices its importance in his own literary evolution.

This episode in *Black Boy* tells us much about readings of gothic literature—those thrilling tales of horror that seemingly have no relationship to reality. Instead of being gateways to other, distant worlds of fantasy, the example of Wright suggests, gothic stories are intimately connected to the culture that produces them. Actually folded within the pages of the newspaper, the gothic tales of Wright's magazine insert should not be read separately from their historical and, specifically, their racial contexts. Thus situated, the gothic tales act as the conduit for Wright's new knowledge of racial politics instead of as an escapist retreat from it. Moreover, in revealing the connection between the gothic and history, Wright implies that gothic tales are enacted in the everyday terrorism of the Ku Klux Klan and that accounts of those terrors can evoke in the reader a response similar to that provoked by a gothic tale (hence, the young Wright's goose bumps on reading the anti-Negro paper). Wright, then, articulates a multivalent relationship between the newspaper and its magazine insert of gothic stories. First, the gothic, like all discourses, needs to be historicized; to read it out of cultural context is to misread it. Second, the gothic can remain continuous with official narratives, even when it apparently contradicts them. The gothic may unveil the ideology of official discourse, but its transformative power can be limited; in Wright's narrative the gothic magazine insert enables the dissemination of the paper's politics. Just as Wright covers over his reasons for quitting the paper, the gothic's effect can simply be repressed. Finally, if the gothic is informed by its historical context, the horrors of history are also articulated through gothic discourse. The brutal and uncanny images of the newspaper signify how history can be coded in gothic terms.

Throughout this study, I will argue for a reading of the gothic as an integral part of a network of historical representation. Claiming that the gothic is intensely engaged with historical concerns, this study contests traditional assessments that classify it as an escapist form. Instead of fleeing reality, the gothic registers its culture's contradictions, presenting a distorted, not a disengaged, version of reality. While this study addresses a number of sites of historical horror—revolution, Indian massacre, the transformation of the marketplace—it is especially concerned with how slavery haunts the American gothic. Instead of making the same mistake as the young Wright, who becomes so enthralled by the thrilling tale that he misses its connection to his culture, *Gothic America* remains mindful of history's horrors and attentive to reading practices that would disavow them.

Defining the American Gothic

The Gothic code is difficult to define, but easy to classify.
—Robert Hemenway, "Gothic Sociology"

The question "How do you define gothic?" has been the necessary starting point for most conversations about this project; the inquiry has less to do, I suspect, with a need for generic precision than with a genuine bafflement about what might constitute the *American* gothic. When modified by *American*, the gothic loses its usual referents. The second most-asked question about this project—"How do you differentiate between the American and the British gothic?"—supports this theory: the canonical British gothic serves as the reference point for readers attempting to locate the less identifiable American version. As a critical category, the American gothic lacks the self-evident validity of its British counterpart.

Several factors contribute to the uncertain status of the American gothic. Unlike the British gothic, which developed during a definable time period (usually marked as beginning with Walpole's *The Castle of Otranto* [1764] and continuing through the 1820s) and has a recognized coterie of authors (Walpole, Radcliffe, Monk Lewis, Godwin, Hogg, Maturin, Mary Shelley), the American gothic, one of several forms that played a role in the development of the early American novel, is less easily specified in terms of a particular time period or group of authors. There was no founding period of gothic literature in America, and given the critical preference for the term *romance*, few authors were designated as gothicists. Even when authors such as Edgar Allan Poe or periods such as the twentieth-century Southern Renaissance are associated with the gothic, they reveal the difficulty of defining the genre in national terms: the American gothic is most recognizable as a regional form. Identified with gothic doom and gloom, the American South serves as the nation's "other," becoming the repository for everything from which the nation wants to disassociate itself.[1] The benighted South is able to support the irrational impulses of the gothic that the nation as a whole, born of Enlightenment ideals, cannot. America's self-mythologization as a nation of hope and harmony directly contradicts the gothic's most basic impulses. The American gothic, as Leslie Fiedler points out, is "a literature of darkness and the grotesque in a land of light and affirmation" (29).

If the American gothic is difficult to understand due to its seemingly antagonistic relationship to America's national identity, it is equally difficult to classify in generic terms. Just as *gothic* unsettles the idea of America, the modifier *American* destabilizes understandings of the gothic. Once imported to America, the gothic's key elements were translated into American terms, and its formulas were also unfixed. As Charles Brockden Brown, one of America's first novelists to use the gothic, argues in his preface to *Edgar Huntly* (1799), "the field of investigation, opened to us by our own country, should differ essentially from those which exist in Europe" (3). "Puerile superstition and exploded manners; Gothic castles and chimeras" might be the materials usually employed in this genre, Brown continues, but the "incidents of Indian hostility, and the perils of the western wilderness, are far more suitable; and, for a native of America to overlook these, would admit of no apology" (3). To be sure, some authors, such as Isaac Mitchell in *The Asylum; or, Alonzo and Melissa* (1811), imported castles to America, but most American authors transformed and hence dislocated British models of the gothic. Combined with other literary forms and adapted to native themes, the American gothic consists of a less coherent set of conventions. Its more flexible form challenges the critically unified gothic genre and demands a reassessment of the gothic's parameters. As a result, a definition of the American gothic depends less on the particular set of conventions it establishes than on those it disrupts. Any attempt to define it without showing how the terms "American" and "gothic" complicate and critique each other curtails the challenge to both terms.[2]

Even the British gothic, against which the American gothic is defined, has proven oddly elusive. From early works such as Edith Birkhead's *The Tale of Terror: A Study of the Gothic Romance* (1921), to more recent studies such as Eve Sedgwick's *The Coherence of Gothic Conventions* (1980), an effort to demarcate the conventions of this genre has been at the heart of criticism of the gothic.[3] The debate between Robert Hume and Robert Platzner in *PMLA* highlights the critical need to define the "essence" of the gothic and the difficulty of doing so. While the two disagree on the central traits, they are "agreed that the 'generic character' of the Gothic novel is hard to deal with" (Hume and Platzner 1971:268). Despite its formulaic and conventional nature, despite its easily listed elements and effects—haunted houses, evil villains, ghosts, gloomy landscapes, madness, terror, suspense, horror—the gothic's parameters and "essence" remain unclear. While easy classification seems to imply a definitional stability, the gothic genre is extremely mutable. Cobbled together of many different forms and obsessed with transgressing boundaries, it represents itself not as stable but as generically impure. As Maggie Kilgour writes, "one of the factors that makes the gothic so shadowy and nebulous a genre, as difficult to define as any gothic ghost, is that it cannot be seen in abstraction from the other literary forms from whose graves it arises.... The form is thus itself a Frankenstein's monster, assembled out of the bits and pieces of the past" (3–4).[4]

Though the gothic foregrounds its generic instability, critics still insist on categorizing it. The tendency toward "generic essentializing"[5] in criticism on the gothic has to do with where this genre ranks in the canon's hierarchy. The drive to order and identify the gothic stems less from a critical desire to discover its particular essence than from a need to differentiate it from other, "higher" literary forms. As Jacques Derrida suggests in his essay "The Law of Genre," the critical desire for generic classification and clarity signals a fear of contagion: the law of genre depends upon the principle of impurity. Categorical generic distinctions aim to ensure the purity of certain individual works or the stature of related genres. Associated with the hackneyed, the feminine, and the popular, the gothic lacks respectability and hence must be quarantined from other literary forms.[6] Elizabeth Napier, for instance, would "delimit the genre with greater strictness," arguing that

> it is essential to make such distinctions in the case of the Gothic because of its peculiar likeness to many of the more searching works that it in part inspired. The Gothic does, in fact, exhibit many of the procedures of fragmentation and disjunction that the romantics ... would elevate to art, but they seldom at this early stage lead to the profound realizations about human consciousness that some critics have asserted that they do. It is with this systematic failure that the present study is concerned. (xiii, 7)

Seeing the gothic as a systematic failure and arguing that it is a cruder anticipation of Romanticism and hence easily distinguishable from it, Napier polices the difference between the two forms. Ironically, the likeness between the gothic and the romantic necessitates that the gothic's boundaries be located and limited. Whether establishing a distinction between the romantic and the gothic or between the popular gothic and the more serious works it inspired, the critical aim is a clean canon.[7]

The desire to quarantine the gothic from higher literary forms is especially prevalent in the scholarship devoted to American literature. Given its historical belatedness, critics are particularly anxious to provide the American literary canon with a respectable foundation. American literature might be "embarrassingly, a gothic fiction," as Leslie Fiedler argues, but critics have made every effort to hide this fact (29). Despite the origins of the American romance in the gothic and historical romance, critics such as Richard Chase in his foundational work *The American Novel and Its Tradition* (1957) have followed Hawthorne's idiosyncratic use of the term in order to define a respectable canon. As Nina Baym has pointed out, before 1860 the term *romance* in America connoted characteristics now associated with the gothic: *romance* designated "pre-modern types of novels . . . which depended on supernatural and marvelous events to resolve their plots and to achieve their effects," along with works of sensational fiction or fictions associated with the "highly wrought, the heavily plotted, the ornately rhetorical, the tremendously exciting and the relentlessly exterior" (1984:437, 438).[8] In American literary criticism, however, the romance has come to be elevated above and separated from its modifier, gothic, rather than recognized as sharing gothic characteristics.

The category of romance dominates the critical discourse within American literature while the term *gothic* is almost fully repressed. For instance, in *The American Novel and Its Tradition*, Richard Chase subsumes gothic under the heading of melodrama:

> The term has taken on a general meaning beyond the Mrs. Radcliffe kind of thing and is often used rather loosely to suggest violence, mysteries, improbabilities, morbid passions, inflated and complex language of any sort. It is a useful word but since, in its general reference, it becomes confused with "melodrama," it seems sensible to use "melodrama" for the general category and reserve "Gothic" for its more limited meaning.

By making the gothic a "subdivision" of melodrama, Chase limits its application (37). More recently, in *Beneath the American Renaissance* (1988), David Reynolds uses the heading "Dark Adventure" to describe gothic works. In both cases, *gothic* is replaced by a broader generic term. This displacement also occurs when *dark* is substituted for *gothic* as the modifier of romance. Chase follows Malcolm Cowley in identifying Charles Brockden Brown as the "originator of that strand of dark romance that runs through the tradition" (31); Reynolds argues that the roots of Dark Adventure are in "European Dark Romanticism" (190).[9] Whether the term *gothic* is displaced in favor of another generic category or the broader, less-specific modifier *dark*, it disappears and is securely segregated from the romance. In American literary criticism, then, there is no need to police the boundaries between romantic and gothic, high and low, since the gothic is erased from the equation altogether.

The replacement of *gothic* with *dark* signifies the critical displacement of the category from discussions of American literature. While the adjective *dark* conjures the atmospheric associations of the gothic, it does not carry the same generic baggage. Unlike the term *gothic*, which connotes "popular," *dark* has come to signify "profound" in American literary criticism. Beginning with Herman Melville's famous discourse on Hawthorne's soul, which is "shrouded in blackness, ten times black," American literature's "power of blackness" has been defined as mystical and metaphysical: the "deep far-away things" in Hawthorne are also the "flashings-forth of the intuitive Truth in him," claims Melville ("Hawthorne and His Mosses," 243, 244). In *The Power of Blackness*, Harry Levin also reads American literature's blackness in weighty symbolic terms. The vision of evil it represents is that of the introspective mind, not some staged fright: the "symbolic character of our greatest fiction," Levin argues, is linked to the "dark wisdom of our deeper minds" (xii). In distinguishing between the "palatable" gothic novels that translate gothic decor into a symbol for the "hidden blackness of the human soul and human society" and those gothic novels that fail to make their "cheapjack machinery" symbolic, Leslie Fiedler's work exemplifies the way that *blackness* is critically weighted: the gothic's superficial, dark spectacles are transformed into the more meaningful symbolism of psychological and moral blackness (28, 27). American literature's *darkness*, then, becomes associated with depth rather than surface, a psychological and metaphysical symbolism rather than cheap tricks.

However, at the same time that the term *blackness* displaces the gothic's unpalatable associations, it is stripped of its racial connotations. By evacuating *darkness* of racial meaning, critics can claim that the blackness that typifies the American romance is, for the most part, symbolic and not societal, a sign of an inner darkness or moral truth. This conjunction between the displacement of the gothic as a critical term and the abstraction of the American romance's blackness is hardly coincidental. As this study demonstrates, the American gothic is haunted by race: resurrecting the term *gothic* reasserts the racial roots of the romance's blackness. Significantly, when race is restored to the *darkness* of American literature, the gothic reappears as a viable category. In *Playing in the Dark* (1992), Toni Morrison not only insists upon restoring race to the *blackness* of American literature, but also reconstructs the American literary canon in terms of the *gothic* romance. Remarking on "how troubled, how frightened and haunted our early and founding literature truly is," Morrison argues that one of the words we have for this haunting is *gothic* (35, 36). Looking at disturbances within the American romance, Morrison reveals how race haunts American literature. Once specified in historical rather than symbolic terms, *darkness* emblematizes the gothic's disruptive potential instead of replacing the term as a more palatable modifier.

By resurrecting the gothic as a critical term in American literary studies, *Gothic America* contributes to the destabilization of traditional readings of the American literary canon, defamiliarizing readings that the romance has ensconced. By insisting on the gothic's intimate relation to the romance, this book views American literature as infiltrated by the popular, the disturbing, and the hauntings of history. Embracing the gothic's generic instability, this study examines how the gothic seeps into other genres and appears in unlikely places. It recognizes that American literature's most cherished children's author, Louisa May Alcott, wrote sensation stories; that one of America's earliest literary critics, John Neal, theorized a uniquely American literature based on the gothic's emotive effects; that gothic moments occur in texts ranging from St. John de Crèvecoeur's Enlightenment fable, *Letters from an American Farmer*, to the realist texts of the slave narrative. It also shows how the gothic infiltrates and informs the canon of American literature: male and female, high and low, supernatural stories and actual histories. *Gothic America* is not genre criticism; rather, it is an exploration of how genre enables and constrains critical readings and canon formation. In response to the question "How do you define gothic?" this study asks other questions: Whose interests and what readings are served by particular definitions of the American gothic? How are traditional readings of American literature unsettled by allowing the gothic to reappear as a viable, if not easily definable, literary category?

Historicizing the American Gothic

While the English Gothic had dealt with physical terror and social horror, the American Gothic would concentrate on mental terror and moral horror.
—Frederick Frank, Introduction to *Through the Pale Door*

When Cathy Davidson poses the question, "Does America have enough of a history to sustain the Gothic's generic challenge to history, its rewriting and unwriting of history?" she exposes the American gothic's problematic status: it is an historical mode operating in what appears to be an historical vacuum (231). The gothic's connection to American history is difficult to identify precisely because of the national and critical myths that America and its literature *have* no history. As exemplified in Frederick Frank's assessment, views of the American gothic rely upon the traditional misreading of American literature as representing, in Richard Poirier's term, "a world elsewhere." Through critical readings of the romance as otherworldly, American literature's exceptionality came to be located in its ahistoricism. As Nina Baym points out, "[m]ost specialists in American literature have accepted the idea that in the absence of history (or a sense of history) as well as a social field, our literature has consistently taken an ahistorical, mythical shape for which the term 'romance' is formally and historically appropriate" (1984:427). Despite the significant body of criticism that situates the British gothic within its cultural context, critics of the American gothic continue to resist historical readings.[10] If the British gothic is read in social terms, the American gothic is viewed within psychological and theological rubrics. Because of America's seeming lack of history and its Puritan heritage, the American gothic, it has been argued, takes a turn inward, away from society and toward the psyche and the hidden blackness of the American soul. As Joseph Bodziock asserts, "the American gothic replaced the social struggle of the European with a Manichean struggle between the moral forces of personal and communal order and the howling wilderness of chaos and moral depravity" (33). Leslie Fiedler, the first critic to discuss the American gothic's peculiarity and to recognize its social impulse, sees the American gothic as "a Calvinist exposé of natural human corruption" (160). For Fiedler, as for many others, the American gothic remains first and foremost an expression of psychological states.

Cathy Davidson and Lawrence Buell are two notable exceptions to this rule. Both argue that the American gothic has a social referent: Davidson sees the early American gothic as a critique of individualism and Buell notes in his study of the "provincial gothic" the "potential inherent in gothic, from the start, to give this irrationalist vision a social ground" (352).[11] Moreover, Karen Halttunen's work on how the "cult of horror" emerged during the late eighteenth century in America and how nineteenth-century gothic literature illuminates redefinitions of pain provides historical frameworks in which to view the development of the American gothic and suggests that it responded to and reinforced certain historical movements. Halttunen's historicizing of the American gothic also reflects a movement toward reading the American gothic in social, not psychological, terms.

Arguing that America does have enough history to sustain the gothic's challenge, this study situates the American gothic within specific sites of historical haunting, most notably slavery. American gothic literature criticizes America's national myth of new-world innocence by voicing the cultural contradictions that undermine the nation's claim to purity and equality. Showing how these contradictions contest and constitute national identity even as they are denied, the gothic tells of the historical horrors that make national identity possible yet must be repressed in order to sustain it.

Throughout this study, I use the term "abject" to signify these historical horrors.[12] The nation's narratives—its foundational fictions and self-mythologizations—are created through a process of displacement: their coherence depends on exclusion. By resurrecting what these narratives repress, the gothic disrupts the dream world of national myth with the nightmares of history. Moreover, in its narrative incoherence, the gothic discloses the instability of America's self-representations; its highly wrought form exposes the artificial foundations of national identity. However, while the gothic reveals what haunts the nation's narratives, it can also work to coalesce those narratives. Like the abject, the gothic serves as the ghost that both helps to run the machine of national identity and disrupts it. The gothic can strengthen as well as critique an idealized national identity.[13]

Arguing that the American gothic exposes the cultural contradictions of national myth, this study attends to the specific effects of this unveiling rather than make essentializing claims about it. Although the gothic is not the only form that articulates abjection, it serves as a primary means of speaking the unspeakable in American literature. Many texts that are not predominantly gothic use gothic effects at key moments to register cultural contradictions. Further, the critical history of the gothic as it is constructed within American literature makes it particularly salient for exposing the alignment of America's literary histories with the nation's idealized myths. This study, then, is concerned with how the gothic challenges the critical narratives of American literary history and with how it unsettles the nation's cultural identity.

While each chapter takes up a specific site of cultural contradiction—the intrusion of slavery into the Enlightenment narrative or the pastoral setting, the violent origins of the nation in Indian massacre, the "angel in the house" unveiled in the public marketplace—the book falls into two sections. The first part focuses on the gothic's role in constructing and contesting the nation's narratives. The first section (chapters 1–3) is concerned with the gothic's relationship to narratives created during the early national period. Beginning with an examination of St. John de Crèvecoeur's *Letters from an American Farmer*, chapter 1, "Haunted by History: Crèvecoeur's National Narrative and the Gothic," focuses on how the gothic disrupts the Enlightenment fable of the early republic with the cultural contradictions—slavery and revolution—that establish the republic yet also threaten its dissolution. Chapter 2, "Diseased Discourse: Charles Brockden Brown's *Arthur Mervyn*," relates the text's subject—the 1793 outbreak of yellow fever in Philadelphia—and the infectious nature of Mervyn's tale to postrevolutionary America's obsession with its own degeneracy. Addressing the reasons Brown chose to write his national narrative in the gothic mode, this chapter examines the possibilities for national well-being and recovery inscribed in the gothic form. Chapter 3, "Literary Nationalism and the Gothic: John Neal's *Logan*," examines the attempts of John Neal, America's first literary critic, to found a national literature upon a literature of the blood. Focusing on his gothic novel *Logan*, which registers the cultural contradiction of Indian massacre, this chapter explores the gothic's place in American literary nationalism and Neal's ghostly presence in the canon of American literature.

The second part of the book (chapters 4–6) broadens its focus to assess why the gothic comes to be identified with marginal groups or regions, focusing on three crucial categories of the gothic: the female, the southern, and the African American. Chapter 4, "The Ghost of Race: Edgar Allan Poe and the Southern Gothic," examines Poe's centrality to studies of the American gothic by problematizing his position in the American literary canon as well as the subgenre with which he comes to be associated—southern gothic. This chapter shows how Poe and the gothic come to bear the burden of race in American literature. Chapter 5, "(Un)Veiling the Marketplace: Nathaniel Hawthorne, Louisa May Alcott, and the Female Gothic," explores the relationship between the sentimental and the gothic modes in nineteenth-century America. Examining Nathaniel Hawthorne's *The Blithedale Romance* and Louisa May Alcott's ghost stories, the chapter shows how the gothic unveils the market forces that lie beneath the surface of the sentimental, specifically, how the newly emerging marketplace of industrial capitalism is depicted in gothic terms. Exploring the commercial exchanges between the sentimental and the gothic as well as between male and female authors in the literary marketplace, the chapter complicates notions of the female gothic by locating the gothic heroine in the marketplace instead of the house. The final chapter, "Haunting Back: Harriet Jacobs, African-American Narrative, and the Gothic," assesses Richard Wright's claim, in his introduction to *Native Son* ("How 'Bigger' Was Born"), that the African American *is* the American gothic, and argues that African-American literature provides a vantage point from which to revise critical readings of the American gothic. Through the African-American version, the gothic's relationship to history is fully revealed. Investigating the horror of slavery in Jacobs's *Incidents in the Life of a Slave Girl* and the African-American expressive tradition she invokes to haunt the master's text, the chapter explores the uses and dangers of the gothic mode for African-American authors as well as its possibilities and limits for resurrecting and representing history.

1

Haunted by History: Crèvecoeur's National Narrative and the Gothic

> For a people who made much of their "newness"—their potential, freedom, and innocence—it is striking how dour, how troubled, how frightened and haunted our early and founding literature truly is.
>
> —Toni Morrison, *Playing in the Dark*

St. John de Crèvecoeur's *Letters from an American Farmer* (1782) is not a self-evident place to begin a discussion of the American gothic. *Letters* has most often been read as an Enlightenment fable of an idealized American identity. My intent is not to argue that *Letters* is a gothic text, but rather to explore the role that the gothic plays in *Letters* and, more broadly, in America's national narratives. If, as Toni Morrison argues, America's founding literature remains troubled and haunted despite its claims to newness and innocence, then what is the source and the effect of this haunting? *Letters*, which begins by depicting America as Edenic and ends by describing it as a ruined bower, articulates the dream of American innocence and the nightmare of American history. This chapter looks at the moments in Letters 9 through 12 when the gothic discourse of decay and degeneracy ruptures the book's Enlightenment vision of balance and order and examines how Crèvecoeur's idealized fable cracks under the weight of history. The gothic gives voice to cultural contradictions that Crèvecoeur's national narrative represses; I focus here on slavery's abject presence in the text and the gothic's role in representing it. Slavery threatens to undo

Crèvecoeur's national narrative just as the gothic, by articulating the abject within American culture, threatens to reveal that America's dearest myths are haunted by history.

The Case of Crèvecoeur

If we forget that fictions are fictive we regress to myth.
—Frank Kermode, *The Sense of an Ending*

Letters opens by presenting the American farmer in the main character of James, who as the embodiment of Jefferson's agrarian yeoman represents the ideal republican citizen, and by discussing the yeoman's proper speech, the plain style.[1] Having been asked to write to a former European guest, farmer James spends most of Letter 1 trying to resolve the question "How should an American write?" before addressing the question "What is an American?" Suffering from a lack of education but not of experience, James has difficulty figuring out "how to collect, digest, and arrange what [he] know[s]" (41). When he is told that writing is like "talking on paper," and that "a Letter is only conversation put down in black and white," his difficulty evaporates, for by writing as he speaks James need not artfully arrange his experience, but merely express it simply and straightforwardly. Indeed, his letters will be so natural and spontaneous that "they will smell of the woods and be a little wild" (41, 44, 41). Like Noah Webster's glorified yeoman, who is not only "the bearer of the true political and economic identity" but also the guardian of a pure, democratic language, James will speak his simple truths in a plain style (Simpson 75). Letter 1, then, first sounds the civic voice through which Crèvecoeur will create his national narrative.

In presenting his narrative as a private correspondence written in the plain style and by a yeoman, Crèvecoeur employs devices central to many foundational narratives of national identity. The persona of the yeoman farmer was prevalent in writings of the period. As the embodiment of the nation, he represented an idealized citizen; through this character the nation could be totalized into a single identity.[2] The plain style, which became the unofficial discourse of the new nation, served as the vehicle through which national identity could be solidified. Seeing language as intimately connected to the social order, the new nation argued that unity could be achieved through linguistic legislation.[3] Like the yeoman's claim to cultural naiveté, the plain style's pretensions of artlessness and central tenet of the subordination of language to idea were crucial to the production of the nation's founding narratives. Calling for the transparent reflection of sense, the plain style not only forswore language that might obscure meaning but also presented itself as a self-evident discourse.[4] Through the plain style, the nation's foundational narratives attained the status of self-evident truths: the founding fathers, as Robert Ferguson argues, used "their faith in the text to stabilize the uncertain world in which they live[d]," subsuming "in the substances of print, proof, style, and form" any and all contradictions. In this way, the unified text, not concrete facts, came to represent reality (1986:4).[5] Making the translation of ideas into language appear effortless, the plain style turns a complex textual maneuver into a spontaneously recorded, self-evident fact. For example, in *Common Sense* (1776), Thomas Paine writes, "in the following pages I offer nothing more than simple facts, plain arguments, and common sense," but his argument depends on an intricate rhetoric and complex ideology (81). Thomas Jefferson's statement about the aims of the *Declaration of Independence*—"to place before mankind the common sense of the subject, in terms so plain and firm as to command their assent"—suggests how the plain style disguised ideology as truth (Ferguson 1986:6). Like the language of myth, the plain style appears as innocent speech.[6]

In answering the question of how an American should write before telling the reader what an American is, *Letters* makes its narrative's style crucial to its substance. Through the plain style—which disguises his public discourse as private, his crafted fable as self-evident—Crèvecoeur fashions a mythic narrative of national identity that appears stable, coherent, and transparent and presents "a world wide open and wallowing in the evident" (Barthes 143). By enticing the reader to believe that what James writes is "all true and real," he turns his fiction of national identity into fact (62).

However, as with many writings of the early national period, *Letters*'s self-proclaimed use of plain style is itself a fiction. Crèvecoeur might present himself in the guise of an illiterate farmer and his public text as a collection of private letters, but these maneuvers are in themselves marks of a self-conscious craftsmanship. At the level of the story, James's style is not as simple as it seems. James learns that writing is a natural and spontaneous process, but also that it is an art, "acquired by habit and by perseverance"; and, even though he claims to be writing an "unaffected and candid" correspondence, he allows the minister and his wife to comment on rough drafts before his letters are presented publicly (45, 49). This tension between James's letters as spontaneous impressions full of "unadorned information" and as crafted revisions is replayed at the level of the text (40). Like James's letters, Crèvecoeur's narrative is presented as a private correspondence written in a "plain and familiar" style by a "simple cultivator of the earth" ("Advertisement," 35, "Dedication," 37). Biographical facts, however, discredit Crèvecoeur's yeoman pretensions (he was an educated French aristocrat and a gentleman farmer in America), while his sophisticated style contradicts his claim to simplicity.[7] Note, for instance, the elevated prose and the periodic nature of his first sentence: "Who would have thought that because I received you with hospitality and kindness, you should imagine me capable of writing with propriety and perspicuity?" (39). Moreover, his use of dialogue, which is meant to enact the idea that writing is like conversation, foregrounds his stylistic maneuvers rather than making them disappear. It is this artful façade of self-evidence that the gothic discourse of the later letters destabilizes.

Just as the first letter sets up the mythic, civic voice of the text that the gothic's degenerate rhetoric will later disrupt, it presents a theory of America's difference from Europe that the gothic vision will collapse. In Letter 1, the minister describes Italy to James as America's degenerate double. Whereas in Italy, the minister says, "all the objects of contemplation, all the reveries of the traveller, must have a reference to ancient generations and to very distant periods clouded with the mist of ages," in America "on the contrary, everything is modern, peaceful, and benign. Here we have had no war to desolate our fields; our religion does not oppress the cultivators; we are strangers to those feudal institutions which have enslaved so many" (42). If Italy is a ruined republic destroyed by war, oppression, and tyranny, then America is a new beginning based on progress, peace, and prosperity. Italy represents a degenerate past; America embodies an ever-progressive future. As the repository of everything America is not, Italy is a necessary "other" that allows James to map an America without contradiction and immune to the forces of history. The absolute distinction between America and Europe is the basis for James's belief that the American "is a new man, who acts upon new principles" (70). However, once James discovers that this strict separation does not hold—that America also has feudal institutions like slavery as well as war—his myth falls back into history.

Throughout the first eight letters, James adheres to the minister's model of America's difference. Using Europe as a foil, James concludes in Letter 3 that Americans "have no princes for whom we toil, starve, and bleed; we are the most perfect society now existing in the world" (67). Moreover, in reply to the letter's query "What is an American?" James insists that an American is not merely a European transported to the new world, but a

European regenerated and transformed: "He is an American, who, leaving behind him all his ancient prejudices and manners, receives new ones from the new mode of life he has embraced, the new government he obeys, and the new rank he holds" (70). However, once James begins to outline America's internal variants instead of merely recording its differences from Europe, his myth-making runs into contradictions. Turning from the industrious Americans who live near the sea and in the middle colonies, James discovers in the frontiersmen of the west "the most hideous part" of American society: they are "a mongrel breed, half civilized, half savage" and live a lawless, "licentious idle life" (72, 77, 78). However, James is able to explain away the frontiersmen's degeneracy by manufacturing spatial and temporal difference. First, he claims that this segment of the population lives at the outermost edges of American society, beyond good government and close to the evils of an unknown wilderness; they are not the "true" representatives of American society, but its "off-casts" (73). Second, and more important, he associates the frontier with the past: "forty years ago, this smiling country was thus inhabited," James states, but "it is now purged, [and] a general decency of manners prevails throughout" (73). With the forward movement of progress, the "most vicious of Americans" vanish, replaced by a "second and better class, the true American freeholders, the most respectable set of people in this part of the world" who will "change in a few years that hitherto barbarous country into a fine, fertile, well-regulated district" (79, 73). Instead of heightening society's impurities, as it would in Europe, "time will efface those stains" in America, replacing the frontiersman's degenerate society with the right order of the yeoman's agrarian republic (79). Through this spatial and temporal dislocation, James not only neutralizes a contradiction that threatens his myth of America's perfection, but also revitalizes the myth by transforming the evils of the past into a testament to America's glorious future.

James's myth might be able to efface America's degenerate precursors, but it cannot prevent a degenerate future. Having finished his tour of the agrarian middle and seafaring northern colonies, James turns his attention in Letter 9 to the southern colonies as he visits Charles Town. Although, as Elayne Rapping points out, James's letters describe a single present, they implicitly trace "the country's development over a period of time" (710). If the frontier represents America's impure past and the middle and northern colonies its virtuous, industrious present, the South signifies America's degenerate future. Instead of finding in Charles Town the even greater perfection his progressive philosophy would predict, James discovers all the signs of a society heading toward ruin. Luxury, a primary symptom of societal corruption in the republican lexicon, abounds. James voices his concern about this vice when he remarks that Charles Town's "climate renders excesses of all kinds very dangerous" (167). Besides threatening to ruin the city, such vice could also infect the entire American society, for as James warned in Letter 4, "A Description of Nantucket," "could the manners of luxurious countries be imported here, like an epidemical disorder they would destroy everything" (125). In fact, luxury is so infectious that James prescribes emigration as its only cure. Signs of the South's excesses serve as a warning that America might not be immune from Europe's diseases after all. As the "centre of our beau monde," the South represents the abject "other" that is supposedly excluded from American identity, but that constitutes its very core (166).

Slavery is the contradiction that collapses James's mythic narrative of America. More than a symptom of possible infection, slavery is the canker that proves the South is suffering from the same degenerative disease as Europe.[8] By destroying the antithesis between Europe and America, slavery undermines the myth of American exceptionalism. Like Europe, America has feudal institutions, a decadent aristocracy, tyranny, and oppression. Plowed by Africans stolen from "harmless, peaceable African neighbourhood[s]," its fields—the very source of its regenerative powers—are like the Roman dominions that "were tilled by the hands of unfortunate people who had once been, like their victors, free, rich, and possessed of every benefit society can confer, until they became subject to the cruel right of war and to lawless force" (168, 173). This contradiction—that the "chosen race" practices a "barbarous custom"—finally forces James's myth back into the fallen history of the world (168, 173). Unable to sustain his reverie, James rails against the horrors of history:

> The history of the earth! Doth it present anything but crimes of the most heinous nature, committed from one end of the world to the other? We observe avarice, rapine, and murder, equally prevailing in all parts. History perpetually tells us of millions of people abandoned to the caprice of the maddest princes, and of whole nations devoted to the blind fury of tyrants. Countries destroyed, nations alternately buried in ruins by other nations, some parts of the world beautifully cultivated, returned again into their pristine state, the fruits of ages of industry, the toil of thousands in a short time destroyed by few! If one corner breathes in peace for a few years, it is, in turn subjected, torn, and levelled; one would almost believe the principles of action in man, considered as the first agent of this planet,

to be poisoned in their most essential parts. We certainly are not that class of beings which we vainly think ourselves to be. (173–74)

Participating in an act practiced in all ages and nations, America is no longer exempt from the poison of history. Like all nations, America will soon be buried in ruins; its destiny is not progress but decline. In Letter 9, the history of the world as a "place of punishment [rather] than of delight" replaces James's myth of new-world perfection, and a bleak meditation on the perverse nature of all men who refuse liberty for power supplants his hopeful inquiry "What, then, is the American, this new man?" (175, 69). Even nature, which in the initial letters is the blueprint for rational order, is ineffectual in this unbalanced world: "Strange order of things!" James wails. "Oh, Nature, where art thou?" (169). Discovering that all his cherished classifications have collapsed, James bears witness to the destruction of his myth.

James's façade of self-evidence also cracks under the stress of history; his reasoned tone gives way to a heightened rhetoric brimming with emotion. As soon as he begins to discuss slavery, James's anguish becomes apparent in his speech: not only is his descriptive narrative replaced by a melancholy meditation, but his style also becomes more intense. Using questions and exclamations, James no longer claims to speak plainly or straightforwardly. Julia Kristeva suggests that the abject is marked by a revolt within language, a crisis of the word or the shattering or impossibility of narrative (208). Such narrative shattering is manifest in James's letter: his plain style disappears and the scene that occasions his tirade and haunts his discourse is not revealed until the end. The narrative difficulty of this letter is related to the cultural contradiction it voices. The abject moment that causes the letter's narrative distortions cannot be easily unveiled; the scene is narratively deflected both before and after its articulation, yet it functions as the subject from which James's narrative cannot return.

The scene he describes is a gothic one.[9] Leaving the daylight world by taking a sheltered path through a pleasant wood, James is horrified to discover not a ghost but a "living spectre," a slave suspended in a cage: "I shudder when I recollect that the birds had already picked out his eyes; his cheek-bones were bare; his arms had been attacked in several places; and his body seemed covered with a multitude of wounds. From the edges of the hollow sockets and from the lacerations with which he was disfigured, the blood slowly dropped and tinged the ground beneath" (178). This hideous sight is rendered even more frightening by its uncanny nature.

Located in a clearing enclosed by shaded woods, the caged slave makes manifest the horror of slavery that the sunny South conceals from the public. Moreover, by fusing contradictory categories, this scene of live burial makes the familiar frightening. The tortured slave is located in the proper pastoral setting but not in his regular place: instead of tilling the ground, fertilizing it with his sweat, he is suspended above it, staining it with his blood. Half-dead and half-alive, a rotting corpse and a Christ figure, the caged slave embodies the abject, "the in-between, the ambiguous, the composite" that disturbs "identity, system, order" (Kristeva 4).[10] What is usually domesticated is here defamiliarized—slavery is not merely a peculiar institution but a living hell. In stark contrast to the familial scene of northern slavery in which James argues that slaves "enjoy as much liberty as their masters" and "participate in many of the benefits of our society without being obliged to bear any of its burthens," the excesses of this scene cannot so easily be fit into America's self-proclaimed identity (171). This gothic scene upsets James's tidy classifications, forcing him to see what they repress. Encapsulating the larger movement of the letters to this point—a pastoral reverie ruptured by the specter of slavery—this scene also makes visible what the national myth naturalizes. Like the pleasant woods, America's mythic image masks a corruption hidden at its core.

James's response to this scene also reveals the limits of the gothic's effect. He states, "I found myself suddenly arrested by the power of affright and terror; my nerves were convulsed; I trembled; I stood motionless, involuntarily contemplating the fate of this Negro in all its dismal latitude" (178). Unwillingly confronted with the abject, James seems powerless to move or act: he wants to "end this dreadful scene of agonizing torture" but he has no ball for his gun (178). Like the caged slave, James is seemingly unable to free himself from the torture and oppression of this scene. However, despite his claims of impotence, James is able to remain in control. Contemplating not the man but his fate, he turns the slave into an abstraction that he can then distance and universalize. Moreover, by identifying himself *as* a victim, James saves himself from having to identify *with* the victim. He might sympathize with the slave, but he chooses finally to ally himself with the master. Mustering the strength to walk away, James travels on to dine at the master's house where he benefits from hospitality made possible by slave labor. Eliding his power in the scene, he hides his complicity; his investment in the system that upholds his rights as property owner makes him unwilling to challenge the planter's right to kill the slave or his rationale for doing so. Indeed, the planter's rationale is so self-evident that James need not repeat it. Like the planter who executes the rebellious slave in the name of self-preservation, James represses the scene of abjection that could destroy his national narrative. He ends the letter with his repudiation of the slave's misery and the scene's implications in an "Adieu" (179).

The gothic scene might be the means of slavery's representation, but when figured as a world apart it also allows for slavery's repression. James, like the reader, can walk away from its horror. However, his introduction of this scene at the end of Letter 9 shows that it cannot be easily forgotten. James writes: "The following scene will, I hope, account for these melancholy reflections and apologize for the gloomy thoughts with which I have filled this letter: my mind is, and always has been, oppressed since I became a witness to it" (177). Paradoxically positioned at the end of the letter yet blamed as the source of his melancholy, the scene is deflected before it makes its ultimate return. As James suggests, it can never be exorcised. It serves as the abject origin and center of his national narrative: the scene constitutes the narrative yet must be denied for it to continue.[11]

Following Letter 9, James attempts to resuscitate his mythic vision and his simple style. However, his recuperative acts contain the traces of trauma. In Letters 10 and 11, the contradictions of Letter 9 are subsumed in evermore-overt literary forms. In Letter 10, what at first seems a description of America's flora and fauna quickly becomes a parable of the destruction James has just witnessed. He depicts America not as a well-ordered paradise but as an Eden penetrated by snakes whose poison contaminates even those who do not come in direct contact with them. While the South contains a greater variety of snakes than the North, James also discovers some on his own land. Echoing the gothic scene of Letter 9, where his walk in the pleasant wood is interrupted by an agitation of the wind that draws his attention to the clearing and the tortured slave, James's pastoral reverie in Letter 10 is interrupted by a scene of warfare:

> As I was one day sitting solitary and pensive in my primitive arbour, my attention was engaged by a strange sort of rustling noise at some paces distant. I looked all around without distinguishing anything, until I climbed one of my great hemp stalks, when to my astonishment I beheld two snakes of considerable length, the one pursuing the other. . . . The aggressor was of the black kind, six feet long; the fugitive was a water snake, nearly of equal dimensions. They soon met, and in the fury of their first encounter, they appeared in an instant firmly twisted together; and whilst their united tails beat the ground, they mutually tried with open jaws to lacerate each other. What a fell aspect did they present! (184)

This spectacle of snakes in mortal combat is a parable of America's embrace of slavery, an entanglement that will end in the nation's destruction. James's earlier description of the black snake as "remarkable for nothing but its industry, agility, beauty, and the art of enticing birds by the power of its eyes," resonates with that of the caged slave in Letter 9, whose eyes have been picked out by birds; however, predator and victim are reversed, suggesting slavery's destructive power (180). Able to fascinate prey with its fiery eyes, the snake threatens any viewer; moreover, once enthralled, "the distracted victim, instead of flying its enemy . . . finally rushes into the jaws of the snake and is swallowed" (183). The roles of spectator and gothic spectacle change places in this letter: the farmer turns into a living corpse and a maniac when he is stung by a copperhead, taking the terrorized position that was once the slave's (181). Instead of offering the slave poison by which to kill himself, the farmer is poisoned by slavery. James may sublimate the scene, containing it in the form of an "anecdote," but slavery's destructive threat continues to haunt his narrative (183).

James's resistance to writing this letter not only emphasizes his desire to repress the scene, but also reveals the way his role as letter writer is structured by unequal power relations. His patron has insisted that he say something about snakes; forced to write despite his claims to "have but very little to observe," James figures himself as coerced instead of free: "Why would you prescribe this task; you know that what we take up ourselves seems always lighter than what is imposed on us by others" (180). His writing, which was first a "debt of gratitude," is here described as oppressive, his kind patron unveiled as a tyrant (39). Writing is not simply talking on paper but a coercive contract; when economic and power dynamics are fully unmasked, the act of writing is implicated in the system of slavery it tries to conceal.

In Letter 11, James's mastery of his mythic vision returns only when he is reinstated in a powerful position. Inserting a letter from a Russian gentleman in place of his own, James reverses the order of the European-American relationship by taking the position of patron. The visiting Russian, indebted to James for a letter of introduction, writes this letter about John Bertram, the botanist, at James's request. As critics have argued, the mythic vision of the *Letters* as a whole can only be recaptured by a new persona; significantly, this persona continues to be haunted by the scene of slavery.[12] The voice that sutures the trauma of the gothic scene also becomes the site of its scar. James's voice might disappear behind the mask of the new persona, but the contradiction of slavery continues to trouble the narrative.

Through this replacement voice, Letter 11 returns to a self-evident vision of America as a society marked by "perfect order and regularity" and by "a diffusive happiness . . . in every part" (188, 187). John Bertram's botany embodies a rational view of nature just as his Quaker religion espouses an Enlightenment view of slavery: by freeing their slaves and treating them as the "companions of [their] labours," the Quakers turn them into a "new set of beings" (196). The Russian gentleman, however, admits that his vision of an America untroubled by slavery is based on repression: he has "no patience to behold" the spectacles of slavery and cannot endure to spend any more time in the southern provinces (197). Moreover, his comparison of Philadelphia to Pompeii links America again to Italy and a threatened ruin. Most important, his suggestion that America and Russia "are perhaps nearer neighbours than we imagine" strengthens the fear of Letter 9: that domestic slavery could easily turn into civil slavery, and the farmer become a slave (189). Drawing a parallel between Russian serfdom and American slavery, the Russian gentleman undermines his glowing vision of America's future with his prediction that Russia, and by extension America, can "never flourish under such impolitic government" (197).

Interrupting James's narrative with the voice of a Russian gentleman, Letter 11 not only continues the discussion of slavery, however displaced, begun in Letter 9 but also unveils the constructed nature of the supposedly self-evident discourse. The once-transparent identification between farmer Crèvecoeur and his persona James comes undone with the addition of this second fictional voice. If Letter 9 cracked the façade of artlessness erected by the civic voice of the first eight letters, then Letters 10 and 11 widen that gap, for even as they attempt to recover the vision of the first eight letters, they reveal the formal maneuvers with which those letters contain the vision's contradictions. After the snake scene, the nature parables of the early letters can no longer be read as merely descriptive. These letters expose the workings of their form and in so doing show language to be an active agent in molding meaning. The gothic scene of Letter 9, then, does not momentarily challenge but rather continues to disturb *Letters*'s self-evident voice.

By Letter 12, all attempts to contain the gothic scene of Letter 9 prove ineffective as the horrors of history, along with an overwrought gothic rhetoric, return. In the gothic nightmare of this final letter, the apocalypse is at hand: with the onslaught of revolution, history and all its corruptions have arrived. No longer free from the wars that desolated the fields of Europe, America now participates in the doom and decline of the old world. Surrounded by a "convulsed and a half-dissolved" society, James finds that the localized infection of Letter 9 has spread throughout the nation, becoming a deadly disease (201). Like his society, James collapses into a heap of ruins: "I resemble, methinks, one of the stones of a ruined arch, still retaining that pristine form which anciently fitted the place I occupied, but the centre is tumbled down; I can be nothing until I am replaced, either in the former circle or in some stronger one" (211).

Once again, the source of his horror in Letter 12 is slavery, specifically the fear that domestic slavery could become civil slavery. Revolution is described as oppressive and tyrannical, not freeing and regenerative; it is a force that will destroy instead of enable individual liberty. James describes himself as one of the "innocent class" who are always "the victims of the few," the oppressed victims who must toil and bleed under the arbitrary power of government (204). "Why has the Master of the world permitted so much indiscriminate evil throughout every part of this poor planet, at all times, and among all kinds of people?" he asks (209–10). By relying on the rhetoric of oppression, however, James performs his own revolutionary act. Figuring himself as impotent victim, he justifies his right to revolt against society. Slavery, which was at the heart of revolutionary rhetoric, serves as the founding discourse of James's rationale even though it must be elided for that rationale to be sustained.[13] By freeing his slaves and asking them to look upon him as an old friend and fellow-laborer, James imagines that he can relinquish the role of master without any consequences: unlike the slave in Letter 9 who killed his overseer, his slaves will not rebel against him. By positioning himself as a caged victim enclosed on all sides by hostile forces, and by denying the revolutionary potential of his slaves, James both appropriates and represses Letter 9's horrifying scene of slavery. The scene might linger in the generalized threats of murderous attacks, yet James harnesses its horror to rebel against history rather than to recognize its contradictions.

James's ordered language also disintegrates in the face of history's return. A republican citizen turned madman, James speaks as a Poe-esque narrator in Letter 12. "I am seized with a fever of the mind," he writes, "I am transported beyond that degree of calmness which is necessary to delineate our thoughts. I feel as if my reason wanted to leave me, as if it would burst its poor weak tenement" (201). James writes in what Richard Hofstadter describes as the American paranoid style. Apocalyptic in expression, this style consists of "heated exaggeration, suspiciousness, and conspiratorial fantasy" (2). Witnessing the destruction of his myth by the invading forces of history, James expresses his conspiratorial nightmare in a frenzied style. "Pardon my repetitions, my wild, my trifling reflections; they proceed from the agitations of my mind and the fulness of my heart" (215–16). Flying from "one erratic thought to another," this letter is guided not by logical connection but by emotion (210); working by stream of consciousness, it consists of a number of "unconnected accounts" (203). The linearity of his argument is shattered, and his rhetoric is unraveled as well:

> Shall I wait to be punished with death, or else to be stripped of all food and raiment, reduced to despair without redress and without hope? Shall those who may escape see everything they hold dear destroyed and gone? Shall those few survivors, lurking in some obscure corner, deplore in vain the fate of their families, mourn over parents either captivated, butchered, or burnt; roam among our wilds and wait for death at the foot of some tree, without a murmur or without a sigh, for the good of the cause? No, it is impossible! (207–8)

Marked by a heated exaggeration, James's style works by accumulation, not balance. His questions build on each other, creating a rhythm that only an exclamation of refusal finally halts. The sentences are not simple but periodic, stacking clause upon clause (punished, stripped, reduced; deplore, mourn, roam) and adjective upon adjective (captivated, butchered, burnt); the paragraphs go on for pages, rarely halting the forward movement of the sentences' rhythm. This cumulative effect constantly pushes James's language, as well as his logic, to the verge of decomposition; his rhetorical plenitude attempts, as Michel Foucault argues of delirious language in general, to fill the void of his madness (106). James's overwrought language screams out its inability to control the contradictions of history, instead of silently reflecting a transparent truth. Unable to sustain his idealized myth of America in the wake of history, James is also unable to write simply in Letter 12; his language is not a sign of social order but a symptom of his society's ruin.

James's revolutionary act turns out, however, to be less a revolt than a retreat. His attempt to restore himself, his family, and his vision of a perfect society takes the form of a nostalgic push into the past as he plans to join an Indian community on the frontier. There, James plans to "cut asunder all former connections and to form new ones" in a society that is not warlike and whose members are "strangers to *our* political disputes and [have] none among themselves" (211, 225). By reversing his progressive philosophy, James hopes to purge himself of the corruptions that have destroyed his society and push himself out of history by reverting to a state "approaching nearer to that of nature" (211).

At the end of Letter 12, however, James's fantasy of a prelapsarian world continues to be haunted by history. His final vision is constantly qualified. Not only does he doubt his ability to turn his dream into fact—"Perhaps my imagination gilds too strongly this distant prospect.... It is easier for me in all the glow of paternal anxiety, reclined on my bed, to form the theory of my future conduct than to reduce my schemes into practice"—but his dream itself is only founded on prayers and hope: "our little society... shall rest, I hope, from all fatigues" (225). As James has already informed the reader, such a hope is ill-founded, for he will never be able to rest in peace: "But let me arrive under the pole, or reach the antipodes, I never can leave behind me the remembrance of the dreadful scenes to which I have been witness; therefore, never can I be happy!" (200). The nightmare of history will continue to haunt his dreams, just as it troubles Letter 12's optimistic ending. Like his previous attempts to regain his original vision, this effort also seems destined to fail. James's gothic nightmare threatens to destroy his dream of America's perfection once again.

Letter 12, then, completes the trajectory toward history and a gothic discourse begun in Letter 9. Registering cultural contradictions instead of erasing them, the gothic ruptures the unified structure of *Letters* and shatters its simple style. In so doing, it unmasks the "fictitious" nature of society and the instability of the systems that sustain it (214). As the repressed side of the national narrative, the gothic exposes its contested and contradictory origins. By representing the unnamed foundation of American culture—the untold misery of the slave—the gothic articulates the abject that constitutes American identity and must be repressed in order for a seamless national narrative to continue. In insisting that the abject can never be fully exorcised, however, the gothic warns that America's national narratives will remain haunted by its history.

Coda: Crèvecoeur's Canonization

He wanted his ideal state. At the same time he wanted to know the other state, the dark, savage mind. He wanted both.
—D. H. Lawrence, *Studies in Classic American Literature*

Crèvecoeur's *Letters from an American Farmer* serves as a useful example of how the gothic has been marginalized in readings of American literature.

From its initial reception to its current canonization, *Letters* has most often been viewed as a fable of innocence and perfection rather than a tale of horror. Published to immediate acclaim, *Letters* was seen as a positive advertisement for America. Benjamin Franklin recommended the book as a "representative voice of the American agrarian experience," and George Washington wrote in 1788: "Perhaps the picture he gives, though founded on fact, is in some instances embellished with rather too flattering circumstances"(Rice 91, 358). Promoting the first English edition as a "genuine production of the American farmer whose name they bear," Crèvecoeur became identified with his own creation; hence the information in his letters was deemed "authentic" ("Advertisement," 35). As Norman Plotkin points out, however, the pessimistic side of Crèvecoeur's vision of the nation was never completely unknown (402). One of the first English reviewers, noting the uneven tone of *Letters*, argued that it must have been written by two different men (Cunliffe 132); moreover, during the first two decades of the text's publication, Letter 9 was reprinted at least as often as Letter 3.[14] The financial failures of the 1793 American edition and of *Voyage dans la Haute Pensylvanie et dans l'état de New-York* (1801), and Crèvecoeur's near-oblivion in the annals of nineteenth-century literature, also suggest the waning cultural power of his agrarian vision.

Letters reclaimed its role as promoter of an idealized American identity at the beginning of the twentieth century. In *The Literary History of the American Revolution* (1897), Moses Coit Tyler resurrects Crèvecoeur to address the question "What is an American?" (349). While acknowledging that the book has two distinct notes, "one of great peace, another of great pain," Tyler foregrounds the optimistic side of the text; he writes of Letter 3, "it is probable that not many passages in these letters were more enjoyed at the time, or are more likely to last in our literature" (351). Following Tyler, many twentieth-century critics have placed *Letters* at the starting point of a uniquely "American" literary tradition, using the famous question of Letter 3 and the utopian impulse that prompts it to codify that tradition.[15] In *Main Currents in American Thought* (1927), Vernon Parrington notes the "dark shadow of civil war" and the bitter invectives of the then-recently recovered letters in *Sketches of Eighteenth Century America* (1925), but he concludes that Crèvecoeur was "a lover of peace and good will," "a friend of man," "an embodiment of the generous spirit of French revolutionary thought, a man whom Jefferson would have liked for a neighbor" (146, 147). In his *Syllabus of American Literature* (1923), William Hastings calls *Letters* "sentimental descriptive essays on American life" (11). Percy

Boynton in *A History of American Literature* (1919) argues that "so enthusiastic was Crèvecoeur over conditions in America, and so certain was he that they never would be disturbed in any unfortunate way, that the twentieth-century reader looks over his pre-Revolution pages with a kind of wistful impatience" (64); Boynton reads slavery as an "external blemish" rather than "a national danger" (65). Robert Spiller includes *Letters* under the heading "The American Dream" in his *Literary History of the United States* (1948), and in *The Literature of the American People* (1951), Arthur Hobson Quinn recognizes *Letters*'s bleaker vision but emphasizes its hopeful themes: "Crèvecoeur did not blink [at] some of the ugly aspects of the life around him, and his description of a caged Negro being tortured to death by birds and insects is horrifyingly realistic. But his best passages usually dealt with simple pleasures which the countryside offered the nature lover or with the tamer aspects of the farmer's life" (132). Even as Letter 3 was canonized as the representative letter of the text, then, *Letters*'s gothic vision of degeneration and destruction was recognized but deemphasized so as not to disrupt the text's overall utopian impulse.

In the 1970s, *Letters* enjoyed renewed critical attention that attempted to counter readings of the book like Leo Marx's, as "delightful, evocative, though finally simple-minded" (108). Arguing against understandings of the book as simply utopian or of Crèvecoeur's persona as transparent, critics read *Letters* as being consciously constructed to serve particular political ends and its author as having multiple personas. The book's internal inconsistencies and contradictions were highlighted along with its pessimism.[16] A reading of *Letters* as figuring the tension between experience and theory, disillusionment and belief, was canonized through the book's classification as a romance. After calling Crèvecoeur's text a "prototypical American Romance" in his introduction to the Penguin edition, Albert Stone deduces that "*Letters* exhibits many of the qualities identified by Richard Chase in *The American Novel and Its Tradition* as characteristic of our finest fiction: idyll or melodrama as modes, the borderland as the locale where actual and imaginary worlds can mingle, alienation and disorder as themes, and, at the end, not development and resolution but persistence of those polarities discovered in American experience" (18). Also working from Chase's influential model, Robert Winston claims that "Crèvecoeur's work *is*, in fact, a germinal romance and needs to be examined as such," for "like his nineteenth-century successors, Crèvecoeur, too, turned to the romance to explore those contradictions, to investigate both the idyllic and the demonic sides of America and thus to present his version of America's 'intermediate identity' through his representative American" (249, 264). While the term *romance* allows Stone to elevate Crèvecoeur's text to canonical status, it enables Winston to set the contending visions of the text in perfect equipoise: instead of destroying the optimistic dream, the gothic nightmare merely offsets it. Indeed, Chase's theory of the romance as two opposing strands—the idyllic dream and the melodramatic disillusionment—influences many interpretations of the text and highlights either two unreconcilable visions (as in Stone's reading) or a neutral middle ground (as in Winston's reading).[17]

The romance's binary opposition of the idyllic and the demonic might make the gothic vision of *Letters* more visible, but it also curtails that vision. By opposing the narrative's two voices instead of showing how they are integrated, critics have tended to segregate the text's gothic from its mythic discourse and hence to deny the gothic's constitutive role in the national narrative. Moreover, by following Chase in reading cultural contradictions in broad symbolic rather than social terms, critics displace history from the gothic. Stone, for instance, follows Bewley in seeing the scene of slavery as a "symbolist statement" (21). While recent assessments of *Letters* have focused much more on the way the two discourses are intertwined from the beginning of the book, they have yet to displace the oppositional romance reading.[18] In *Literature in America* (1989), Peter Conn writes that Crèvecoeur's "reports include an acknowledgment of the 'horrors of slavery' and affecting descriptions of white planter brutality," but he concludes that "for most of their length, however, De Crèvecoeur's essays render an idealized vision of the New World, offering images of peace and plenty not unlike the promotional literature of two centuries earlier" (95). Once again, the horror of slavery is recognized only to be repressed by the book's mythic vision. Norman Grabo's complaint that critics have yet to face the disillusionment of the text suggests the extent to which the gothic discourse of *Letters* continues to be recuperated and signals an anxiety about the persistent power of the text's mythic discourse (1991:160).

Indeed, even the recovery of letters (in the 1925 edition of *Sketches of Eighteenth Century America*) that were excluded by the English publisher from the final manuscript "on grounds of structural and or thematic incompatibility"—letters written during the revolution, and more critical and pessimistic in tone—has not unseated the optimistic reading of *Letters* (Putz 115). *Sketches*, as David Robinson aptly puts it, has served as *Letters*'s "shadow text" (18). With its contending voices and pessimistic, violent tone, *Sketches* highlights the gothic impulse of *Letters*; however, it has been seen as a "startling contrast" to *Letters* rather than as its logical extension

(Philbrick 1988:151).[19] Labeling six out of the seven letters in *Sketches* "narratives of atrocity," Thomas Philbrick argues that "the world that the Pine Hill manuscripts illuminate is the obverse of that which *Letters from an American Farmer* celebrates" (1976:27); Marcus Cunliffe states that "the *Sketches* make strange reading when set beside the *Letters*" (134). The latest and definitive edition of these excised letters, Dennis Moore's *More Letters from an American Farmer* (1995), may focus critical attention on the continuity of the letters, but *Letters*'s canonization as a mythic vision of America, linked as it is to an overarching structure of American literature, will not be easy to displace.

Focusing on the gothic discourse of *Letters* makes a different view of the text and, by extension, of America's literary tradition visible. When Crèvecoeur's tale of horror rather than his Enlightenment fable is taken as the starting point for an American literary tradition, a fundamentally different account of America's literary history results. With the emergence of the gothic, the cultural contradictions that haunt America's self-image but have often been critically relegated to the shadows in readings of the American literary canon come to light. Reading the gothic as the site of history and showing how the gothic scene of slavery continues to trouble the text reveals *Letters*'s national narrative to be constituted by the very contradictions its façade of self-evidence disavows. If *Letters from an American Farmer* has been the progenitor of mythic themes of American newness and innocence, it is also a useful primer on how the gothic haunts America's national narratives with the horrors of history—specifically, the specter of slavery.

2

Diseased Discourse: Charles Brockden Brown's *Arthur Mervyn*

> This city had grown ancient and fallen into ruin in two months since early August, when the first cases of fever appeared. Something in the bricks, mortar, beams and stones had gone soft, had lost its permanence.... Membranes that preserved the integrity of substances and shapes, kept each in its proper place, were worn thin. He could poke his finger through yellowed skin.... What should be separated was running together. Threatened to burst. Nothing contained the way it was supposed to be. No clear lines of demarcation. A mongrel city.... An awful void opening around him, preparing itself to hold explosions of bile, vomit, gushing bowels, ooze, sludge, seepage.
> —John Edgar Wideman, "Fever"

Like the short story "Fever,"[1] which employs the yellow fever as a metaphor for Philadelphia's social sickness, racism, Charles Brockden Brown's *Arthur Mervyn* (1800) uses the 1793 yellow fever outbreak in Philadelphia to meditate upon the social health of postrevolutionary America. Describing a city that has fallen into ruins and lost its ability to distinguish between the living and the dead, friend and stranger, sincerity and seduction, *Arthur Mervyn* warns that the new nation already suffers from a disease that leads to decay and disorder—the disease of commerce. In making this diagnosis, *Arthur Mervyn* articulates its culture's central contradiction and greatest fear: that a republic with a commercial society at its core cannot remain healthy. The Revolution had allowed America to escape the corruption of England's commercial society, but with the growth of its own capitalist economy and its reliance on the institution of slavery, the new nation soon faced a similar threat from within.

By intertwining the opposing discourses of progress and decay, *Arthur Mervyn* articulates its culture's contradictory responses to this threat. Attempting to reconcile the classical notion of a republic with the reality of its modern, commercial society, America in the 1790s was both buoyed by a liberal ideology that believed in the benefits of commerce and troubled by the vestiges of a civic republicanism that feared commerce was an infection.[2] The novel's Enlightenment narrative of progress, stability, and success argues for the benefits and civilizing influence of commerce. The novel's gothic counternarrative of disease, degeneracy, and decay warns of commerce's corrupting effects. However, by refusing to separate the sincere self-made man from the confidence man, truth from lies, hard cash from counterfeit bills, *Arthur Mervyn* collapses these narratives, confounding all distinctions between virtue and vice, health and illness. *Arthur Mervyn* horrifies precisely because it upholds the paradox that the Enlightenment narrative of good health may finally be indistinguishable from the gothic narrative of disease.

Completed during the feverish two-year period in which Brown wrote his four major gothic novels, *Arthur Mervyn* serves as an index of Brown's contradictory diagnosis of the period and his assessment of its cure: the first nine chapters of part 1 were published in serial form during the the summer of 1798, before the publication of *Wieland* (September 1798) and *Ormond* (February 1799); part 2 was published in August of 1800, almost a year after the publication of *Edgar Huntly* (August 1799).[3] Describing himself as a "story-telling moralist," Charles Brockden Brown hoped that his fiction would be useful in reforming his society ("Walstein's School," 135). As Brown states in the preface to *Arthur Mervyn*, the moral observer, who is allied with the physician, uses humble narrative to inculcate mankind with the lessons of justice and humanity. Brown writes his national narratives in the gothic form with the hope that by exposing the nation's ills his fictions will offer a cure. However, even as *Arthur Mervyn* proclaims the curative power of narrative, it delineates narrative's infectious properties. In *Arthur Mervyn*, stories do not purge disorder but liberate it; they do not tidy experience, but complicate it. Intent on reforming, not aggravating, the nation's ills, Brown retreated from his gothic fictions after *Arthur Mervyn*. Focusing on the relationship between tale-telling and well-being, this chapter examines how the novel's contending narratives encode the possibilities for the nation's health and recovery from the corruptions of commerce.

The Plague of Commerce

> The revolutionary world contained . . . the capitalist seeds of its own destruction.
> —Michael Paul Rogin, *Fathers and Children*

In August of 1793, yellow fever returned to Philadelphia for the first time in thirty years. By the end of the month, between 104 and 325 people had died; by mid-November, 10 to 15 percent of Philadelphia's population had died of the fever and 20,000 people had fled the city (Pernick 241). Decimating the nation's capital, the yellow fever seemed to give final proof of the country's degeneracy. Those fearful that the new nation was already ailing during the early 1790s found further cause for alarm in the return of this plague. In a republic that believed that individual well-being reflected the state of the body politic, the yellow fever epidemic forecast a bleak future.[4]

Because the yellow fever gave concrete form to political fears, the debate surrounding it is a useful starting point for understanding the period's various self-diagnoses. As Martin Pernick shows, the medical debate about the yellow fever divided along party lines. The Republicans, who thought that the health of the country depended on the well-being of each citizen, believed that the fever had domestic causes. The unhealthy location of the city, its stagnant sewers, and the rotting coffee on its docks were all possible sources of contamination. The Federalists, who depended on a strong immune system—the central government—to protect the republic's health, argued that the fever was a foreign disease, imported by 2,000 French refugees fleeing the black revolution in St. Domingue, who arrived in Philadelphia at the end of the summer. Each side read its own anxieties into the yellow fever. The Republicans worried that the disorder emanated from the nation's growing cities; the Federalists feared that it was transmitted by contact with contagious French revolutionaries and, by metonymic association, insurrectionary slaves. Each side advocated a different cure: the Republicans, who became associated with Dr. Benjamin Rush's revolutionary (and quite fatal) cure of bloodletting, argued for sanitary reform; the Federalists, who advocated a traditional program of stimulants such as quinine bark, wine, and cold baths, called for a quarantine to exclude French radicals and limit trade with French islands (Pernick 244). While a political compromise was reached when both solutions were initiated, the debate surrounding the yellow fever was a contest for control of the nation's character: a healthy identity made possible by purgation or by quarantine.

Arthur Mervyn participates in the ongoing debate during the 1790s about the source of the nation's ill health and its possible cure.[5] The novel opens with Doctor Stevens discovering Arthur, disabled by sickness, in the middle of fever-ridden Philadelphia. Arthur, the representative republican citizen, has had his rustic simplicity shattered by the city. He has been physically infected with yellow fever, and his simple agrarian values have been polluted by the gold fever of commerce. Begun in 1798 in the middle of a national bout of speculation that resulted in numerous defaults and insolvencies, *Arthur Mervyn* sees the fever issuing from the nation's commercial economy.[6] In the novel, yellow fever represents both social anarchy resulting from sickness and flux and breakdown brought on by mercantile revolutions. From Wortley's loss of his fortune and Carlton's imprisonment for debt to Thetford's usury and Welbeck's fraud, economic disasters and financial intrigues permeate this novel, and no character is immune to their effects. Responding to its culture's belief that the characters of the economy and the society were symbiotically related, the novel proclaims the nation severely ill.

Arthur's two entrances into the city in part 1 demonstrate that the only difference between Philadelphia's yellow fever and gold fever is one of degree: Arthur's commercial confusion is exaggerated by his illness. When Arthur first enters the city, at night, he is mesmerized by the lamps on Market Street that present the city as "a spectacle enchanting and new" (27). On his second visit, the lamps are illuminated as before, but this time he meets ghostlike figures, wrapped in cloaks and casting suspicious glances (139). The night world of spectacle and magic that symbolizes commercial Philadelphia is transformed in Arthur's second visit into a gothic underworld of phantoms and pestilence. During the outbreak of yellow fever, the commercial man is turned into a ghost: Arthur finds Wallace looking like an "apparition of the dead" and Welbeck to be a specter returned from the grave (166, 191). The shadowy world of the slave economy is also made manifest during the fever. As Bill Christophersen has shown, blacks appear frequently during the yellow fever sections as hearsedrivers and servants, their wellness an insurrectionary warning (104–5).[7] The yellow fever scenes also unveil the city's dependence on black labor. The fever, then, materializes the phantoms that already exist in the commercial world. The commercial man, who in manipulating money seemingly fashions himself out of nothing, is an apparition; the urban marketplace, dependent on black labor, is metonymically connected to the slave economy; the commercial city, which works by magic and appearance, is already a gothic underworld.

Even before the yellow fever, the degenerate world of the city is described in gothic terms. Full of secrecy and suspicion, coincidence and complexity, the commercial city operates like a gothic realm as it turns appearance into reality. The gothic villain of this apparitional world is Welbeck, the economic man. Serving as a sorcerer, a grand manipulator of money, Welbeck signifies the commodified self: a fluid social persona produced through a series of transactional performances. Just as he converts worthless paper into a fortune through counterfeiting, Welbeck coins himself as a personage of opulence and rank by hiding his past and forging a fictional identity. For Welbeck, reputation—public credit—replaces all private value. Representing in his aristocratic Englishness the vices of a fully developed commercial society—rampant individualism, speculative wealth, indolence, sensual excess—Welbeck embodies both the degenerate past that the nation has fled and the corruption that haunts its future.

If the commercial world is associated with the gothic, so are the narratives it produces. Throughout *Arthur Mervyn*, the twin paper revolutions of credit and printing are conflated. People tell tales to earn credit for their character and writing is implicated in commercial transactions: the Carltons make their living by the pen, "binding fast the bargains which others made," and Wortley warns Stevens that fortunes may be demolished by "four strokes of a pen" (261, 227). In the commercial world, stories and money are both fictions that circulate without stable referents, earning credit through exchange. The meaning of the tale, like the value of paper money, is only an agreed-upon fiction. Writing in the commercial society is also associated with illness. The artist figures in the book are associated with the commodified self and are also disfigured or ill: Welbeck, who plots to plagiarize a text, has a maimed hand; Clavering, an actor who is skillful with a pencil, dies of fever. Moreover, the novel constantly remarks that writing's sedentary labor is unhealthy. Writing and storytelling, then, are not only economic activities in the novel but also potential carriers of disease.

The gothic's narrative devices of secrecy and dissimulation underwrite speculation and credit in the commercial world. Welbeck, whose narratives obscure rather than reveal, depends on silence and an empty eloquence to earn him the wealth he already claims. Welbeck enjoins Arthur to conceal his knowledge about his past, since Welbeck can only continue to reproduce himself if his stories cannot be traced. Like money, his life story gains credit by circulating. Whereas secrecy encourages an endless series of speculations, exposure short-circuits that process; Arthur's exposure of Welbeck's story, which "shut[s] every avenue to [his] return to honor," not the loss of money, finally kills Welbeck (259). Welbeck *is* the tale he tells.

Like a gothic text, which is spun out of a secret and consists of a series of narratives rather than a single story, Welbeck's life-story depends not on mimesis but on multiplicity.

This correlation between gothic narrative and commercial society is not particular to *Arthur Mervyn*. Historically, the gothic novel arose in the eighteenth century from an emerging market economy and not only facilitated the consolidation of a middle-class identity, but also was itself highly commercialized. As Andrea Henderson shows, its repetitive and superficial form exposes the workings of the commercial economy. Making "character a matter of surface, display, and 'consumption' by others," the gothic novel records a market-based model of identity (Henderson 226). Working by coincidence and repetition, the gothic novel presents a world that functions relationally, accruing value through external signs rather than intrinsic identity. The gothic novel's self-referentiality, exemplified by its complicated tissue of texts, produces a reality from appearance rather than concrete referents. In its narrative form, then, the gothic novel reconfigures what creates it: the phantasmic world of the market.

In part 1, the conflation of commerce, narrative, disease, and the gothic is exemplified by the tale of Lodi. Welbeck first meets Lodi, a French-speaking Italian, by chance on the street. Dying of yellow fever, Lodi tells Welbeck his story and then bequeaths him money and a manuscript to give to his sister, Clemenza. The money comes from the sale of his father's estate in Guadeloupe, where Lodi's father has been killed by one of his slaves. The manuscript, written in Italian, is a family memoir of the Ducal House of Visconti. Welbeck, who is on the brink of suicide when he meets young Lodi, is revived by this mission. Turning himself into Clemenza's guardian, he appropriates both the money and the manuscript, deciding to claim authorship of the work by translating and expanding it and then publishing it under his own name. Eager for literary fame and opulence, Welbeck gains both credit and credibility from Lodi.

This substory exemplifies many of the novel's obsessive themes. First, it equates money and words, showing them to function similarly. Like money that is easily stolen, the written word is easily disassociated from its author and reappropriated for another's use. The detachable nature of words makes them, like money, prone to corruption. Second, the scene associates this corruption with the mysterious transmissions that occur in a gothic text. An ancient Italian narrative transported across time and space, and undergoing translation, Lodi's manuscript resembles a gothic novel with no verifiable origin and a suspect purity. Third, the story argues that words, like money, are diseased: both issue from yellow fever. Finally, the substory associates that disease not just with a market economy but with the specific commercial activity of slavery.

Indeed, slavery haunts the economic activities of the entire novel. Welbeck's commercial venture, which intersects many of the novel's subplots, is deeply implicated in slavery: the ship in which he has invested is captured by the British because two French mulattoes were carrying contraband on the vessel. We later learn that the ship's captain, a man named Watson, is returning from St. Domingo (in one version of the story) or Jamaica (in another version) with bills of exchange from selling a friend's estate there.[8] This scene—the loss of an American ship to the British because of the treachery of the French and blacks—harbors the nation's many contradictory anxieties: the fear of becoming economically degenerate like the British, of losing the commercial competition with England, of French revolutionaries and the contagion of liberty, of the competition a newly emancipated France might offer for America's foreign markets, and of slave insurrection that not only sends diseased money into the American economy but that might also, if it occurs domestically, destroy America's commercial society from within. While the novel consistently displaces discussion of the nation's domestic economy onto the international scene, the specter of slavery lurks in every economic transaction. Money from slave societies ubiquitously circulates to America, revealing America's international and domestic economic dependence on slavery. This money, tainted by disease and issuing from destruction, makes suspect the foundations of the American economy. As David Brion Davis argues, slavery contradicted the early republic's liberal commercial model: "The entire rhetoric of liberalism reassured individuals that their own true freedom could not run counter to the best interests of anyone else; but the connection between slavery and economic success dramatized contradictions in the very meaning of liberty" (1975:85–86). In the tale of Lodi, slavery threatens to destroy the nation in contradictory ways: its commerce is figured as corrupting, yet its interruption by slave revolt is even more frightening. Slavery, like commerce in general, threatens to undermine the nation through both its success and its failure.

The transmission of Lodi's manuscript and money to Arthur in the second half of part 1 reveals how seriously infected Arthur has become by the commercial contagion of the city. The contagion begins when Welbeck hires Arthur as his amanuensis. When Arthur does not get a chance to work on the Lodi manuscript in the city, he takes it with him to the country and begins translating it for his own edification. As he works on the gothic tale of Italian banditti who discover treasure while hiding in a tomb, Arthur himself finds $20,000 glued into the leaves of the book. Arthur sets out for the city to return the money to Clemenza, whom he decides is the rightful owner, only to run into Welbeck again. In the penultimate scene in part 1, Arthur, sick with yellow fever in Welbeck's bedroom, burns the money, believing Welbeck's story that it is actually counterfeit. Welbeck then tells him that the notes were genuine; "the tale of their forgery was false" (210).

As this scene dissolves any distinction between the counterfeit and the real, it collapses the difference between evil and benevolence. Through a series of reversals, Arthur's good intentions become analogous to Welbeck's evil plots. To begin with, Arthur is the one who is sick in this scene; he threatens to infect Welbeck, who stays to minister to him. Moreover, in trying to protect Clemenza from the evils of counterfeit money, he denies her, as did Welbeck, her inheritance. His benevolent act—to return sound money to a rightful owner—seems, as Welbeck states, not only ridiculous but also criminal in a commercial world: as a representative fiction, money is already counterfeit; unlike property, it has no rightful owner, only a current possessor; and it is useless unless it circulates. By burning the money, Arthur denies both Clemenza and society its potentially beneficial effects. In a world that operates by appearance, not truth, motives do not matter—only their effects.

Arthur's good intentions not only short-circuit the commercial economy but also come to replicate it. His commercial fantasies mirror Welbeck's actual transactions. Imagining that his resemblance to young Lodi will make Clemenza fall in love with him, Arthur dreams of the wealth he will secure through marriage. Arthur's sentimental story looks like Welbeck's gothic plot: where Welbeck seduces Clemenza by acting as her guardian and steals her money, Arthur would seduce her into marrying him by acting as her brother and thus inherit the money. Arthur's translation of the Lodi text also mirrors Welbeck's plans for plagiarizing it. While Arthur claims the translation to be only the "business" of his "leisure" and a profit to his mind, he actualizes Welbeck's fantasy, gaining money from his work (125). Despite his intentions, Arthur's actions are deeply rooted in the commercial economy. His success in manipulating the market, however, is as problematic as his failure since it signals the corruption of the agrarian man by commerce. Arthur represents the nation's double bind: the need for both a successful commercial economy and for freedom from corruption.

The work of part 2 is to find a solution to this dilemma in the form of a commercial republicanism. Before Arthur can be purged of his commercial corruption, however, he must return to a proper narrative form, for if the city has infected his character, it has also debased his language. "When the night is remembered," Arthur muses, "how like a vision will it appear. If I tell the tale by a kitchen fire, my veracity will be disputed. I shall be ranked with the story tellers of Shirauz and Bagdad" (35). The night world of the city has taught Arthur a language that operates through concealment and multiplicity rather than disclosure and mimesis, and threatens to undermine not only the economic health of the nation but also its linguistic foundations. In a nation created through an act of verbal fiat—a *declaration* of independence—and founded through print, language played a powerful role in the credibility of the national identity. Since language was perceived to be organically connected to the workings of postrevolutionary American society, the corruption of the nation's language, like its economic excess, could also threaten national stability.[9] As the bearer of the nation's political, economic, and linguistic identity, Arthur, the citizen yeoman, must be economically healthy and must also speak a stable language grounded in simplicity, self-evidence, and sincerity.

To rid Arthur of commerce's corruptions, Doctor Stevens prescribes a cure similar to Republican bloodletting: the catharsis of tale-telling. By confessing his youthful errors in a simple, self-evident tale, Arthur will credit his character. Against Welbeck's poisonous prescription of secrecy, Stevens offers Arthur its antidote—disclosure. By relearning Stevens's self-evident language, a discourse of facts and truth, Arthur can be restored to a world that operates by science, not magic; that believes that the self is stable and that language reflects its referent; a world, in short, where the gaping gothic hole between reality and appearance has been closed. Adhering to the "moral treatment" that gained ascendancy in the 1790s from the age's optimism in reform and that urged patients to minister to themselves and form internal self-control, Stevens believes that he can restore Arthur to good health through narrative.[10] Seeing storytelling as a way to institute order and create virtue, instead of as a carrier of disease, Stevens is optimistic about the efficacy of language.[11] Against Welbeck's gothic narrative, which is not only associated with the market but also a carrier of its diseases, Stevens offers an Enlightenment narrative of good health.

Having taken Stevens's cure, Arthur can claim to "have been restored to life and to health" at the end of part 1 (214). In fact, Arthur's recovery seems so successful that Stevens plans to fit him for the "practice of physic" (220).

Stevens's belief in Arthur's well-being, however, relies on not a reasoned diagnosis but a leap of faith. Instead of examining his patient, Stevens simply trusts Arthur's own proclamation of good health. Stevens makes this leap of faith because of his large investment in Arthur's recovery; if Stevens cannot trust Arthur's artless tale and wholesome appearance, then he too will fall into Welbeck's gothic world. "If Mervyn has deceived me," Stevens proclaims, "there is an end to my confidence in human nature. All limits to dissimulation, and all distinction between vice and virtue will be effaced" (248–49); the entire republican experiment will be doomed to failure.[12]

The question of Arthur's recovery is also central to the critical debate about *Arthur Mervyn*. The novel offers two conflicting readings of Arthur: he is either cured by Stevens, become once again a stable citizen who serves public virtue, acts by reason, and speaks a self-evident language, or he remains infected with Welbeck's gothic world view, an economic man who serves private interest, is ruled by passion, and spreads a diseased discourse. While the novel leaves the question of Arthur's recovery ambiguous, the critical debate tends to try to make sense of its contradictions by reducing the novel to a single discourse: Arthur, as America, is either healthy or unhealthy.[13] The critical debate, however, depends on a dichotomy that the novel proposes and then subverts. Ultimately, the novel argues that the difference between health and infection does not depend upon material well-being but on how that well-being is credited. By showing that the Enlightenment narrative, like the gothic, is constituted by the commercial and operates by credit, *Arthur Mervyn* collapses the difference between confidence and contagion, making the Enlightenment narrative of good health indistinguishable from the gothic narrative of disease. Whereas in *Letters from an American Farmer* the gothic disturbed the Enlightenment narrative, in *Arthur Mervyn* it threatens to dismantle it altogether.

Tainted Tales

> He has told a tale, that had all the appearances of truth—
> —Charles Brockden Brown, *Edgar Huntly*

Part 2, which begins "here ended the narrative of Mervyn," has been read as problematic (218). If Mervyn's narrative is complete, why is part 2 necessary? And why does it begin by offering an ending, yet delay closure for two hundred pages until Mervyn finally decides to put down his pen? If part 1 has chronicled the fall and rise of Arthur Mervyn through his contamination and cure, then what role does part 2 serve, besides example of Brown's excess? Critics like Jane Tompkins and Norman Grabo read part 2 as the Enlightenment cure to part 1's gothic malady.[14] If part 1 depicts an abject world that brims with bile and operates through secrecy, then part 2 describes a clean and proper world that overflows with benevolence and is based on openness; if in part 1 Arthur answers to Welbeck's orders, in part 2 he follows Stevens's prescriptions. The novel, then, seems to move from disorder to order as Arthur returns from sickness to health.

As Arthur circulates in part 2, returning bills of exchange and telling his story, he seems the model of financial and narrative health. Economically, he represents the liberal ideal of commercial republicanism which, believing the market to be based on Enlightenment principles, trusted that commerce could lead to progressive and virtuous ends.[15] The self-regulating individual operating in the market would naturally stimulate a harmony of interests beneficial to all. Self-interest would lead to the public good; individual freedom would generate prosperity. If the market had a moral base in the individual, then, it would operate by the law of virtue. Purged not of commerce but of its corruptions, Arthur does not return to the farm but continues to operate in the marketplace; however, instead of spreading contagion he dispenses benevolence. He returns money to its rightful owners, serves as the protector of several women, and tells truthful tales that fill in gaps. In part 2, Arthur seems to symbolize the social ethic of the self-made individual. Instead of rejecting commerce, he sees his fall as fortunate: "My knowledge of Welbeck has been useful to me. It has enabled me to be useful to others. I look back upon that allotment of my destiny which first led me to his door, with gratitude and pleasure" (357–58). Part 2, then, seems to be an advertisement for commerce's civilizing and beneficial effects.

However, part 2 suggests an opposing reading: the Enlightenment narrative of economic good health continues to be haunted by the gothic narrative of commercial corruption. Not only has the fever spread to the countryside in the form of disease and commerce (the Hadwin farm is mortgaged and Arthur's father's farm has been sold to finance a land speculation scheme), but Arthur, despite his intentions, finds himself hopelessly entangled in and infected by the commercial economy. Arthur might optimistically argue that he is immune to the vicissitudes of his environment, but part 2 shows that he is still contaminated: "My spirits were high, and I saw nothing in the world before me but sunshine and prosperity. I was conscious that my happiness depended not on the revolutions of nature or the caprice of man. All without was, indeed, vicissitude and uncertainty; but within my bosom was a centre not to be shaken or removed. My purposes were honest and steadfast" (312). Arthur's refrain in part 2—"I come to confer a benefit not perpetrate an injury"—reveals the way benevolence and evil continue to be indistinguishable in the second half of the novel (319). Intending to do good, Arthur spreads destruction: he might be honest and steadfast, but the society he operates in is not. Whether Arthur acts as a well-intentioned citizen or a confidence man, he still passes on pestilence. By showing that the individual, despite his virtue, is ruled by the market, part 2 does not outline a movement from illness to health but further collapses their distinction, revealing the commercial defense of liberal republicanism to be untenable: rather than operating by rational principles, the marketplace is a gothic underworld full of corruption and disorder.

In part 2, Arthur takes two journeys: the first to the countryside to check on the Hadwins and Clemenza and the second to Baltimore to return Watson's money. As he travels through the country and from house to house, he resembles a gothic wanderer who brings destruction and death. In scene after scene, Arthur breaks into a house intending to do good, only to bring death. Entering three abject realms on his first journey—the fever-infested farmhouse, the whorehouse, and the debtor's prison—Arthur is either impotent to cure disease or he hastens its progression: mistaking Arthur for her fiancé Wallace, Susan Hadwin, who is already emaciated from the fever, "[sinks] upon the floor without signs of life" (274); breaking into Mrs. Villar's house, Arthur discovers Clemenza "sickly and pale," and watches her infant die (324); finding Welbeck a "monument of ruin," Arthur is accused of being the author of his miseries (335). At the very best, Arthur's benevolence is thwarted by a diseased world that runs on money, not good intentions, and on duplicity rather than sincerity. Arthur wants to save Clemenza from the whorehouse, but he has no money to give her for another house; he wants to point out the path of honor and safety to her through his tale, but they do not speak the same language. He wants to bring Susan a nondefective tale about Wallace, but he cannot discover Wallace's whereabouts or predict that Susan will mistake him for Wallace. In a commercial world where all actions are embedded in a web of exchange, Arthur has no control over the outcome of his intentions. The doubling that haunted Arthur in part 1 (his resemblance to Clavering and young Lodi) and signified his status as a commercial, serial self is further exaggerated in part 2 as he becomes the ghostly representative of other characters. Arthur shows that even if the self is stable—which is highly uncertain in Arthur's case since he is ruled by passion—it cannot regulate the marketplace, which constantly disrupts that self and its intentions.

Despite his motives, then, Arthur serves in part 2 as the agent of disruption and the carrier of diseased discourse.[16] Arthur's second journey emphasizes the disorderly and destructive operations of the market. Having received Watson's bills of exchange from Welbeck on his deathbed, along with Welbeck's instructions to return them to their rightful owners, Arthur heads off to Baltimore. His second journey, however, is no more successful than his first. His good intentions have ill effects: Mrs. Watson shrieks and swoons upon being told of Watson's death and her children run around the room terrified; Mrs. Maurice responds to Arthur's news by crying, "O! I am sick; sick to death" (381). Once again, Arthur is turned into an apparition. Hoping to locate Mrs. Watson's house the following day, Arthur terrifies her black slave when she sees him in the window. He may mean to proceed cautiously and openly with Mrs. Watson, but he ends up acting impulsively and appearing secretive. After he leaves Mrs. Watson, he states, "I had started up before this woman as if from the pores of the ground. I had vanished with the same celerity, but had left her in possession of proofs sufficient that I was neither spectre nor demon" (375). This claim is yet another example of the spectral nature of credit. As the apparition that appears out of nowhere to aid or destroy and whose proof of existence lies only in bills of exchange, Arthur symbolizes commercial society. His constant intrusions upon private property and his insistence that people listen to his story show Arthur's alliance with a market society that insists on exchange, no matter how disruptive, and that obeys no rules.

Arthur's inability to control the market realm he represents is especially evident in his visit to the Maurice home. Taken to be a creditor, Arthur is shut out of the house. Only after he breaks in and makes clear that he is Watson's representative is he allowed to speak with Mrs. Maurice. Even then he is suspiciously questioned about the papers' origins and his role in Watson's embezzlement plot. Arthur is treated as the market representative that he is: the disruptive force that has more likely come to collect money than to distribute it. Serving as Eliza's representative in part 2 when he helps to place her in another home, and as Clemenza's when he asks Achsa Fielding to supply her with the means of subsistence through him, Arthur is not an agent but a conduit and messenger; like money, he is only the bearer, not the owner, of value. Hence, he cannot control his own value, which is produced through exchange. In some cases, as with Mrs. Watson, who invites him into her house and with whom he feels an "electrical sympathy," he may be pleased with the exchange; in others, as with Mrs. Maurice, who distrusts him, he may not: "I expected to witness the tears of gratitude and the caresses of affection. What had I found? Nothing but sordidness, stupidity, and illiberal suspicion" (374, 382). Moreover, he cannot regulate whether the money he delivers will be used virtuously or not. Mrs. Watson's humble home will be benefited whereas the Maurice's luxurious house will not be favorably changed; the money will not improve, and indeed might worsen, the mother's character. Instead of raising the Maurices from a level of indigence as he did the Watsons, Arthur has only conferred pleasure upon them. Unregulated exchange, then, is not necessarily beneficial.

The problem of how to control commerce's corrupting effects continues to trouble part 2. As the means of commercial exchange, Arthur cannot remain unpolluted: part 2 insists that there is no way to participate in the commercial economy without becoming corrupt. Arthur's continued allegiance to Welbeck in part 2 emphasizes his contamination. It is Welbeck, not Stevens, who in a deathbed conversion instructs Arthur to return Watson's money. Given Welbeck's suspect advice in part 1 as well as his counterfeit bills, Arthur's benevolence issues from a contaminated source: by making restorations with bills of exchange from Welbeck, Arthur could be circulating counterfeit money. Moreover, by setting out on his journey immediately after Welbeck's death, Arthur serves as Welbeck's representative in part 2, disseminating his money and doing his bidding. The source as well as the benefit of Arthur's benevolence seems suspect at best.

The scene of Arthur's departure to Baltimore in a stagecoach further underscores the contamination of his journey. Traveling with "a sallow Frenchman from Saint Domingo, his fiddle-case, an ape, and two female blacks," Arthur begins his journey south (370). Associated with yellow fever and revolution as well as slavery, Arthur's traveling companions represent the specters of commercial corruption. Once again, the domestic corruption of slavery is given an international face. Arthur spends time indulging his scientific racism by differentiating the features of his "*four* companions" before looking outside at the country (370). However, as the journey unfolds and Arthur enters two slave-owning households, his ability to demarcate breaks down. The international problem becomes domestic as Arthur, operating as his own one-man revolution, infuses money into a slave society. The contrast between Mrs. Watson's slave, treated as part of the family, and Mrs. Maurice's slaves, treated with contempt, marks a difference between a viable and a corrupt slave society only to collapse it: Arthur gives money to the luxurious and corrupt slave plantation as well as to the humble home. Once circulated, money cannot be controlled; the corruptions of the slave economy spread throughout the entire system, implicating the North as well as the South.

In part 2, then, Arthur is no longer merely infected with commerce's corruption, but actively dispersing it. Whereas in part 1 he was duped into intruding in other people's houses, in part 2 he breaks into them. Whereas in part 1 he was unwilling to circulate Welbeck's bills, in part 2 he liberally disseminates them. Whether Arthur circulates money for benevolent or selfish ends, he finally cannot regulate its effects. The question of Arthur's private virtue is not the issue, for even if the republican citizen is not a powder keg of passion, egotism, and self-interest, the market society within which he functions operates in these terms. If part 2 shows that commerce is always contaminated, it also insists that any individual who lives in the plague world is necessarily sick: one cannot participate in commerce and remain immune to its corruptions.

Discourse is also diseased in part 2. Arthur may claim to be the spokesman for a self-evident language when he argues that an "honest front and a straight story will be sufficient" and tries to reform his incoherent and imperfect tales from part 1, but he actually spreads a diseased and disruptive discourse (349). Like the tale of the yellow fever, which makes its hearer grow pale and temporarily indisposed, Arthur's tales have bodily effects: Watson's wife, for instance, faints after hearing of her husband's death, and Welbeck dies after exposure to Arthur's life-story. Like Eliza's letter, which infects Arthur with her own sadness, his tales contaminate his listeners. By telling Stevens his tale, he draws the doctor into a complicated web of commercial transactions, just as Welbeck's story drew Arthur: Stevens must decide what to do with his knowledge of Watson's death. Moreover, Arthur's excessive openness in part 2—he is not only "willing but eager to communicate" his story—replicates the disruption it aims to eradicate (260). As he breaks into house after house accosting people with his tale, Arthur's "unaccountable behaviour" and "singular language" break ordinary rules and make him look mad: "Your language and ideas are those of a lunatic," Mrs. Wentworth states (319, 362). Instead of bringing enlightenment, Arthur's discourse, which looks unstable and unaccountable, is not credited; his innocent brow and voluble tongue are as suspect as his former secrecy. Indeed, throughout part 2 Arthur's excessive speech appears to be merely the obverse of his secrecy. As Arthur's simple and artless tale burgeons into a "long and various" account, his virtuous disclosure comes to resemble the market world's diseased discourse (260).

Arthur's narrative is constantly challenged and discredited in part 2 by contending tales. Stevens gets a different version of Arthur's agrarian origins from one of the Mervyns' neighbors, Mrs. Althorpe. She tells him that Arthur was idle, had illicit "commerce" with his father's second wife, stole his father's money, and ran away to the city (236). In Mrs. Althorpe's version, Arthur's past resembles that of Welbeck, who also was idle, seduced a woman, and ran away with her money to the city to create himself anew. Arthur attempts to counter this version of his childhood with a truthful tale. However, his tale, which tries to account for his motives, operates by the logic of the market world rather than the rules of self-evidence. In telling Stevens repeatedly "it is true" that he hated school and took up the spade and the hoe rarely, but explaining "these were my motives," Arthur espouses Stevens's doctrine of self-evidence, based on fact and truth: if he can only make his motives clear, then their effects will be properly understood (341–42). However, even as it attempts to make a stable connection between motive and effect, his narrative reveals their radical disjuncture. The very need to produce a counternarrative shows that the world does not operate by self-evidence but credit, since the same facts produce very different versions of reality. In a world of appearance where motive and effect are disjoined, Arthur's efforts to relocate reference not only appear singular and strange, but also replicate the very disjuncture they hope to heal. Arguing that "it was not me whom they hated and despised" but "the phantom that passed under my name, which existed only in their imagination," Arthur relies on the logic of the market world to regain his credit: he must paradoxically double himself in order to reclaim a stable identity (340). Arthur's narrative also multiplies as it proclaims its truthful status; as the narrative form of part 2 exemplifies, the closer Arthur's story seems to approach the truth, the more it appears to be produced.

The structural change between part 1 and part 2—a movement from relative order to disorder—encodes the increased commercial infection in the novel's own narrative form. Part 1, which consists of a series of framed narratives—Welbeck's tale nested within Arthur's, which is enclosed within Stevens's—immediately calls into question the "simplicity" and "straightforwardness" of Arthur's tale. However, even though it proliferates into many tales, part 1 remains coherent since it is controlled by Stevens's framing perspective. Serving as the narrator of the frame tale, Stevens stands as the last teller in the chain of transmissions; he subsumes Welbeck's gothic narrative within his Enlightenment frame and stems its infections. In part 2, the tale-telling structure is horizontal, not vertical. Lacking a controlling perspective, part 2 consists of competing and conflicting reports; instead of nicely contained tales, it is composed of an episodic plot that contagiously replicates itself; instead of a single teller and a single listener, it abounds with listeners and tellers; instead of being told in one sitting, Arthur's story is related in bits and pieces; instead of talking face to face, Arthur resorts to writing his story in a letter. By foregrounding the mediated, fragmented, and conflicted nature of Arthur's tale, part 2 exposes what remains relatively hidden in part 1: the suspect foundations of Arthur's self-evident tale.[17]

Paradoxically, even as the text proclaims its self-evident status, it unveils its Welbeckian operations: the closer the text comes to its origins, the more unstable it becomes. Part 2 careens out of control precisely when Stevens's authorial perspective drops out of the text. Midway through part 2, as Arthur sets off on his journey to Baltimore, he picks up Stevens's thread, writing what remains of his story in a letter to Stevens. Instituting *Arthur* as the text's *author* shatters the novel's consistent point of view and undermines its authority. Since Arthur takes up Stevens's thread when he sets out on his journey as Welbeck's representative, the narrative becomes implicated in commerce's corruptions: the text, like the market, has no stable foundation but instead consists of a series of transactions. The final turn of the screw, however, occurs when Arthur's letter to Stevens breaks off with a long dash, unmasking Arthur as the author behind the entire text, not just sections of part 2. As the novel opens out to the present, the reader learns that it is the written narrative of Arthur's life that Mrs. Wentworth requested, and that therefore the entire story flows from Arthur's pen. Just as Welbeck plans to revise Lodi's narrative and make it his own, Arthur edits and adds to his life-story, which has already been written down by Stevens: "Luckily, my friend Stevens has saved me more than half the trouble," Arthur writes, "He has done me the favor to compile much of my history with his own hand.... It has saved me a world of writing. I had only to take up the broken thread, and bring it down to the period of my present happiness" (412). Our text is not Stevens's account of Arthur's story but Arthur's version of Stevens's written narrative of Arthur's oral autobiography. In a neat reversal, as Cathy Davidson points out, Stevens becomes Arthur's scribe just as Arthur was once Welbeck's (244). Moreover, Stevens and Arthur inscribe each other.

With the revelation of Arthur's authorship, the credibility of the text is undermined. By disclosing its true author, the text would seem to unveil its origin and claim a self-evident status; however, by exposing its many layers the text reveals its own mediated and fictional nature.[18] The text invalidates its own claims to mimesis by reminding the reader that the tale we have been reading is a representation of reality, a written version of Arthur's life. Moreover, in revealing that Arthur, like Welbeck, has literally become the tale he tells, the novel exposes its own lack of foundation: its author is a fictional character, and Arthur's disclosure of his authorship exposes the novel's continued connection to a commercial world where words can be detached from authors, character is produced by a tale, and truth is merely a function of credit. The dash that ends Arthur's manuscript and connects the novel to the present, then, symbolizes the disjuncture that the text has been trying unsuccessfully to heal: the gaping gothic hole between appearance and reality.

Arthur's disclosure of the text's secret underscores how his entire narrative has been tainted by a gothic discourse of secrecy and appearance. Arthur's words have hidden a secret even when they have seemed to disclose all. The last, gothic scene of part 1, which takes place right before Arthur's declaration of good health, calls into question both his truthful tale and his assertion of wellness, and exposes the commercial connections between disclosure and secrecy. After describing his ascent into the dark recesses of Welbeck's attic, Arthur ends his narrative with another dash, telling Stevens "there is nothing which I more detest, than equivocation and mystery. . . . I would willingly escape the accusation, but confess that I am hopeless of escaping it" (212–13). Instead of omitting the scene, Arthur confesses both that he is keeping a secret and that he cannot escape it. His disclosure not only fails to reveal the truth but also emphasizes his enthrallment to secrecy; it shows the hole in his narrative and argues that the narrative can never be made whole. Moreover, his confession exposes how the excessive disclosures of part 2 might conceal as easily as they reveal. The gothic hole that concludes part 1, then, undermines Arthur's claim to a consistent story even before the conflicting tales of part 2, since he continues to practice Welbeck's diseased discourse under the cover of Stevens's self-evident cure.

By showing that disclosure produces another tale rather than a truth, the story of the secret rather than the secret itself, this scene exposes the fictional and commercial foundations of Stevens's self-evident discourse. In this scene, disclosure earns Arthur's story credit and interest. By sacrificing the secret of the mystery, if not the mystery itself, Arthur hopes to convince Stevens that his story is sincere; by tantalizing the listener with his open secret, Arthur creates interest in his narrative: "the interval, though short, and the scrutiny, though hasty," Arthur says, "furnished matter which my curiosity devoured with unspeakable eagerness, and from which consequences may hereafter flow, deciding on my peace and my life" (213). Arthur's confession does not bring closure to part 1 but acts as an advertisement for part 2, which promises to make his narrative whole. The excesses of part 2, however, represent the endless narratives that can be spun from such a secret. While part 2 does not make anything further of this particular secret, it is constantly exposing the holes in Arthur's narrative in part 1. Arthur's revelation is simply another hole that demands yet another round of interpretation. Part 2, like the entire novel, is a commercial narrative that gains credit through circulation rather than closure.

The gothic moment at the end of part 1, which exposes the void in Arthur's tale, is emblematic of the commercial operations of the entire novel. The novel might aspire to the self-evident performativity of the Enlightenment narrative, but by constantly foregrounding the way its performance is produced, it unveils the gothic hole at the center. The Enlightenment narrative keeps secret what the gothic one discloses: that any narrative operating in the commercial world has no stronger foundation than credit. Stevens's confidence is merely a leap of faith over the gothic void that exposes this fact. By refusing to veil the gothic disjuncture between appearance and reality, *Arthur Mervyn* may fail to achieve its cure, but by continuing to circulate it gains credit. Arthur's narrative finally is not an integrated tale of good health but a commercial account pockmarked with holes.

If *Arthur Mervyn* begins by espousing a faith in reform, then it concludes by arguing for skepticism. Given the corruptions of the commercial world, the nation and its narratives will remain diseased. Indeed, the novel presents an even more alarming diagnosis of Arthur's ailments. Not a localized infection, Arthur's sickness is genetic; he belongs to a race "whose existence some inherent property has limited to the short space of twenty years" (135). Since "the seeds of an early and lingering death are sown in [his] constitution," even if he is cured of yellow fever, he is "unalterably fated to perish by *consumption*" (135). The new republic also carries the commercial seeds of its own destruction. Haunted by the corruption at its core—the specter of slavery—the nation, the novel warns, may not outlive its youth.

The novel's conclusion, a love story, shows that the novel's troubling revelations will not be put to rest. The sentimental world might seem to offer the healing salve of love and marriage, but it too operates by the rules of the market. In seeing Achsa as a substitute for his mother, and in only being able to imagine loving a copy of her, Arthur reveals his love to be not authentic but illusory: he does not love Achsa herself but her representation. Marriage, which the novel describes as a "contract awful and irrevocable," can provide Arthur first and foremost with money; he asks, "Has she property? Is she rich?" before "Has she virtue?" (297). However, Achsa's money, like her virtue, is tainted. Arthur meets her in a whorehouse, and she is a "mother but not a wife" (360). Moreover, her money is suspect: what she inherits from her father, a Portuguese Jew, most likely issued from the slave trade, and much of it was lost through speculation.[19] Described by Stevens as "a foreigner: independent of controul, and rich," she represents the old age of Europe's commercial economy and the contagion of its many revolutions: at twenty-five she is considerably older than Arthur, who at eighteen is the same age as the new republic; she is associated with commercial revolutions through her father and with the contagion of liberty through her former husband, a French revolutionary (432). Love further involves Arthur in the vagaries of the commercial world. At the end of the novel, when Arthur states that his love has "infected [him] with these unworthy terrors," love is represented as yet another carrier of disease; it increases rather than allays his fears (445).

The novel does not conclude on a note of confidence. Arthur's dream that Achsa's husband has come back from the dead to kill him haunts his rosy picture of their future, and Achsa can only provisionally hope that their happiness "may be so" (445). The novel's repressive final move—to disarm Arthur of his disruptive discourse—marks the ending's skepticism. The difficulty that Arthur has in abjuring his pen parallels the difficulty of the novel's own closure: "Lie there, snug in thy leathern case, till I call for thee, and that will not be very soon. I believe I will abjure thy company till all is settled with my love. Yes: I *will* abjure thee, so let *this* be thy last office, till Mervyn has been made the happiest of men" (446). The novel concludes by forcibly enacting the closure that has been deferred. Like the nation, which by instituting the Sedition Act in 1798 defensively opted to ward off language's potentially anarchic effects instead of trusting its reformative powers, the novel concludes by curtailing the disruptive discourse that proliferates in part 2.[20] Seeing language as diseased and disruptive, as equally capable of destroying the nation and reforming it, the novel, like its culture, retreats from its initial cure. Silence, not storytelling, is the text's final prescription.

The Return to Repression

Brown brought the gothic novel to America and abandoned it.
— Paul Witherington, "Benevolence and the 'Utmost Stretch'"

Although *Arthur Mervyn* never unmasks its real author, Charles Brockden Brown, it serves as a self-reflexive meditation on Brown's own tale-telling. *Arthur Mervyn* comes to the same conclusion as Brown's other gothic novels: that language itself is diseased and partakes in, rather than purges, disorder. By exposing the corruptions of the novel's form and its circulation within the commercial economy, *Arthur Mervyn* diagnoses the dis-ease of American culture without offering a cure. *Arthur Mervyn* not only fails to reform society but even threatens to destroy it altogether; by unveiling the illusory foundations of the Enlightenment narrative, Brown's gothic narrative threatens to undermine the nation's stability.

Brown retreats from this revelation—that his narratives might be subverting rather than reforming his society—in horror at the end of the century. Finding language to be a force for revolution instead of restoration, a commercially corrupting instead of a purifying agent, Brown turns to the more comforting and publicly sanctioned genres of sentimentalism, pamphleteering, and historical fiction.[21] By 1803, Brown rejects his fictional tales altogether: "I have written much, but take much blame to myself for something which I have written, and take no praise for any thing. I should enjoy a larger share of my own respect, at the present moment," he writes, "if nothing had ever flowed from my pen, the production of which could be traced to me" ("Editor's Address," 4). Like the skeptical doctor figures—Mr. Cambridge in *Wieland* and Saresfield in *Edgar Huntly*, both of whom speak for repression rather than reform—Brown attempts to repress his earlier diseased discourse.[22] With the end of *Arthur Mervyn*, Brown begins the new century not confidently cured of his gothic fears, but conservatively containing them.

However, just as Brown's endings seem to present cures yet ultimately offer only uneasy remissions from disease—Clara begins a new life in Europe only to face the terrors of the French Revolution, Clithero drowns but may have swum to safety, Arthur may marry but has not yet—Brown's own act of repression is not complete. His critical reputation credits the very thing he wants to repress: his gothic fictions. Brown may attempt to move from Welbeck's to Stevens's camp, but as with Arthur, his success depends upon how the move is credited. Brown's critical reputation remains grounded in the gothic; his name more than any other author's (with the exception of Poe) signifies the gothic in American literature. Despite his foreclosure of it, Brown's diseased discourse continues to circulate. He finally cannot escape the commercial revelations of his gothic narratives since authorial reputations, like national narratives, are only matters of credit.

3

Literary Nationalism and the Gothic: John Neal's *Logan*

> One merit the writer may at least claim; that of calling forth the passions and engaging the sympathy of the reader, by means hitherto unemployed by preceding authors. Puerile superstition and exploded manners; Gothic castles and chimeras, are the materials usually employed for this end. The incidents of Indian hostility, and the perils of the western wilderness, are far more suitable; and, for a native of America to overlook these, would admit of no apology.
> —Charles Brockden Brown, *Edgar Huntly*

John Neal (1793–1876), one of America's early literary critics and a novelist in his own right, took up Charles Brockden Brown's call for an American literature that grew "out of the condition of our country" (*Edgar Huntly*, 3).[1] In response to Sydney Smith's taunt in the *Edinburgh Review* (1820), "who reads an American book?" (79), Neal wrote a series of articles on American writers in *Blackwood's Magazine* (1824–25) under the pseudonym Carter Holmes, which, as he would later claim, "was not so much a *nom de plume* as a *nom de guerre*" (qtd. in Lease 1972:48). Neal's stated aim in these articles was to make a "DECLARATION OF INDEPENDENCE, in the great REPUBLIC OF LETTERS" ("Unpublished Preface," xviii). Concluding that "with two exceptions, or at the most three, there is no American writer who would not pass just as readily for an English writer," Neal called for an American literature based on native materials and a colloquial language (*American Writers*, 29). Rejecting the stilted prose of Irving, whom he called the American Addison, and the derivative form of

Cooper, whom he labeled the American Scott, Neal sought to write a North American story: "a brave, hearty, original book, brimful of descriptive truth—of historical and familiar truth; crowded with real American character; alive with American peculiarities; got up after no model, however excellent; woven to no pattern, however beautiful; in imitation of nobody, however great" (*American Writers*, 205).[2]

To write his own North American story, Neal paradoxically turned to a British form, the gothic novel. Like Brown, Neal found the gothic useful in calling forth the passions of his readers. The gothic served Neal's aim of assaulting conventional literary rules by capturing authentic emotions in a forceful language. Moreover, its Godwinian strain allowed Neal, a self-proclaimed social reformer, to explore a multitude of cultural problems ranging from dueling and capital punishment to slavery and women's rights. Neal's wildest gothic experiment, *Logan* (1822), deals with Indian massacre. *Logan* not only registers the cultural contradiction of Indian removal and extermination, but also articulates this national narrative as gothic. If *Letters from an American Farmer* shows how the gothic disturbs the American myth and *Arthur Mervyn* reveals how the Enlightenment narrative of good health is indistinguishable from a gothic narrative of disease, *Logan* discloses that national identity is founded on the gothic. The novel argues that the abjection of the Indian lies at the heart of a national narrative of expansion and consolidation, and that this narrative depends on a set of gothic conventions for intelligibility. Neal's argument for a uniquely American literature written as a literature of blood and excessive emotion makes him crucial to an understanding of the gothic's role within America's developing literary nationalism, and his marginal status within the American literary canon he helped to establish illuminates the gothic's underacknowledged role in the creation of America's national narratives.

Native Materials

> The Indian's demise became perfectly representative of America's potential antiquity even as it authorized a progressive futurity.
> —Eric Sundquist, *The Literature of Expansion and Race*

The gothic played a central role in America's movement toward literary nationalism. Since the gothic novel was popular in England during the early national period, American literature was often measured against its conventions. As Benjamin Spencer argues, "the inventory of stock properties for the

Gothic imagination was endlessly reiterated by antebellum critics as a point of departure for assessing native liabilities and assets" (83).[3] Writing about *The Spy* in *The North American Review* (1822), for instance, William Howard Gardiner agrees that America is "destitute of all sorts of romantic association," and he is "by no means sure that a first rate horror, of the most imaginative kind, might not be invented without the aid of Gothic architecture, or Italian scenery"—even as he defends American literature (253, 254). He writes, "Here are no 'gorgeous palaces and cloud-capped towers;' no monuments of Gothic pride, mouldering in solitary grandeur; no mysterious hiding places to cover deeds of darkness from the light of the broad sun . . . no traces of the slow and wasteful hand of time. You look at the face of a fair country, and it tells you no tale of days that are gone by. . . . How are you to get over this familiarity of things, yet fresh in their newest gloss?" (252–53). America's lack of gothic subjects, particularly a ruined past, is constantly remarked upon by early American writers and critics and continues to trouble authors as late as Hawthorne and James. As Hawthorne puts it in his preface to *The Marble Faun* (1860), "No author, without a trial, can conceive of the difficulty of writing a romance about a country where there is no shadow, no antiquity, no mystery, no picturesque and gloomy wrong, nor anything but a common-place prosperity, in broad and simple daylight, as is happily the case with my dear native land" (3). While Hawthorne complains about the lack of gothic materials in America, he turns this lack into the sign of the country's uniqueness as a commonplace, daylight world with no gloomy past.

The ideological maneuver that eventually based America's distinctiveness on its difference from rather than its connection to the gothic, however, was still under negotiation during the early national period. The gothic's conventions were rejected as inconsequential to and incompatible with the American project of literary nationalism, yet they were adopted for that project once set in an American context. Neal, for instance, argues that American literature does not need the gothic trappings of an antiquated past when it has such a powerful present:

> We have no old castles—no banditti—no shadow of a thousand years to penetrate—but what of that. . . . I would take up the tale, with the events of this very day—and I would dare to say, to them that, questioned me.— Lo! here is proof, that we want no traditions—no antiquity—nothing but tolerable power, to tell you a tale that shall thrill to your marrow—and that too, without borrowing from anybody, or imitating anybody. . . . He who shall first dare to grapple with the *present*, will triumph, in this country. Remember, my prediction. (*Randolph* 2:208).

Neal insists that a gothic effect—"a tale that shall thrill to your marrow"—can be achieved by means other than the traditional gothic elements, and he turns to the Indian to provide that effect. By making the Indian the representative of America's antiquated past and a sublime force of terror in his novel *Logan*, Neal appropriates the gothic's effects for a distinctive American literature while rejecting its traditional characteristics. Along with many early American writers, Brown included, Neal did not simply reject the gothic as incompatible with American principles; instead, he saw the gothic as suitable for adaptation to the American scene.

The gothicized Indian provided the nation with a distinctive literary asset as well as a politically useful cultural image. Though America did not have crumbling castles and antiquated traditions, it did have in the Indian a symbol of a ruined and conquered past. As Roy Harvey Pearce argues, the progressive philosophy of "savagism," used to justify America's manifest destiny, relegated the Indian to symbolic status: "To study him was to study the past. To civilize him was to triumph over the past. To kill him was to kill the past" (49). By associating the Indian's childlike and savage nature with an underdeveloped, archaic state, savagism argued that in the wake of progress's inevitable forward movement Indians were doomed to extinction unless they could be civilized and brought into the present.[4] The cultural discourse of savagism, which enabled the policies of civilization and removal, intersected with a literary discourse that took the Indian as the native material for a past specifically coded as gothic. This correlation achieved two corresponding goals: it doomed the Indian to inevitable distinction in the present and it created a unique antiquity that could be appropriated by an emerging American literature. By identifying its exceptionality with the Indian—as Theodore Dehon claims in in his 1807 Phi Beta Kappa address, "Upon the Importance of Literature to Our Country"—American literature could be original and new and still compare favorably to a British gothic model (Pattee 1935:353).[5] By providing the materials for a past that assured the nation an exceptional literature as well as a progressive future, the Indian simultaneously enabled America's literary flowering and its consolidation of a national identity.

As America's "native" material, the Indian gave American literature a distinctive feature that could be easily transcribed into gothic terms. After Gardiner lists America's lack of gothic materials in his review of *The Spy*, he offers Indians and their history as one possible substitute. He states: "We are confident that the savage warrior ... is no mean instrument of the sublime and terrible of human agency" and that the "aera of the Indian wars" are "peculiarly well fitted for historical romance" (258, 255). Arguing that instead of constructing "a second castle of Otranto," American literature should erect "its native elegance and strength on American soil, and of materials exclusively [its] own," Gardiner turns to the Indian as one source of America's romantic material: "it scarcely needs to be asserted, that the Indians themselves are a highly poetical people.... At the present day, enough is known of our aborigines to afford the ground-work of invention, enough is concealed to leave full play for the warmest imagination" (254, 257–58). Promoting "domestic literature" in *The Atlantic Magazine* (1824), R. C. Sands also depicts the Indian as America's chief gothic material: "If scenes of unparalleled torture and indefatigable endurance, persevering vengeance, and unfailing friendship, hair-breadth escapes, and sudden ambush; if the horrors of the gloomy forests and unexplored caverns, tenanted by the most terrible of banditti; if faith in wild predictions, and entire submission of the soul to the power of ancient legends and visionary prophecies, are useful to the poet or romancer, here they may be found in abundance and endless variety" (132–33). Sands insists that it is the "creative faculty" that is "wanting," not "the materials to be wrought upon" (132). In *Tom Hanson, the Avenger* (1847), Samuel Young takes this argument one step further when he claims that the new world not only has romantic associations but is even more gothic than the old: "Talk, ye philanthropists, of barbarity in the Dark Ages: tell of the tyranny of superstition, of the horrors of civil wars: tell of France and her bloody scenes, when frantic with revolutionary frenzy. Yea, summon more, and let all fail in rendering a comparison to those terrible scenes of bloodshed and havoc perpetrated in the New World, amid a wilderness infested with devils in human shape" (qtd. in Barnett 35–36). The Indian, demonized as a devil, and the wilderness, turned into a bloody landscape, not only replace but exceed their British types.

The translation of the Indian into gothic form solved the problem of how to create a uniquely American literature and also provided a discourse that justified the nation's expansion.[6] Turning the Indian into a ghost in the literary landscape, as Freneau did in "The Indian Burying Ground" (1788), helped to naturalize the Indian's disappearance from the American landscape. Described as devils and banditti—Andrew Jackson states in 1811, "*The blood of our murdered countrymen must be revenged.* The banditti ought to be swept from the face of the earth"—the Indian was demonized through gothic symbols that in turn justified white aggression (qtd. in Sheehan 206). Thomas McKenney's argument—that one obstacle to white benevolence toward Indians was the horror stories about them that whites heard as children—shows how the gothic was utilized for nation building:

> Which of us has not listened with sensations of horror to nursery stories that are told of the Indian and his cruelties? In our infant mind, he stood for the Moloch of our country. We have been made to hear his yell; and to our eyes have been presented his tall, gaunt form, with the skins of beasts dangling round his limbs, and his eyes like fire, eager to find some new victim on which to fasten himself, and glut his appetite for blood....
>
> And thus were we, on our part, alienated from the Indian; and it was natural we should be—for amidst descriptions of savage barbarity like these, it was not to be expected that our feelings should be kind towards the authors of them. (233–34)

Taught from infancy to see the Indian as a gothic monster, Americans were predisposed to accept Indian extermination as justified. Pictured by Brantz Mayer in his history of *Logan* (1851) as demons who inscribe "their wild red marks in the memory of white men by deeds of cruelty and blood alone" and as "transient as phantoms of mingled romance and horror" whose "only permanent and consecrated resting place" is the grave, the Indian was projected as both a gothic villain and a shadowy past (25). Displacing the Indian from the present into a remote past identified him as a phantom that had already vanished. In his Second Address to Congress (1830), Andrew Jackson shows how the Indian, pictured as a buried past, can be transformed from an actual threat into a gothic effect: "Humanity has often wept over the fate of the aborigines of this country . . . one by one have many powerful tribes disappeared from the earth. To follow to the tomb the last of his race and to tread on the graves of extinct nations excite melancholy reflections. But true philanthropy reconciles the mind to these vicissitudes as it does to the extinction of one generation to make room for another" (Richardson 1083–84). The Indian is at once a source of the sentimental and the sublime: the nation weeps nostalgically over his disappearance and is excited by the graves that mark his extinction. If, as Mogen, Sanders, and Karpinksi argue, the frontier is an "intrinsically gothic symbol in American literature," it is because the gothic's alliance with the frontier was culturally produced to support a national (literary) identity (15).[7]

John Neal is central to an examination of the alliance between the literary production of the gothic and American cultural identity. Neal wrote *Logan* at the beginning of the period (the 1820s and 30s) of the Indian's prominence in American literature. Like his culture, Neal appropriated the

Indian for his own brand of literary nationalism. In his short story, "Otter-Bag, the Oneida Chief" (1829), Neal writes:

> There may be no such ruins in America as are found in Europe, or in Asia, or in Africa; but other ruins there are of a prodigious magnitude—the ruins of a mighty people. There may be no places . . . that have been sanctified by song and story, age after age . . . no piles of barbarian architecture . . . no half buried city . . . no prodigies of the mist—of that beautiful dim vapor, the twilight of another world, the atmosphere of tradition, through which the bannered palaces, the rocky fortresses, and the haughty piles of Europe loom with a most unearthly grandeur. But if there are no such things in America, there are things which are to be found nowhere else on earth now—the live wreck of a prodigious empire that has departed from before our face within the memory of man; the last of a people who have no history, and who but the other day were in possession of a quarter of the whole earth. (5–6)

Written before the Removal Act of 1830, "Otter-Bag" pictures the Indian, still visible in the American landscape and the national mind, as part of a vanished past. The Indian is only present as a trace: a "skeleton of a race that is no more" that the white man digs up in the wilderness (5). The "live wreck" of the Indian nations provides the ruins and the romantic atmosphere of an antiquated past. Neal's description of the Indians as a people who "have no history" underscores his appropriative gesture: divested of their history, Indians can be used for the cause of literary nationalism.

Neal takes the Indian not only as the native material for a distinctive American literature but also as the prototype for its indigenous style. Arguing that instead of adhering to polite rules, American literature should be written in a bold style and a natural idiom, Neal calls for a literature of the blood and heart, to be connected to emotion and natural expression and for which the Indian's "savageness" was to provide the passion—rather than a literature of the brain, which he associated with reason, artificial effort, and skill.[8] The passion and the natural eloquence of the Indian's colloquial speech made it a useful model for a literature of the blood, whose bold power and passionate expression was to agitate readers and make them feel the full force of the scene. As the narrator says of the Indian in "Otter-Bag": "his language is remarkable for sobriety, for a severe and familiar plainness—not for bold ornament nor metaphor. It abounds with short, strong phraseology, and abruptness. . . . His thoughts are eloquent, but never in the way that ours are, with beauty of speech—they are so with a sort of barbarous candor, and straightforwardness. They are full of passion—full of energy" (12). Inventing the Indian's speech, which he paradoxically mythologized as both eloquent and rough, and adopting it for his own theories of American literature, Neal argues that the Indian's uncorrupted, untamed style should constitute the voice of a new American literature.

Neal's literature of blood is also allied with the gothic's formal characteristics. As Eugenia DeLamotte comments, many writers "seeking a fresh language for 'the truth of the human heart' " turn to the "tired vocabulary of Gothicism" (5). The gothic's affective nature—"its primary formal aim is the emotional and psychological involvement of the reader," as George Haggerty states—helps Neal to excite his reader's emotions (18). Like Brown, who writes in *Edgar Huntly*, "thou wilt catch from my story every horror and every sympathy which it paints," Neal wants his reader to feel the immediacy and intensity of his emotional effect; like Brown, he turns to the gothic to achieve this (6). Eve Sedgwick's description of the gothic underscores its emotive characteristics: "Writing in blood, writing in flesh—even when the formulas are figurative, they represent a special access of the authoritative, inalienable, and immediate; the writing of blood and flesh never lies. What the writing gains in immediacy, though, it loses in denotative range, since writing that cannot lie is only barely writing" (1986:154).

Neal's desire to create a literature of emotional truth led him to create a gothic literature that was not only bloody but wild. Writing rapidly and refusing to revise in order to avoid any deadening of emotion, Neal wanted to appall his reader with an unprecedented emotional intensity: "I am impatient," he wrote to his publisher, Carey and Lea, in 1822, "and therefore would have you come down upon them (the publick) clap after clap, before they can get their breath. They are startled at the celerity of the Scotch novelist—let us appal them—if we can" (qtd. in Lease 1972:40).[9] Like Brown, who writes in *Edgar Huntly*, "in proportion as I gain power over words, shall I lose dominion over sentiments" (5), Neal argues that a literature full of emotional truth would be spontaneous and disorderly: "The want of arrangement; the incoherency . . . the want of method, and manifest design, in this tale . . . [is] for the purpose of showing how people really do talk, in this world of ours; and, with a hope of putting to shame, in some measure, the cold, artificial beauty of classical writing" (*Errata*, v–vi). An unrevised narrative, Neal claims, is the most authentic. Along with its "savage" subject, then, the form of Neal's native American literature is also untamed.

In his North American tale *Logan*, Neal employs the excesses of the gothic and the sublime effect of the Indian. By basing his nationalist literary agenda on the gothicized Indian, Neal makes the gothic's role within a narrative of nationhood founded on Indian civilization and removal strikingly visible. Neal's articulation of America as not separate from but associated with the gothic reveals the gothic's place in establishing and disrupting America's literary and national identities. Neal's gothic novel of Indian massacre, *Logan*, is interesting precisely because it shows how the gothic can work oppositionally: it both coalesces and contests a national narrative of Indian extermination.

A Family Massacre

> *Logan* is not a nice story. Superstition, supernatural suggestions, brutality, sensuality, colossal hatred, delirium, rape, insanity, murder are the stuff out of which Neal weaves a Gothic tapestry never quite paralleled by Charles Brockden Brown or Poe.
>
> —Alexander Cowie, *The Rise of the Novel*

Subtitled "A Family History," John Neal's *Logan* examines white–Indian relationships on the prerevolutionary American frontier through the complex intraconnections of the Logan family. It takes for its central plot the life of the historical figure Logan (Tah-guh-jute [c.1725–1780]), Chief of the Mingos. The half-breed son of a Cayuga Indian mother and a white French father (who was himself captured as a child, raised as an Oneida Indian, and later made chief), Logan was a friend to whites until his family was massacred in 1774 by a group of frontier traders during a border skirmish in the Ohio Valley. In retaliation, Logan led a number of raids that precipitated the conflict known as Lord Dunmore's War (1774). His speech to Lord Dunmore during the peace negotiations, made famous by inclusion in Jefferson's *Notes on the State of Virginia* (1787), sums up his grievances against the white man:

> I appeal to any white man to say, if ever he entered Logan's cabin hungry, and he gave him not meat; if ever he came cold and naked, and he clothed him not. During the course of the last long and bloody war, Logan remained idle in his cabin, an advocate for peace. Such was my love for whites, that my countrymen pointed as they passed, and said, "Logan is the friend of white men." I had even thought to have lived with you, but for the injuries of one man. Col. Cresap, the last spring, in cold blood, and unprovoked, murdered all the relations of Logan, not sparing even my women and children. There runs not a drop of my blood in the veins of

any living creature. This called on me for revenge. I have sought it: I have killed many: I have fully glutted my vengeance. For my country, I rejoice at the beams of peace. But do not harbour a thought that mine is the joy of fear. Logan never felt fear. He will not turn on his heel to save his life. Who is there to mourn for Logan? —Not one.   (Jefferson 100)

Logan's lament is a tale of race relations gone wrong, of white encroachment and Indian revenge, of peace earned only at the price of extermination.

Neal uses Logan's culturally resonant story—a story disseminated not only in Jefferson's *Notes* but also printed widely after 1775 and well into the middle of the nineteenth century as an example of Indian eloquence and nobility (Pearce 79)—as the Ur-text for his American tale.[10] Telescoping a national history through the lens of a family chronicle, Neal takes the moment of family massacre as the primal scene for the nation and his novel. Narrated by the last of the Mingos, on his deathbed, in a letter from London dated December 31, 1820 at midnight, the story opens with the massacre of Logan's family by white settlers: "The shot rang, and many generations mingled their blood at his feet" (1:7). In response, Logan, a British noble turned Indian, takes up the hatchet against the white man. He begets a son whom he feeds with white men's blood and whom he makes into a warrior. He then disappears, leaving his son to fulfill his malediction upon the whites.

All of this happens just within the first few pages of the eight-hundred-page novel. A full summary of the novel would reveal it as incoherent and excessive—*Logan* is Neal at his most unrestrained. Faced with disconnected scenes and unexpected revelations, the reader struggles to follow the intricacies of this "broken and long, long narrative" (2:328). Neal acknowledges *Logan*'s excesses when he describes it as "an experiment" whose "rambling incoherency, passion, and extravagance" he hopes to control in his next novel (*Seventy-Six*, v). His pseudonymous self-assessment in *American Writers* describes *Logan* as follows:

> *Logan* is full of power—eloquence—poetry—instinct, with a more than mortal extravagance: Yet so crowded—so incoherent . . . —so outrageously overdone, that no-body *can* read it entirely through. Parts are without a parallel for passionate beauty; —power of language: deep tenderness, poetry—yet every page—almost every paragraph, in turn, is rank with corruption, —the terrible corruption of genius. —It should be taken, as people take opium. A grain may exhilarate—more may stupify—much will be death.   (168–69)[11]

According to Neal, *Logan* is an untamable narrative that is so intense as to be unreadable. Elevating emotional effect over coherence, the novel excites its reader to death.

Most critics agree with Neal's self-assessment.[12] Commenting on Neal's singular style, one contemporary reviewer writes of *Logan*: "it is like the raving of a bedlamite. There are words in it, but no sense" (*Magazine of Foreign Literature* [1823], qtd. in Cairns 208). Other critics argue that *Logan*'s gothic excesses are so absurd that they even surpass the atrocities of Brown: Neal's "dramatis personae are . . . atrocious two-legged nightmares, such as might have been engendered in the brains of Edgar Huntly, if he had washed down raw panther collop with new Yankee rum, and slept in the reeking skin" (*The British Critic* [1826], 71). Edgar Allan Poe writes that he hardly knew "how to account for the repeated failures of John Neal as regards the *construction* of his works. His art is great and of a high character—but it is massive and undetailed. He seems to be either deficient in a sense of completeness, or unstable in temperament; so that he becomes wearied with his work before getting it done" (*Marginalia* [1849], 184–85). In "A Fable for Critics" (1848), James Russell Lowell argues that Neal "wants balance": "Broke the strings of his lyre out by striking too hard,/And cracked half the notes of a truly fine voice,/Because song drew less instant attention than noise" (134). Lillie Loshe makes a similar assessment when she states that "apart from his general incoherency, his fatal defect was a total lack of any idea when to stop. One always has a vision of him gaily writing away until the ink bottle runs dry, and then scrawling in pencil a few deaths and an insanity or two in order to end the matter" (94).[13]

Indeed, between incest and miscegenation, murders and massacres, madness and apparitions, ladies in distress and towering villains, mistaken identities and revived corpses—to name just a few—Neal overloads his novel with gothic devices. His extravagance causes the charge normally leveled against the gothic novel—that it is artistically flawed—to be amplified against Neal's work. *Logan*'s incoherence has hindered critics from analyzing the novel. For example, Louise Barnett argues that despite its elements of the frontier romance, *Logan* does not merit attention in terms of that genre's development because it is so "incoherently plotted as to defy discussion" (69).[14] Yet it is through the book's incoherent plotting and gothic excesses that the ideological maneuvers of the frontier novel are made apparent. *Logan*'s disjunctive and repetitious form registers its culture's contradictions.

Logan's demonization of the Indian and association of the Logan tribe with an extinguished past makes it symptomatic of its culture. Neal uses the gothic novel's excess violence and fascination with bloodlines to map the nation's history through a single family and answer the question: Who will inherit America? While the novel eventually resolves that the revolutionary American, not the Indian, is the rightful possessor, it also shows how that inheritance is an appropriation of Indian attributes as well as land. By having a British nobleman adopt the collective tribal name, Logan, the novel repossesses Indian identity for the white man. The narrator says that Logan "was Indian—Indian! body and soul! heart and spirit! blood and thought" (1:95). A white man posing as an Indian, Logan claims the legitimacy of Indian blood, and hence a rightful inheritance. The novel performs a similar maneuver when it appropriates the Indian's sublime attributes to legitimize itself as a North American story. Logan is superhuman and inaccessible; he is an evil spirit and a man of blood: "The Indian [Logan] stood before him like an apparition. . . . He stood motionless and apalling; the bleak, barren, and iron aspect of a man, from head to foot strong and sinewed with desperation, and hardened in the blood and sweat of calamity and trial" (1:16). Besides adopting the Indian's horrible effect for his American story, Neal describes the Indian as doomed to death. The novel begins with the narrator—the last of the Mingos—signing off from his deathbed: "I—I—I have done—the blood of the red man is growing cold—farewell—farewell forever!—" (1:4). Within the story, Harold, Logan's son, is also destined to die: a prophet figure Harold meets in the woods tells him, "Thou art accursed forever, and ever—thou and thine— thy death shall be a death of violence!" (1:178). The novel, then, participates in its culture's discourse, turning the Indian into a fiend whose demise is foreordained as a way to consolidate national identity and found an exceptional American literature.

However, in its excessiveness and lack of control the novel exposes the contradictions inherent in this ideological maneuver. Instead of naturalizing a national narrative that assures the Indian's removal, Neal's gothic novel unveils the process of abjection that generates that narrative, and in so doing disrupts it. The novel's repeated massacre scenes and its structural interchangeability articulate a narrative of violence and degeneration rather than civilization and progress. Instead of policing the boundaries between Indian and American, the novel collapses them. Even as it attempts to constitute an American identity, the novel's gothic form obsessively marks the transgression of boundaries between self and other, showing the construction of an inviolate identity to be impossible. Through the "failure" of its form, then, *Logan* reveals how national identity is created through abjection: the Indian that constitutes national identity must be expelled and denied for it to operate smoothly.[15]

Instead of developing linearly, volume 1 is structured by the repeated moment of massacre. In volume 1, no fewer than twelve massacre scenes occur, most recounting the death of a family or an entire tribe. As *The Monthly Magazine or British Register* (1823) remarks, "every chapter [is] covered with blood or heaving with the throes of lacerated flesh" (qtd. in Cairns 209). Besides having a sensational effect—the narrator tells the reader, "Your hand should be upon the hilt of your dagger. Your heart should rattle against your ribs; you should breathe seldom and hard while you listen to me" (1:137)—the reiterated violence emphasizes a single point: the breakdown of social order and, in particular, familial identity. In *Logan* a "sacrificial crisis" is at hand. According to René Girard's formulation,

> the sacrificial crisis ... coincides with the disappearance of the difference between impure violence and purifying violence. When this difference has been effaced, purification is no longer possible and impure, contagious, reciprocal violence spreads through the community.... The sacrificial distinction, the distinction between the pure and impure, cannot be obliterated without obliterating all other differences as well. One and the same process of violent reciprocity engulfs the whole. The sacrificial crisis can be defined, therefore, as a crisis of distinctions—that is, a crisis affecting the cultural order. (49)

Logan is full of an impure and unchecked violence. Instead of offering the purification on which Richard Slotkin's theory of regeneration through violence depends, volume 1 anxiously argues that violence may not solidify American identity but instead expose its foundations to be impure. If the distinction between the savage and the self no longer holds, then national identity is destroyed. In *Logan*, massacre is an act of asserting that identity; however, its repetition also signals the uncertainty of its success.

The novel centers the crisis of distinction in the family. The first massacre of whites graphically illuminates the social breakdown that accompanies the collapse of differentiation. Up in arms after the spectral appearance of Logan in the garrison, the white soldiers in their terror and confusion mistake their own families for savages and fire upon them:

> The soldiers having forgotten, it would seem, that the block houses were constructed for no other purpose than the protection of the women and children, all at once took it into their heads, that this was only a new strategem of the enemy, and that the terrified creatures who were com-

ing in under the rain and fire of their riflemen, desperate from excess of terror, were savages in disguise.... Thus the terror of a midnight alarm, came nigh de-populating a beautiful little village, making fathers and husbands the murderers of all that they loved on earth. (1:23)

Here, white murders white, husband kills wife, and terrified victim is transformed into terrifying villain. The violence that is supposed to save the village ends by decimating it. Instead of solidifying national identity, this scene of massacre reveals the fear that whites might be the victims, not the victors, of violence. The soldiers' strategic forgetting and unfounded reading of their families as savages in disguise reveal their excessive terror of being massacred. By collapsing the difference between invader and family, this scene shows how the Indian functions as both a projection and a disavowal of white fear.[16] In a world of mistaken and indistinguishable identity, there is no purifying violence since the sacrificial victim looks too much like the self. Similar incidents of misrecognition and self-destruction recur throughout the novel. In his effort to kill his enemy, Logan, Harold almost commits patricide; in his haste to defend himself against another enemy, he discovers himself "red with the blood of his brother" (1:216). In volume 1, violence is not purifying but self-consuming.

The crisis of distinction in *Logan* is also evident in the Logan family proper. The family consists of two branches, one British and one American. Logan, originally George of Salisbury, has English offspring, Caroline and Oscar, by his British wife and an American child, Harold, by his Indian wife. Through its family history, or what Donald Sears calls its "family fiasco," the narrative pushes its culture's discourse of familial identification with the Indian to its limit (42).[17] In *Logan*, the Indian (Harold) is the blood brother of the white man (Oscar). The narrator emphasizes the blood connection between the two races in describing Logan's descendants: "The blood of this race was afterwards mingled with that of their white neighbours, and produced, in their remote descendants, a family neither Indian nor white; neither savage nor civilized" (1:9). The two races are linked not only through a single father—Logan, the white man turned Indian—but also through other coincidental connections. Through absurd doublings (Harold and Oscar become demonic doubles), transgressive desires (Harold rapes his foster father's wife, Elvira, and Logan and Harold are betrothed to the same woman, Leona), and confusion of identity (Elvira mistakes Harold for her lover, Oscar, and Harold mistakes Elvira for his lover, Leona), Neal's gothic novel exposes likeness and breaks down racial boundaries. Everyone comes to belong to the same family in this book.

Perhaps the most obvious way that the two races are made indistinguishable is through the split identities of the novel's main characters, Logan and Harold. Although both consider themselves Indian, they both also have white identities: Logan is a former British nobleman, and Harold is an attaché to the governor of a British garrison. Each contains attributes of the savage and the civilized: Harold is wicked but has the "rashness and obstinacy of a hero" (1:47), and Logan is a "great savage" (1:12). Harold in turn defends and attacks the white man; Logan is both a red man in "body and soul" and a white man "all over—body and soul" (1:95, 63). While Logan's and Harold's ambiguous identities and shifting alliances might be attributed to the novel's inconsistency, they can more usefully be read as symptomatic of its impulse to break down boundaries. The confused identities and family revelations of this gothic tale reveal the impossibility of forging familial, and hence national, boundaries.

The novel's narrative structure encodes its crisis of differentiation. The gaps and disjunctions between scenes and the structural interchangeability of characters dissolve separations and underscore the absence of boundaries. The narrative coheres through repetition of the massacre scene rather than by linear plot development. Moreover, Neal's stylistic intensity—his use of parentheses, dashes of different lengths, ellipses of various types, italics, and exclamations—registers the narrative's emotional excesses. The novel's typographical techniques also destabilize language. Haunted by Logan, Harold exclaims: "Logan—accursed be the recollection!—It rises like a spectre before me, and menaces me even now. Look! look!—Spirit of the wilderness! * * Man of blood! * * whence art thou? * * why comest thou upon me? * * I feel thine unhallowed approach * * * Oh, shield me, love—his cold hand is near me: —oh, how cold!" (1:231).[18] Through innovative stylistic techniques that capture excessive emotion and structural devices that resist differentiation, *Logan* rejects a seamless narrative of national identity based on differentiation in favor of an incoherent narrative of indistinguishable identity.

By announcing its failure to mark both stylistic and thematic boundaries, *Logan* exposes the impurity at the core of national identity: the savage is part of the self. The differentiation between savage and self, however, must be reproduced in order for the novel to be resolved. Volume 2 seeks to contain the contagious, impure violence of volume 1 by working out a blueprint for a new social order. If volume 1 is about extermination and massacre, volume 2 is about civilization. In volume 2, Harold is civilized: his passion is tamed and he is transformed from a savage into a Christian and a republican: "Yes, and the red arm, the ensanguined forehead, and the lofty eye of the young savage—the unsparing and deadly harnessing of his spirit have all passed away. He is a man now, and a christian. Calamity hath tamed him" (2:257). Becoming an Indian leader, Harold moves from bloodshed to diplomacy: "beware of murder; but give *them* battle in their churches, at their fire sides, funerals—" Logan tells him before he dies (1:110). In volume 2, Harold goes to England to "learn all that white men know" in order to "return and emancipate the Indians" (1:110).

Harold's civilization clarifies his ambiguous identity, taming his savage self and turning him into an American. By the end of the story Harold identifies himself as follows: "I was born an American, of an Indian: an Englishman was my father, a daughter of Logan my mother" (2:276). The American is a half-breed: half English, half Indian. However, in order to claim his new identity Harold must reject both the corruption of the Englishman and the savagery of the Indian. Transformed from bloodthirsty demon into noble savage, Harold can become a representative republican. "Thou art indeed, a child of nature," he is told, "a republican after God's own heart" (2:106). Moreover, by rejecting the degenerate example of his British brother Oscar, he can become the proper leader of his people. Volume 2, then, locates an American identity differentiated from that of its parents. Moreover, it argues that the "true" American is neither a savage demon nor a gothic villain.

In volume 2, the American gothic tale of massacre and mayhem turns into a British gothic story of moldering family mansions, murder, and betrayal. The sacrificial crisis of volume 1 turns into a sexual free-for-all in volume 2, with incest and violent desire, rather than massacre, serving as the symbol of cultural disorder. Oscar, who plays the gothic villain, represents the passion that Harold must purge from himself: "Mayest thou have all the virtues of thy blood," Harold is told, and "none of its . . . *vices*. Remember thy father—thy brother—do thou rightly, as thou wouldst shun their sorrow" (2:100). Unlike Oscar, whose excessive passion and evil demons lead him to commit incest with his sister, try to murder his lover, Elvira, and attempt suicide, Harold learns to tame his desires. This personal transformation also signals a new social order. Unlike Oscar, who plots to overthrow the state and precipitate a revolution, Harold advocates nonviolent reform.[19] Sure that he would "quake now at the sound of our own war whoop," Harold prepares to lead his people "forth, from barbarianism and ignorance, to liberty and light" (2:326; 1:232). Having tamed his personal passion, Harold is no longer a political menace. The Indian transformed into a republican citizen proves the nation's progressive philosophy: the Indian, once civilized, is no longer a national threat.

In the end, with family boundaries reconstituted, the novel's progressive narrative is restored. Civilization seems to have solved the sacrificial crisis. With their destructive passions purged, everyone returns to their rightful partner: Leona, an Indian princess civilized through an education in France, is reunited with Harold; Elvira, a British aristocrat, is again paired with Oscar. The narrator describes this foursome as follows: "Oscar's proud nature is bowed to the earth—he is now the very apostle of sorrow and humiliation. . . . The fiery and impatient spirit of Harold too, is curbed and subdued. He is now another, and a nobler creature. The two brothers are christians now, as well as men; brave, cool, and wise: and even the untamed, untameable Leona, hath learnt to bear herself meekly" (2:325–26). These pairings resolve several issues. First, the problem of miscegenation—another blurring of boundaries in the novel—is erased. The previous couplings of Harold and Elvira and Leona and Oscar are suppressed as the white couple and the Indian couple are reconstituted—even Leopold, the child of Elvira and Harold's miscegenous pairing, conveniently dies of the croup. Civilization, it would seem, does not allow for assimilation. Having restored the proper bloodlines, the novel can finally conclude.

Yet it does not end. Instead, the specter of Logan reappears and the moment of massacre returns with a vengeance. The violence that the narrative's resolution disavows is resurrected in the form of Logan, the unappeased ghost of the American landscape, and the civilizing project of volume 2 is undercut by the final massacre scene. As Lillie Loshe puts it, "the tale ends in an epidemic of death and insanity" (93). Upon returning to America, the new family order disintegrates with the appearance of Logan, who is still alive. In his madness, more monster than man, Logan, who has spent the past years on a murderous rampage to avenge his family's deaths, kills Harold just before Oscar kills him. In an attempt to defend his family, Logan ends up destroying it: he kills his son in the act of avenging his son's death; Oscar murders his father in an attempt to save his brother. Moreover, by the end of the scene the entire family is dead: Harold from Logan's bullet, Logan by Oscar's hand, Leona from shock, Oscar from madness, and Elvira from a broken heart. There is no regeneration through violence in this ending, no purification—only the blood of extermination. The past rises up to strike down the present. The narrative of progress is once again disrupted by a narrative of degeneration.

This penultimate ending, which the narrator "struggle[s] to postpone," registers the cultural contradictions that constitute national identity: the nation remains haunted by the moment of massacre (2:327). Oscar's dream of a "great eagle sitting calmly on [a] rock, with his black, shining eyes, and talons clotted with flesh and blood," perched vulturelike over the dead carcass of an Indian (Harold), symbolizes America nourished by the blood of Indians (2:329–30). The gothic ending, which disrupts the neat resolution of volume 2, resurrects the violent origins that the national narrative of Indian disappearance disavows. By foregrounding the difficulty of its own resolution, *Logan* articulates the gothic intrusions that disrupt the civilized narrative of national identity. Moreover, the ending exemplifies its culture's movement away from a narrative of civilization toward one of removal and extermination.[20] In *Logan*, the Indian, however civilized, is destined to die on American soil.

The novel's final ending restores order by prophesying American victory and renewal. The final massacre of the book—the American Revolution—does produce regeneration through violence. The conclusion, which completes the narrator's frame tale, replaces the penultimate ending of national self-destruction with the assurance of America's coming greatness. The eagle is now pictured "breaking onward, through cloud and storm, even to the four corners of the sky" (2:339). Writing from England, the narrator identifies himself as "AN AMERICAN" rather than the last of the Mingos (2:338); thus the ending elides the differences between white American and native American identity: in their opposition to England, both are subsumed under the single heading of "American." Moreover, the internal conflict between Indians and whites is replaced by the civil war between England and America. The narrator accuses the British of having "trod upon our shores ... and poured out your vials of wrath upon a poor, manacled, and bleeding people, till the very earth reddened to its centre" (2:341). While the conflict between the white American and the Indian is still being waged at the moment Neal writes *Logan*, the revolution has already been resolved. Setting its action in the prerevolutionary past justifies *Logan*'s sacrificial crisis of white–Indian massacre through the already realized American revolution. The British are both blamed for Indian extermination and pictured as the oppressive past that has already been overthrown. The American is born out of the bloodshed between the British and the Indian; yet with both sides vanquished—the British have been conquered on the field of battle, and the narrator, the last of the Mingos, is destined to die—the American can inherit the battlefield without taking any responsibility for the bloodshed.

Written at midnight on December 31st, the ending assures the nation a progressive future as well as an identity cleansed of blood.

Logan, then, operates in contradictory ways. Its gothic narrative of excessive violence exposes the bloody ground of the nation; however, its opposing narrative of civilization and progress expels the "savage" from its borders. The Indian who helps to generate a uniquely American identity must finally be denied in order for that identity to be sustained: the "brave children of the west" in the conclusion are American, not Indian (2:338). *Logan*'s narrative of nationhood is finally no different from its culture's narratives of Indian civilization and removal. In both, the Indian is subsumed into and destroyed by the national narratives that he helps to create.

Though *Logan*'s conclusion seeks to consolidate an "American" identity, its excesses expose too much about the contested and contradictory nature of this identity and make it an unsuitable model for the project of nation building. Neal's literature of the blood is finally too uncivilized to represent a new American literature. As Neal's marginal status in America's literary history shows, he is rejected as too wild. Like the Indian who must make way for the civilized man, Neal is only remembered, if remembered at all, as a literary precursor to or a rude prototype of America's "true" literary flowering. Reviewing Neal's canonization as half wildman, half genius, this chapter concludes by examining how the Indian and the gothic—the very attributes that fostered America's literary nationalism—also come to be disavowed.

The Corruption of Genius

No figure in American literature more startling than John Neal. The state of Maine that was to produce a Jack Downing and an Artemus Ward tried her prentice hand first on him. Energy and persistence amazing; conceit, self-consciousness, egotism at every point; ignorance colossal; and with it all a personality that was commanding. At every point in his biography paradox, at every point genius, though genius of a type that must be especially defined.
—Fred Lewis Pattee, Introduction to *American Writers*

In his assessment of John Neal, Fred Lewis Pattee summarizes the central tenets of Neal's reputation. First, Neal's personality is emphasized; critics tend to elevate the man over his work. Associated by Pattee with other nineteenth-century literary showmen, P. T. Barnum and David Crockett, Neal the man is seen as "more interesting and more significant than his novels" (Loshe 94).[21] Second, Neal is described as a trailblazer whose experimentation cleared the way for others, although his prematurity dooms his work to obscurity. Picturing Neal as the wild frontiersman preceding the civilized productions of the farmer, Donald Sears writes, "certainly, he belonged to the generation of those born too early for the major accomplishments of American letters. Those who followed would produce riper crops from the land he mapped and partially cleared" (122). Neal is noted, for instance, as anticipating Whitman's prose-poetic rhythms and Twain's colloquialism. Finally, he is identified by Pattee as a "genius," but of a "type that must be especially defined" (1937:3). Neal's genius, remarked upon by virtually all commentators on his work, is full of originality and brilliance; yet it is also, as Neal himself states, seen to be "rank with corruption" (*American Writers*, 169).[22] Neal's excesses pervert the promise of his genius, turning him into a failure, a freak, or a madman.[23] As Griswold writes, one rises "from the perusal of [Neal's] works with a feeling of regret at the waste of talents, which might, under a just direction and steady application, have gained enduring honour for their possessor and his country" (315). Lacking control, Neal's creative power fails to be transformed into enduring art. His genius may be original, but his madness reveals it to be uncivilized. The construction of Neal's "genius," then, positions him in America's literary history as a wild precursor who embodies originality and passion but lacks refinement.

In his rawness and his excess, identified with the Indian whose cultural identity he appropriated, Neal serves as a savage origin of America's literary nationalism that remains unclaimed.[24] Pattee, for instance, describes him as "a wild Indian in full war-gear . . . with a manuscript" (1935:283). Lease's title, "That Wild Fellow John Neal," also connects Neal with the savage. The source of the title, Hawthorne's remark about Neal in 1845, exemplifies Neal's canonization as the wild precursor: "How slowly our literature grows up! Most of our writers of promise have come to untimely ends. There was that wild fellow, John Neal, who almost turned my boyish brain with his romances; he surely has long been dead, else he never could keep himself so quiet" (*Mosses*, 378). Hawthorne proclaims Neal one of America's early writers of promise yet assumes he is dead (Neal actually outlived Hawthorne by many years). Moreover, Hawthorne differentiates himself from Neal by marking his maturity as a turning away from Neal's gothic romances. Neal, like the Indian with whom he identified, is seen as an immature phase of America's literary nationalism and associated with a dead past. Subsumed by a narrative of literary progress, Neal is no longer recognized as part of the literary tradition he helped establish.

The Indian has also been left out of critical readings of American literature. Lucy Maddox argues, "the one significant blind spot in *most* readings of nineteenth-century American literature has been the failure to take seriously the presence of the American Indians as a factor in the shaping of the literature" (174).[25] The Indian, as Maddox points out, does not fit comfortably into a reading of American literature as "civilized" (178); this holds true for critics of the nineteenth century as well as those of the present day. Indeed, as early as the 1820s many critics were arguing that the Indian was inappropriate material for a "civilized" literature. In 1825, *The North American Review* (volume 20) states that there "is so little of the romantic and of the truly poetical in the native Indian character, that we doubt whether a poem of high order can ever be woven out of the materials afforded. The Indian has a lofty and commanding spirit, but its deeply marked traits are few, stern, and uniform, never running into those delicate and innumerable shades, which are spread over the surface of civilised society, giving the fullest scope to poetic invention, and opening a store of incidents inexhaustible, and obedient to the call of fancy" (211). In *Views and Reviews* (1846), Simms also argues that writers should civilize their Indian materials: "Their dark and gloomy mythologies . . . will receive some softening lights, some subduing touches, from the all-endowing spells of genius" (85). The Indian and the gothic imagery—"dark and gloomy mythologies"—associated with him are viewed as antagonistic to American literature's prospects and principles. Once assets of America's literary nationalism, the Indian and the gothic quickly become liabilities of a more established canon. Yet as American literature's unacknowledged origins, the gothic and the Indian continue to be hauntingly present.

Resurrecting John Neal from the shadows of America's literary past makes these origins manifest. If Neal, rather than Emerson, is taken as the voice of America's literary independence, the roles of the gothic and the Indian in American literature are no longer obscured. Neal also fills a gap in the genealogy of American gothicism that begins with Brown and reaches its apogee with Poe, allowing their careers to be read as part of a continuous tradition rather than as aberrations. Operating as a "ghost in the machine" of American literature, Neal is a figure who helps to generate it but who remains unseen and unaccounted for (Morrison 1989:11). Rematerialized, he enables the location of other subjects—the Indian and the gothic—that have also vanished from the American critical landscape.

4

The Ghost of Race: Edgar Allan Poe and the Southern Gothic

> Monk Lewis once was asked how he came, in one of his acted plays, to introduce *black* banditti, when, in the country where the scene was laid, black people were quite unknown. His answer was: "I introduced them because I truly anticipated that blacks would have more *effect* on my audience than whites—and if I had taken it into my head that, by making them sky-blue the effect would have been greater, why sky-blue they should have been."
> —Letter from Edgar Allan Poe, June 26, 1849

Poe's reiteration of Monk Lewis's disingenuous remarks, which claims that the gothic's hauntings are merely formalistic effects, foregrounds the need to locate the gothic's effects in history. Monk Lewis might explain that his choice of black banditti arose from an innate understanding of his audience, but his own history indicates otherwise. As the son of a slaveholder with two plantations in Jamaica and some seven hundred slaves, Lewis could not help but be cognizant of the cultural context of his aesthetic choice.[1] Indeed, the gothic's "blackness" has strong historical connections to slavery: many male gothicists supported slavery, and the rise of the gothic novel in England (1790–1830) occurred during a period of increased debate over it.[2] As Kari Winter has shown in *Subjects of Slavery, Agents of Change*, gothic novels actively engaged issues of slavery. The terror of possession, the iconography of entrapment and imprisonment, and the familial transgressions found in the gothic novel were also present in the slave system. Given the historical context of the gothic novel (*le roman noir*), its characteristic blackness needs to be examined in terms of slavery and, more generally, ideologies of race.

Like Monk Lewis, who denied the racial referents of his gothic effects, criticism of the gothic has often failed to view its most striking and constant symbolic opposition—black/white—in racial terms. It has taken critics of African-American literature to point out, as Robert Hemenway does in an article on Charles Chesnutt's collection of ghost stories, *The Conjure Woman*, that the gothic's oppositional symbolism carries "a sociological burden even when there is no conscious intention of racial statement" (106). Since the gothic's "color imagery . . . coincide[s] with the mythology of race prevalent in Western culture," Hemenway argues, it leaves "racial fantasies to reverberate in the Gothic effect" (101). According to Hemenway, the gothic's supernatural effects are recurringly haunted by fantasies of race.

In both Toni Morrison's gothic novel, *Beloved*, and her critical works, *Playing in the Dark: Whiteness and the Literary Imagination* and "Unspeakable Things Unspoken: The Afro-American Presence in American Literature," Morrison argues further that the *realities* as well as the fantasies of race inform American literature as a whole and, more specifically, its gothic romances. Insisting that the "blackness, ten times black" in American literature does not "derive its force from its appeals to that Calvinistic sense of Innate Depravity and Original sin," as Melville famously stated ("Hawthorne and His Mosses," 243), but from its social context, Morrison calls for race to be restored to American literature. She insists that we reexamine the founding nineteenth-century works of the American canon for the "unspeakable things unspoken," looking "for the ways in which the presence of Afro-Americans has shaped the choices, the language, the structure—the meaning of so much American literature. A search, in other words, for the ghost in the machine" (1989:11). Morrison's re-visioning of American literature anchors it securely in the context of slavery and the imaginative (re)production of race:

> Black slavery enriched the country's creative possibilities. For in that construction of blackness *and* enslavement could be found not only the not-free but also, with the dramatic polarity created by skin color, the projection of the not-me. The result was a playground for the imagination. What rose up out of collective needs to allay internal fears and to rationalize external exploitation was an American Africanism—a fabricated brew of darkness, otherness, alarm, and desire that is uniquely American. (1992:38)

Morrison shows that the American gothic's blackness needs to be historicized not only in terms of slavery but also, more important, in terms of the racial fantasies that haunt it. Moreover, in showing race to be largely a construct of the white imagination, she insists that the gothic's "whiteness" be historicized as well: the shadow is also a surrogate, a projection of whiteness in blackface.[3]

This chapter takes up Morrison's call not only by placing the gothic's blackness in historical context but also by refusing to let the ghost of whiteness disappear through reification. Focusing on the figure who Morrison argues is the most important writer of American Africanism, Edgar Allan Poe, it explores the connections between the American gothic and race and discusses how these two terms become inextricably connected through a regional identification with the South. As the canonical representative of the South and the gothic, Poe becomes the figure through whom romance and race are linked.[4]

Harry Levin argues in *The Power of Blackness* that the blackness of American literature is symbolic rather than social and that our "greatest" authors were "visionaries rather than materialists, rather symbolists than realists," but the symbolic takes on a specific social inflection in Poe (35). Levin writes that while "for Hawthorne, black and white more or less conventionally symbolize theological and moral values, for Poe, whose symbols claim to be actualities, they are charged with basic associations which are psychological and social" (120). "The continual presence of darkness in human shape, as a tangible reminder of the fears and impulsions that it has come to symbolize" creates in Poe "a sensibility which seems distinctively Southern" (233). Whereas the blackness of Melville's and Hawthorne's gothic romances is equated with Calvinistic depravity, the proper subject for the southern writer and the southern gothic, Levin argues, is slavery. In *Love and Death in the American Novel*, Leslie Fiedler also locates the gothic's blackness in the South: "It is, indeed, to be expected that our first eminent southern author discover that the proper subject for American gothic is the black man, from whose shadow we have not yet emerged" (397). While Fiedler suggests that the American gothic is about race, he carefully identifies its racial blackness with a southern author. Race only becomes central in the gothic tales of southern, not northern, writers: Melville, who shares "the bafflement of his American protagonist; a Northerner like Captain Delano" and who "finds the problem of slavery and the Negro a little exotic, a gothic horror in an almost theatrical sense of the word," is "quite unlike Poe who found this particular theme at the very center of his own experience" (401). Poe, who is rarely historicized in any other terms, is made to take up the burden of race.

Richard Gray states that "when Poe tries to describe his vision of evil, the darkness at the heart of things . . . it is noticeable that he sometimes adopts the familiar southern strategy of associating that vision with black people," showing how the gothic's blackness becomes noticeable as a southern strategy (1991:83). The gothic, like race, seems to become most visible in a southern locale. Indeed, the South's "peculiar" identity has not only been defined by its particular racial history, but has also often been depicted in gothic terms: the South is a benighted landscape, heavy with history and haunted by the ghosts of slavery.[5] The South's oppositional image—its gothic excesses and social transgressions—has served as the nation's safety valve: as the repository for everything the nation is *not*, the South purges contrary impulses. More perceived idea than social reality, the imaginary South functions as the nation's "dark" other. By so closely associating the gothic with the South, the American literary tradition neutralizes the gothic's threat to national identity. As merely a regional strategy, the gothic's horrifying hauntings, especially those dealing with race, can be contained. It is necessary not only to unveil the complex intertwinings of romance and race but also to explore how these discourses become regionally inflected.

Since it is through Edgar Allan Poe that the South and the gothic become inextricably linked and that race most often enters readings of nineteenth-century American literature, I will use Poe's problematic status within the American literary canon to explore how the southern gothic and its blackness are demonized and domesticated. Instead of reducing Poe's gothic tales to southern stories or his meditations on the problem of racial identity to a racial phobia, this chapter shows how the gothic offers Poe a complex and complementary notation with which to explore the racial discourse of his period, a discourse concerned as much with perfect whiteness as terrifying blackness. Outlining the parameters of Poe's (de)canonization, it examines how race and the gothic come to be identified as merely southern problems and argues for an opposing, *American* gothic tradition that refuses to bury race prematurely in the South.

Placing Poe

> The problem of Poe, fascinating as it is, lies quite outside the main current of American thought, and it may be left with the psychologist and the belletrist with whom it belongs.
>
> —Vernon Parrington, *Main Currents in American Thought*

Poe's problematic position within the American literary canon reveals his complex connections to region and race. An absent presence, Poe is a ghost in the critical machinery of canon formation, a figure through which much cultural work gets done. Poe most often functions as the demonized "other" who must be exorcised from the "mainstream" of our "classic" American literature: "It is to save our faces that we've given him a crazy reputation," William Carlos Williams writes, "a writer from whose classic accuracies we have not known how else to escape" (216). While Poe, it would seem, can have no place in the canon, he constantly poses a problem to it.

Five months after his death, the *Southern Literary Messenger* captured the problem when it memorialized him as follows: "Edgar Allan Poe . . . the true head of American literature—it is the verdict of other nations and after times that we speak here—died of drink, friendless and alone, in the common wards of a Baltimore hospital" (March 1850:178). Poe's position in the corpus of American literature—let alone his status as its head—has, from the beginning, been problematized by the mythography of his own drunken corpse and by the diseased bodies and living dead that haunt his stories. In both his life and his work, Poe would seem to lie far outside the American mainstream. If he represents anything at all, it is American literature's irrational bodily impulses. The "after times" have judged Poe harshly; he remains relegated to the "common wards" and alienated from the community of American literature's founding fathers: Emerson, Thoreau, Hawthorne, Melville, Whitman. In *American Renaissance*, which places these authors at the center of a newly consolidated American literature, F. O. Matthiessen buries Poe in a footnote. He explains Poe's exclusion from his "group" as follows: "The reason is more fundamental than that his work fell mainly in the decade of 1835–45; for it relates at very few points to the main assumptions about literature that were held by any of my group. Poe was bitterly hostile to democracy, and in that respect could serve as a revelatory contrast" (xii). As the exception to the rule—the embodiment of everything American literature is *not*—Poe reveals the parameters of a more "authentic" American literature. As a ghost who haunts the American literary canon, Poe becomes a necessary—and useful—evil, as Harold Bloom writes: "I can think of no American writer, down to this moment, at once so inevitable and so dubious" (3).

Poe's dubiousness, I argue, is the very reason for his inevitability: it is through Poe that a number of "dubious" aspects of American literature are demonized, then exorcised from the mainstream American canon. As an excused aberration, Poe becomes the representative of a number of problems that the American literary tradition recognizes but refuses to claim. For instance, through Poe, popular literature can enter the canon without threatening the hard-won, highbrow status of our "classic" American literature. As Bloom argues, "Poe's survival raises perpetually the issue as to whether literary merit and canonical status necessarily go together" (3). Through Poe, as well, a more gothic vision of America comes into view. However, in reading Poe's gothic tales as the projections of his own peculiar psychology instead of as a comment on his culture, critics easily contain his disturbing vision of American society. If Poe is merely a case for psychologists, as Parrington argues (2:58), or if "he gazed in fascinated reverie upon objects that seemed to swim in 'an atmosphere peculiar to themselves,'" as Feidelson states (2), then his particular perspective is not troubling for, as Levin claims, "Poe came by his own strangeness naturally" (102).

Even when Poe's diseased vision is read as a symptom of a larger cultural malaise, it remains quarantined from "mainstream" America and comes to be identified with another "problem"—the South. Indeed, Poe's strangeness seems to arise from his placement in the alienated space of the South. When F. O. Matthiessen claims that Poe was "bitterly hostile to democracy," he implies a connection between Poe's politics and his regional identification. This connection is made explicit in Matthiessen's entry on Poe in Spiller's *Literary History of the United States*: "He was so eager to prove himself a Virginian that he followed Allan's tradition, which was that of Marshall and not that of Jefferson. Poe went so far as to deplore the French Revolution, to defend slavery as 'the basis of all our institutions,' and to assume the scorn held by the propertied class for the democratic 'mob'" (328). Poe's politics, especially his racial politics, are an obsessive theme of much Poe criticism. More than with many other authors, critics look to Poe's politics to read the racial images in his work.[6] For instance, despite his arguments against authorial intention, John Carlos Rowe states, "My argument is on the face of it simple: Poe was a proslavery Southerner and should be reassessed as such in whatever approach we take to his life and writings" (117). After discussing Poe's "deliberate sectional prejudice," Harold Beaver writes in his introduction to the Penguin edition of *Pym*: "The conscious political intent—of this there can be no doubt—was to forestall the degree zero, the South Pole itself, of racial prejudice" (14, 25). This critical view stems partially from Poe's compelling biography (as Levin argues, "If Hawthorne is the man to whom nothing whatsoever has happened, Poe is the man to whom nearly everything happens" [102]), but more fully from a desire to place Poe in an identifiable position. If Poe's blackness can be positioned in the proslavery South, then his "racial phobia," as Levin calls it, can be limited to that region (121). Once placed in "this world," Poe's peculiar history has only to do with the South, not with the nation.

If Poe must be securely located in the South and politically "pinned down" in order to be accepted as the crazy cousin of the American literary tradition, he must be historically evacuated and regionally disassociated to become a charter member. In order to claim Poe for a national tradition, as G. R. Thompson wants to do in *The Columbia Literary History of the United States*, critics must strip Poe of his southern associations and turn him into an "antiregionalist." Instead of addressing the South, Thompson argues that Poe "focuses on the integrity of the work of art in terms of the ideal—a metaphysical ideal of 'pure' poetry, an aesthetic ideal of total unity of effect in both poetry and fiction" (277). Through form, Poe transcends his region and its politics.

The southern literary establishment also focuses on Poe's art rather than his relationship to his social setting in its effort to claim Poe and his national status for its literary tradition. While Poe is canonized as a southerner in virtually all of the major southern anthologies, his lack of specifiable regional identification is constantly remarked upon. In *The Mind of the South*, W. J. Cash calls Poe "only half a Southerner" (93); and Allen Tate states that while he is "a gentleman and a Southerner, he was not quite, perhaps, a Southern gentleman" (41). In a literary tradition that claims distinctiveness based on its unique social conditions, Poe, who spent significant time outside of the South and sets few of his stories there, never quite fits the profile of the southern writer. As Montrose Moses's chapter heading in *The Literature of the South*—"A Southern Mystery: An Author With and Without a Country—Poe"—suggests, Poe's southernness remains suspect (276).

Despite his suspicious roots, Poe becomes the necessary cornerstone of a southern literary tradition precisely because of his national status. As "one of the chief glories of the literature of our nation and our race," he becomes the "greatest ornament of Southern literature" (*The Library of Southern Literature*, 4089). Louis Rubin explains Poe's paradoxical position as follows: "We confront the obvious fact that of all the antebellum Southern authors it is Poe whose writings are *least* grounded in the particularities, settings and issues of the place he grew up in, and equally *most* lastingly a part of world literature" (147). Ironically, it is the southern literary establishment that has so much difficulty placing Poe in the South: Rubin, for instance, insists "Poe wrote almost *nothing* about the South, or about living there, or about Southern history and Southern society, or for that matter about any kind of history whatever" (152). If Poe becomes a proslavery voice from a nonsouthern perspective, he must be evacuated from that perspective by the southern literary establishment. This move can be traced to the argument, popularized by Allen Tate, that in the South, art and politics are not only separate spheres, but that politics hinders the growth of art. Louis Rubin sums up the argument: "The presence of African slavery was incompatible with the growth of an important literature in the Old South" (17). As the only producer of "art" during that period, Poe could not have derived his blackness from his cultural context.

Displaced from his social context, Poe is southernized by his art. As Ellen Glasgow argues in *A Certain Measure*, Poe's literary techniques are identifiably southern. "Poe is, to a large extent, a distillation of the Southern," she writes. "The formalism of his tone, the classical element in his poetry and in many of his stories, the drift toward rhetoric, the aloof and elusive intensity,—all these qualities are Southern" (132–33).[7] Poe could also be saved through his criticism, much of which was published in an identifiable place, the *Southern Literary Messenger*. Edwin Mims and Bruce Payne state in *Southern Prose and Poetry for Schools* that "it is in his critical writing that Poe's Southern bent of mind was most notably evinced" (6). Moreover, Poe's gothic form could make him a forerunner of the Southern Renaissance, and hence an ancestor of southern literature's "true" flowering. It is the ahistorical, symbolist, and more respectable Poe who is finally adopted into the southern literary tradition.

Poe, then, poses a problem for both the southern and the national literary traditions. From the southern perspective, the problem can be solved by claiming his art for southern literature while displacing him—along with the rest of that literature—from southern history. From the national perspective, the problem of Poe can be solved either by defining him in oppositional terms—identifying him with slavery and the South—or by removing his history and regional identification entirely. In both cases, Poe's regional identification is deployed to read his gothic romances in relation to race. Instead of trying to solve the problem of Poe or locate him in any single place, I will argue that it is Poe's regional (mis)placement and (dis)location that make him significant. Reading him as William Carlos Williams suggests, as a "genius intimately shaped by his locality and time," I will look at how his gothic tales are engaged with a national, not regional, discourse on race (216).

The Voyage South:
The Narrative of Arthur Gordon Pym

> ... a geometry of conflict written in gothic notation.
> —Kenneth Dauber, "The Problem of Poe"

At the end of *The Narrative of Arthur Gordon Pym* (1838), the editor's note interprets the hieroglyphic chasms that Pym encounters on the island of Tsalal as "to be shady," "to be white," and "the region of the south" (207–8). This code has been critically read as an indicator of Poe's prowhite racism. My contention is that *Pym*'s racial codings—as well as the critical deciphering of these codings—have much to tell us about nineteenth-century racial discourse and our own readings of it. As Poe's most-often-historicized work, *Pym* reveals how a racial reading of Poe depends on the cipher of the South. For when *Pym* is not universalized as a psychological voyage into the maelstrom of the mind, it is historicized as a social voyage with a very particular destination, the American South; like Poe's position in the canon, *Pym* either transcends its social context or gets mired in a regional reading. As Harry Levin writes, "The 'constant tendency to the south' in *The Narrative of Arthur Gordon Pym* takes on a special inflection, when we are mindful of the Southern self-consciousness of the author" (120). Once viewed through the regional marker of the South, *Pym*'s obsession with "whiteness" and "blackness" turns into a straightforward proslavery allegory. Hence, John Carlos Rowe argues: "I make no claim for originality here; the interpretation of *Pym* as a thinly disguised allegory of Poe's manifesto 'Keep the South White' belongs to others" (126). This critical consensus, however, relies upon a circular argument: *Pym* is at once the sign and the signifier of Poe's southern racism. That is, critics read *Pym* as a projection of its author's southernness *and* they use it as evidence for Poe's southern racist position. Because Poe's authorial position on race is absent in much of his critical and personal writing, *Pym* is often projected as the articulation of that silence. For instance, in an attempt to "turn up a surer meaning at the level of Poe's intention" after his own reading of *Pym*'s allegory as racist, Sidney Kaplan asks: "Does all this seem improbable? Is it possible that the critic who flayed allegory as used by Hawthorne because the technique was too artificial and transparent could himself be guilty of the heresy of an allegorical and didactic damning of the Negro from the beginning to the end of time? I will not labor the point that Poe, as critic and fictionist, was no friend of the Negro. This is common knowledge" (xvi, xxiii). Kaplan's attempt to reconcile his own allegorical reading of *Pym* with

Poe's critical resistance to such a reading is solved by the "common knowledge" of Poe's southern positioning. It would seem that Poe's racism, as well as his text's, can be assumed once they are located in the South.

Pym, I argue, resists such an allegorical reading. For even as the editor's note deciphers the narrative code, it insists that any such reading is a function of critical desire. While the note claims that "conclusions such as these open a wide field for speculation and exciting conjecture," it also cautions that "they should be regarded, perhaps, in connection with some of the most faintly detailed incidents of the narrative; . . . in no visible manner is this chain of connection complete" (208). By obsessively giving *Pym* a regional reading, critics attempt to complete the chain, but this reduces Poe's complex meditation on race to proslavery cant. While I do not deny Poe's regional identification or his politics, I do want to complicate them by reading them in the context of a national discourse on race. I am *not* arguing that Poe should not be historicized or seen in terms of a proslavery sentiment; I *am* taking issue with how this historicization occurs. The implicit equation of Poe's southernness and his proslavery politics belies the complex investments that critics have in a national discourse of racial purity. As Larry Tise argues, a proslavery position is not inherently southern, it is merely canonized as such: "The ready ascription of proslavery writings and, as a consequence, proslavery ideas to southerners and particularly to southern sectionalists has blinded historians to the actualities of proslavery history" (3). Reading a proslavery stance or Poe in terms of a regional, not national, discourse might raise critical comfort levels, but it does little to explain how discourses of race operate in Poe's tales. Moreover, to historicize *Pym* merely in terms of slavery is to miss its engagement with larger nineteenth-century racial ideologies. The debate over Poe's racism needs to be reconstructed along less oppositional lines so that critics who attempt to historicize Poe as other than a proslavery southerner are not accused of being apologists for that vision. I suggest, to quote Hazel Carby, "that instead of searching for cultural purity we acknowledge cultural complexity" (1989:42). We need to historicize Poe within a network of multiple discourses on race—personal, regional, national—while also noting how these discourses intersect with and are influenced by others such as gender and class.[8] Rather than demonizing Poe's reflections on race or quarantining them to the South, I will argue that *Pym* records a complex and often contradictory vision of race and sets in motion a national, not just a regional, racial discourse.

That national discourse is evident even in *Pym*'s southern publication. In the same edition of *The Southern Literary Messenger* (January 1837) that included the first installment of *The Narrative of Arthur Gordon Pym*, there was a review of Jeremiah Reynolds's address to Congress arguing for a South Sea Exploring Expedition. Stating that "the public mind is at length thoroughly alive on the subject," the review summed up the history of Reynolds's endeavors (he had petitioned Congress in 1828 only to be turned down) and the reasons for such a voyage: commercial expansion and patriotic duty (68). While the initial impetus for the voyage originated in a theory put forward by John Symmes in 1818—that the earth was hollow, made up of a number of concentric spheres and accessed by openings at the poles—by the 1830s, Reynolds, Symmes's protegé, had refashioned this theory to more pragmatic ends: "Indeed, while there remains a spot of untrodden earth accessible to man," Reynolds states in his address, "no enlightened, and especially commercial and free people, should withhold its contributions for exploring it, wherever that spot may be found on the earth, from the equator to the poles" (qtd. in *Southern Literary Messenger* [January 1837], 70). Supported by northern, southern, and western states alike, the voyage was seen as a national endeavor: "The enterprize should be national in its object, and sustained by the national means,—belongs of right to no individual, or set of individuals, but to the country and the whole country" (*Southern Literary Messenger* [January 1837], 72).

Arising out of this voyage—which aimed "to study man in his physical and mental powers, in his manners, habits, disposition, and social and political relations; and above all, in the philosophy of his language, in order to trace his origin from the early families of the old world"—and others like it during this period of trafficking in information instead of bodies, was a new theory of race (*Southern Literary Messenger* [January 1837], 71). From the eighteenth century through the 1830s, monogenism, the belief in the original sameness of men, was the dominant racial ideology. Dr. Samuel Stanhope Smith, whose *Essay on the Causes of the Variety of Complexion and Figure in the Human Species* (1787, enlarged edition 1810) established the unity of human species and attributed the differences between races to environmental causes, was the central spokesperson for this theory. Echoing Smith's claims for the superficiality of racial difference, John Drayton, the governor of South Carolina, wrote in his 1802 *View of South-Carolina* that he agreed "with the doctor, in the principle which he has endeavoured to support, viz. 'that all mankind have originally descended from one pair; and that a difference of complexion is only produced by change of situation, and a combination of other circumstances" (25–26). Though there were dissenters as early as 1784 (see, for instance, John Pinkerton's *Dissertation on the Origin of the Scythians* or *Goths* [1787]), the theory held its ground well into the 1830s and 40s. However, it was with the publication of Dr. Samuel George Morton's *Crania Americana* (1839) and *Crania Aegyptiaca* (1844) that polygenism, the belief in the innate difference between the races, began to be taken seriously. As Reginald Horsman points out, however, it was not until the 1850s that an inherent inequality between the races was accepted as scientific fact (134). Moreover, this acceptance was not regionally based: "The overt intellectual argument for innate black inferiority," Horsman states, "was being developed in America before the full surge of abolitionism, it was not restricted to the South in the 1830s and 1840s, and it was not peculiar to those who wished to defend slavery" (122). Although Morton's work sold especially well in the South, and the cause of polygenism was taken up by a southern physician, Josiah C. Nott, to defend slavery and to prove that environmental conditions cannot change a white man into a Negro, much of the South resisted the new theory since it directly contradicted biblical knowledge. Indeed, there was a strong national resistance to the notion of polygenism well into the 1840s. Charles Pickering, the chief naturalist of the U.S. Exploring Expedition and a close friend of Morton's, was censored in his 1845 report to Congress when he attempted to argue that the races had different origins. Congress responded to his report by stating that it was "extremely necessary to be cautious in publishing any new philosophical inquires relative to the History of man," since they were wishing to avoid "anything that might shock the public mind" (qtd. in Stanton 343).

This gradual shift from monogenism to polygenism—as Nancy Stepan summarizes it, from a "sense of man as primarily a social being, governed by social laws and standing apart from nature, to a sense of man as primarily a biological being, embedded in nature and governed by biological laws"—was occurring on the national level as Poe wrote *Pym* (4). To read *Pym* as merely a southern manifesto is to misread its national implications; moreover, to read it as an allegory of racial difference is to project upon it an 1850s discourse of polygenism. *Pym*'s narrative of racial convertibility, I argue, more fully engages the earlier discourse of monogenism. The novel insists that identities are fluid (for example, Pym says to Augustus, "It is probable, indeed, that our intimate communion had resulted in a partial interchange of character" [65]), claims that character can change according to environment (the white crew turns to cannibalism when the ship becomes disabled), and constantly inverts and collapses the poles of "black" and "white" (Peters is first demon, then savior). *Pym* registers the fear that the self can easily become the other.

Indeed, as Joan Dayan puts it, the "story depends upon a crisis of color" (1991:108). With striking reversals and exaggerated racial taxonomies, *Pym* constantly crosses the color line. Death, the ultimate moment of boundary collapse, serves as the central metaphor for this crisis. Characters are described as being, paradoxically, paler than death, and once-white bodies turn black in death. Augustus, for instance, is characterized in his death as a "mass of putrefaction," (142) so without definition and boundaries that his limbs fall off at a simple grasp; his arm is also described as turning "completely black from the wrist to the shoulder" as he dies (142). Later, when the surviving castaways spot what they first assume is a rescue ship, only to realize that it is a ghost ship piloted by corpses, each body is described as having "very dark skin" and the most "brilliantly white teeth" (123). In death, even the brightest white can turn "very dark." What happens to the body in death exemplifies the crisis of color inherent in the racial philosophy of monogenism. Dr. John Mitchell of Virginia makes this connection explicit when he observes that "where any Body loses its white Colour, it of course turns black, without any other Cause concurring, but a bare loss of its Whiteness.... From whence we may justly infer, 1. That there is not so great, unnatural, and unaccountable a Difference between Negroes and white People, as to make it impossible for both ever to have been descended from the same Stock" (qtd. in Jordon 247). Mitchell's conclusion, that "however different, and opposite to one another, these two Colours of Black and White may appear to be to the Unskillful, yet they will be found to differ from one another only in Degree," is similar to *Pym*'s (247). For even as *Pym*'s color symbolism seems constantly to create difference, it elides that difference by articulating a discourse of racial identity that is constructed, and hence vulnerable to change.

Pym's insistence on the constructed nature of race is especially evident in the episode when Pym decides to "represent the corpse of Rogers" in order to trick the mutineers (108). Pym dresses himself in Rogers's shirt, which "was of a singular form and character, and easily recognizable," equips himself with a false stomach "in imitation of the horrible deformity of the swollen corpse," and then gives "the same appearance to [his] hands by drawing on a pair of white woolen mittens" (108–9). Peters finishes off the simulacrum by "arrang[ing] [Pym's] face," rubbing it with white chalk and splotching it with blood in order to imitate the "chalky whiteness" of Rogers's corpse (107). Made up in "white face," Pym views himself in a mirror and states: "I was so impressed with a sense of vague awe at my appearance, and at the recollection of the terrific reality which I was thus representing, that I was seized with a violent tremor, and could scarcely summon resolution to go on with my part" (109). Unable to recognize himself, shocked by his own "otherness," the actor becomes as frightened of his transformation as his audience will soon be. Pym's gothic trick re-presents reality so terrifically that it threatens to challenge that reality. Described as a matter of appearance or of role-playing, racial identity becomes performative. Poe's readers, who were themselves audiences to racial transformations in the minstrel shows, might be similarly disturbed by the way race, as only a function of make-up, could be made up. As Eric Lott writes in his study on blackface minstrelsy, "The blackface phenomenon was virtually constituted by such slippages, positives turning to negatives, selves into others, and back again" (124). Like one of its sources, Benjamin Morrell's *Four Voyages* (1832), which recounts a scene where a native has to satisfy himself that the white narrator is also "constructed of bones and flesh, like his own race, and that the white paint could not be rubbed off [his] ebony skin," *Pym* shows that whiteness is as much a construct as blackness and, in doing so, registers a fear that racial identity is fluid, not fixed (397).

The reproduction of race in this episode highlights the production of race throughout the text. The focus on imitation and appearance is central from the very opening of the story. Pym's preface, which is obsessed with how to give his account the "*appearance* of that truth it would really possess," problematizes notions of truth and reality (55). In *Pym*, truth must be produced; reality is only an effect. Similarly, race is only a representation. This is evident in the discussions of both blackness and whiteness in the text. The stereotypical images of blackness can be read, as Joan Dayan argues, as exaggeration that dramatizes "the fact of appropriation, and thereby undefines the definitions that mattered to civilized society" (1994:250). As the preface points out, excess undermines authenticity: the wild and marvelous nature of Pym's story makes him fear that readers will see it as an "ingenious fiction" (55). If exaggeration has the effect of artifice instead of truth, then the novel's stereotypical descriptions of the natives of Tsalal, its insistence on their total blackness, could actually work to expose the artifice of race instead of merely reinforcing racial difference. Just as the happy, minstrel image of the natives is proved false when their plot to kill the crew is revealed, so too might all racial images be revealed as "put on."

This reading, of course, does not take into account the many ways that the novel deploys and reinforces racial stereotypes even as it reveals race to be a social invention. *Pym* reproduces racial fantasy even while pointing out that it is merely a representation. This contradictory position is more evident in *Pym*'s depiction of whiteness. On one hand, as in the episode of Rogers's corpse, whiteness is terrifying and all-powerful. Its effect allows Pym to reverse positions, turning his nonwhite captors into "the most pitiable objects of horror and utter despair" (112). Whiteness's terrifying power is most strikingly evident in the final scene of the novel, a point to which I will return. On the other hand, despite its reinforcing the power of whiteness, the story registers a fear of losing one's whiteness and becoming like those "silent and disgusting images," the black corpses on the ghost ship (124). The difference between the "very dark" corpses and their "brilliantly white teeth" reinforces the novel's contradictory stance. Its meditation on difference paradoxically registers a fear of delineating racial identity: black skin might harbor the vestiges of whiteness. Instead of policing the color line, *Pym* transgresses it, exploiting rather than allaying readers' fears.

The ghost story Pym tells echoes the effects of its frame tale, Poe's own gothic tale, *Pym*. In order to set the stage for the "terrific appearance of Rogers' corpse," Peters and Augustus tell ghost stories that "wound up [their audience] to the highest pitch of nervous excitement" (111). After Pym makes his grand entrance, dressed as Rogers, "without uttering a syllable," he reflects upon the audience's reaction:

> The intense effect produced by this sudden apparition is not at all to be wondered at when the various circumstances are taken into consideration. Usually, in cases of a similar nature, there is left in the mind of the spectator some glimmering of doubt as to the reality of the vision before his eyes; a degree of hope, however feeble, that he is the victim of chicanery, and that the apparition is not actually a visitant from the world of shadows. It is not too much to say that such remnants of doubt have been at the bottom of almost every such visitation, and that the appalling horror which has sometimes been brought about, is to be attributed, even in the cases most in point, and where most suffering has been experienced, more to a kind of anticipative horror, lest the apparition *might possibly be* real, than to an unwavering belief in its reality. But, in the present instance, it will be seen immediately, that in the minds of the mutineers there was not even the shadow of a basis upon which to rest a doubt that the apparition of Rogers was indeed a revivification of his disgusting corpse, or at least its spiritual image. (111–12)

This passage, a treatise on the gothic's intense effects, foregrounds the difficulty of explaining away the gothic's appalling horror. By substituting an analysis of the effect for the effect itself, the scientific discourse of this passage attempts a rational explanation of the supernatural event. However, this metonymic substitution fails: the excessive explanation cannot completely cover the gap of doubt that always remains. Like Monk Lewis's rationale for his gothic's effect, Pym's explanation is unable to capture fully his haunting impression. It is in this gap—this schism between the scientific and the supernatural—that *Pym* gains its effect, for the "vision" before its spectators' eyes is not only a revivified corpse but also a "visitant from the world of shadows"—the ghost of race. *Pym*'s gothic effects are always haunted by race. Its scientific discourse might attempt to make sense of race by creating safely segregated categories and by rationalizing its actualities, but the novel's gothic effects reveal science's failure to account fully for its haunting visitations. The hope that this tale of racial convertibility is only chicanery is modulated by the fear that it might be all too true.

Perfect Whiteness

> If we follow through on the self-reflexive nature of these encounters with Africanism, it falls clear: images of blackness can be evil *and* protective, rebellious *and* forgiving, fearful *and* desirable—all of the self-contradictory features of the self. Whiteness, alone, is mute, meaningless, unfathomable, pointless, frozen, veiled, curtained, dreaded, senseless, implacable. Or so our writers seem to say.
>
> —Toni Morrison, *Playing in the Dark*

Pym has often been read as a patchwork text, made up of many different narrative modes. Indeed, the book seems to break in half, moving from the gothic tale of sea-voyaging horrors to a scientific account of the South Seas once Pym is picked up by the *Jane Guy*. The gothic tale collapses the boundaries between appearance and reality, death and life, desire and terror, black and white, but the second half of the story seems more interested in reestablishing stable categories and reinforcing a straightforward allegory of racial difference. The gothic tale of racial convertibility turns into a sociological study of slavery, including a model of racial segregation and polarization. For example, Pym observes as the ship travels south that the variation of the sea "uniformly decreased," and describes the water as made up of a "number of distinct veins" that do "not commingle" (166, 172). The allegory of segregation is made clear in the conclusion: "Nothing *white* was to be found at Tsalal, and nothing otherwise in the subsequent voyage to the region beyond" (208). Intent on the "purest white imaginable" and the most "brilliant black," this section of the story reasserts the color line that the previous section collapsed (151). On Tsalal the natives' insides match their outsides: their teeth are black like their jet-black skin. The signs seem excessively clear.

Yet as we have seen, such excess can actually collapse instead of create difference. Indeed, the natives are not what they appear to be. Their exaggerated childlike innocence—"Upon getting alongside the chief evinced symptoms of extreme surprise and delight, clapping his hands, slapping his thighs and breast, and laughing obstreperously"—turns out to be a mask (168). Another insurrection occurs, this time on the island rather than on the ship, and once again destabilizes the poles of black and white. The dark chasm in which Pym, along with Peters, is buried alive on the island of Tsalal represents the color line that is constantly being crossed in the novel. The same fissure that marks difference also threatens to collapse that difference. Pym might believe that through scientific and commercial expertise the proper hierarchy between white and black has been reestablished, but when he finds himself entombed in blackness, Pym, like the book's audience, is confronted with the fact that he cannot escape "blackness."

The extent to which *Pym* continues to collapse the categories of black and white in this section is made clearer with an understanding of how the novel rewrites one of its sources, *Symzonia* by John Cleves Symmes. Written in 1820, *Symzonia* is Symmes's imaginative projection of his hollow-earth theory. Like Pym's voyage south, *Symzonia* is concerned with commercial imperialism and its attendant racial taxonomies. Captain Seaborn, the protagonist of the novel, states: "I felt perfectly satisfied that I had only to find an opening in the 'icy hoop' through which I could dash with my vessel, to discover a region where seals could be taken as fast as they could be stripped and cured" (30). The novel traces Seaborn's voyage to the inside of the earth, where he encounters a race of perfectly white beings whom he calls the internals. In a reversal of the usual colonial contact, Captain Seaborn bows to the natives and remarks upon his own inferiority: "I am considered fair for an American, and my skin was always in my own country thought to be one of the finest and whitest. But when one of the internals placed his arm, always exposed to the weather, by the side of mine, the difference was truly mortifying. I was not a white man, compared to him" (110). Stating that "the sootiest African does not differ more from us in darkness of skin and grossness of features, than this man did from me in fairness of complexion and delicacy of form," Captain Seaborn registers his fear that he may be more black than white (108).

While *Symzonia* adheres to racist stereotypes (Seaborn claims that "it was [his] dark and hideous appearance that created so much distrust amongst these beautiful natives" [107]), it also claims that those stereotypes are not fixed. Indeed, even as the novel argues that external signs are signifiers of internal behavior (the "gross sensuality, intemperate passions and beastly habits of the externals" are indicated by their darker skin; the "appearance, manners, conduct and expression of countenance of [the internals]" perfectly accord with his "ideas of purity and goodness" [134, 117]), it shows just how changeable these signs are. Moreover, in its description of the outcast tribe relegated, because of participation in the "contaminating intercourse" of trade, to a land in the north where the intense heat has turned them dark, *Symzonia* argues that any race—even the most perfectly white—can degenerate into brutes: "The influence of their gross appetites and of the climate," Seaborn explains, "causes them to lose their fairness of complexion and beauty of form and feature. They become dark coloured, ill favoured, and mis-shapen men, not much superior to the brute creation" (167, 132). The seafaring life, which also darkens Seaborn's skin, threatens a similar fate for him; Seaborn's addiction to trade makes him assume that the externals are descended from this exiled tribe. Judged by the Symzonians to be contaminated, the externals are another fallen race turned "black" from the crime of trade, specifically slavery. Seaborn states that "it appeared that we were of a race who had either wholly fallen from virtue, or were at least very much under the influence of the worst passions of our nature [since] . . . we were guilty of enslaving our fellow-men for the purpose of procuring the means of gratifying our sensual appetites" (196).

Preaching an antislavery message even as it enforces racist stereotypes, *Symzonia* reflects the contradictory positions that a single text can hold. While on the one hand it claims that slavery is contaminating and argues for the fluidity of racial identity, on the other hand it reinforces racial hierarchies: races might be socially constructed, the novel argues, but the more advanced and developed one is always white. Monogenism, it turns out, is potentially no less racist a philosophy than polygenism. Like *Pym*, then, *Symzonia* reinforces racial stereotyping even as it argues for the constructed nature of identity; moreover, its obsession with "perfect" whiteness, like *Pym*'s, underscores the fear that one might not after all be pure.

But *Pym*'s difference from *Symzonia* is more telling. Against the hierarchical philosophy of *Symzonia*'s monogenism, *Pym* insists that whiteness is only the obverse of blackness. For instance, the novel replays the scene of Seaborn's first contact with the internals by making the natives recoil from Pym and his crew with the same horror. *Pym* places whites in the position of the "other": "It was quite evident that they had never before seen any of the white race—from whose complexion, indeed, they appeared to recoil" (169). More important, by refiguring the voyage to the center of the earth as a voyage into blackness, the novel argues that Pym's voyage to selfhood has more to do with discovering how whiteness relates to blackness than with how Pym himself reflects a "perfect whiteness."

Journeying to the center of the island, Pym and Peters, his half-breed companion, are literally buried alive in the black granite caverns of Tsalal. Here, Seaborn's and his crew's fear of plunging through the earth's hole into "total darkness," to "never be able to find their way out again" becomes a reality for Pym (91). He finds himself "envelop[ed]" in a "blackness of darkness," a "quantity of loose earth, which was . . . threatening to bury [him] entirely" (182). By deciding to pause at this moment of dissolution (Pym states that he thought "the whole foundations of the solid globe were suddenly rent asunder, and that the day of universal dissolution was at hand" [182]), *Pym* takes *Symzonia*'s fears to their nightmarish ends. Moreover, when Pym finally plunges through the hole, it is into the saving arms of his alter ego, the "dusky, fiendish" Peters (198). Pym discovers himself through blackness, not whiteness; indeed, as Toni Morrison has argued, the black shadow often becomes the reflexive surrogate through which whites meditate upon the self (1992:17). *Pym*, then, not only points out how whiteness is constructed in relation to blackness, but also shows how white identity is mediated through a combined desire for and dread of blackness. Pym's fear of falling into the abyss is matched only by his longing for this plunge: "my whole soul was pervaded with *a longing to fall*; a desire, a yearning, a passion utterly uncontrollable" (198). Beneath the surface of the world, there exists not a more perfect version of the white self, but the black self—both loathed and desired—with which Pym must come to terms.

The novel's ending, where Pym is drawn into another abyss, this time to be met by a shrouded figure of "perfect whiteness," seems to retreat from the more complicated notion of racial identity set forth by the rest of the book. For instance, Sidney Kaplan reads the ending as Pym's rushing "away from the Black into the embracing arms of the comforting White" (xxii). I argue, however, that the ending is less an evasion of than a repeat engagement with the issues of the previous, live-burial scene and, indeed, of the novel as a whole. The ending not only echoes Pym's plunge into the arms of the "filmy figure" of Peters, but it also reiterates the complexity of fear and desire: the figure of "perfect whiteness" both blocks and embraces (198, 206). Like the shrouded figure, the ending embraces the comforting illusion of pure whiteness while revealing the limitations of this embrace; it reaffirms that race is merely a fantasy, a projection, an illusion—a white curtain, a shrouded figure.

The complex production of whiteness is the focus of the ending. An external projection, not an internal identification—everything is described as white but Pym himself—whiteness is less a fact of Pym's self-identity than an imaginative wish fulfillment. In his descriptions of Nu-Nu's strange response to the white that surrounds him, Pym not only denies his own fear ("The Polar winter appeared to be coming on—but coming without its terrors," he claims [204]) by projecting it onto Nu-Nu's black body, but also reaffirms the power of whiteness by reading terror as its byproduct. However, Pym's fantasy of "perfect whiteness" continues to be mediated through blackness. First, his white imaginary is only visible next to the dark: "The darkness had materially increased, relieved only by the glare of the water thrown back from the white curtain before us" (205). Second, Nu-Nu's black body regulates the terms of his engagement with this projection: "Here-upon Nu-Nu stirred in the bottom of the boat; but upon touching him, we found his spirit departed. And now we rushed into the embraces of the cataract, where a chasm threw itself open to receive us. But there arose in our pathway a shrouded human figure, very far larger in its proportions than any dweller among men. And the hue of the skin of the figure was of the perfect whiteness of the snow" (206). In its conclusion, *Pym* seems to argue that blackness blocks whiteness, since Pym cannot rush into the embracing white arms as long as Nu-Nu is alive. As a result, the novel seems to reinstate the color line, exorcising blackness in order to embrace whiteness. However, the ending can also be read in precisely the opposite way: whiteness can only be embraced through blackness. Given the timing of Nu-Nu's death, it is also possible to see the shrouded figure at the end as his spiritual revivification. Pym might be embracing precisely what he hopes to evade.

The difficulty of pinning down *Pym*'s ending reflects the contradictory impulses of the novel as a whole. The ending, like the tale itself, desires "perfect whiteness" yet reveals its impossibility. While the ending makes clear the costs of such an illusion—the terror for blacks, the numbness for whites—it still finds comfort in the hollow reflection of whiteness. Pym's role as the living dead throughout the story exemplifies the novel's position: like Pym, who keeps hoping for a rebirth even as he is buried alive, *Pym* keeps trying to resolve the issue of race. The conclusion's final words—"*I have graven it within the hills, and my vengeance upon the dust within the rock*"—however, warn that the ghost of race will continue to return (208).

I suggest, then, that *Pym*'s obsession with whiteness has less to do with a simple message of white supremacy than with a complex, and even at times contradictory, claim that while white might be "right," it is neither perfect nor pure. I also suggest that readings of *Pym*'s racial discourse are often the projections of one of our most comforting critical illusions: that the terror of race exists only in the South. We need to ask how regional stereotypes allow a particular racial discourse to be canonized, how race is recognized regionally while exorcised nationally. We need to be able to articulate regional difference across the color line while also recognizing the pervasiveness of white racism. Poe's (mis)placement is useful precisely because his ghostly position can dislocate traditional critical paradigms. We must then, as Morrison argues, recognize the ghost of race in all its haunts: "All of us, readers and writers, are bereft when criticism remains too polite or too fearful to notice a disrupting darkness before its eyes" (1992:91). Instead of sleeping with comforting illusions of race as only a regional specter, we must remain awake to the nightmares of race that haunt our national literature.

5

(Un)Veiling the Marketplace: Nathaniel Hawthorne, Louisa May Alcott, and the Female Gothic

> The narrative, on the other hand, is always umbilicated to the Lady—fascinating and abject object of the telling.
> —Julia Kristeva, *Powers of Horror*

The gothic has been depicted by feminist critics as a female genre: written by, for, and about women. Since Ellen Moers's groundbreaking essay on *Frankenstein*, "The Female Gothic" (1976), the gothic has served as a useful site for feminist revisions of female identity and resistance to patriarchal power.[1] However, despite this revisionary trend, many readings of the female gothic continue to imprison it within the private sphere, viewing it either in psychological terms or solely in terms of domestic ideology. In this chapter, I locate the female gothic in relation to the public sphere of the nineteenth-century American marketplace. By dissolving the boundaries between public and private spheres, the female gothic in mid-nineteenth-century America does more than expose female entrapment within and rebellion against a patriarchal culture; it also reflects how the anxieties and dislocations of a new commodity culture were mediated through the female body. The female gothic, I argue, has as much to do with economic concerns as with gender. As the "abject object of the telling," the gothic heroine embodies the very thing she is supposed to hide: the marketplace.[2]

The American gothic has traditionally been defined through gender rather than economic issues. Leslie Fiedler, for example, argues that while the British gothic is concerned with class conflict, the American gothic is marked by its "chary treatment of women and of sex" (31). The "terrible Female" dominates Fiedler's reading: the fear of and flight from the abject woman—"that strategy of evasion, that flight from society to nature, from the world of women to the haunts of womenless men"—distinguishes the American gothic and "sets our novel apart from that of the rest of the Western world" (76). In Fiedler's reading, the abject woman represents the societal issues that America's gothic romances claim to escape and transcend. While the gender investments of Fiedler's model are openly visible, its class concerns are more veiled. Fiedler's own canon-creation, which replays the flight from the abject woman, reveals the class fears at the heart of his gendered model of American literature. Against a subliterary sentimental tradition of "scribbling women," Fiedler sets forth a serious gothic line associated with men. Arguing that "the gothic ... spurred on those serious American writers whom the example of the sentimental had only galled" (126), Fiedler names Charles Brockden Brown and the gothic as the starting point of American literary tradition, relegating Susanna Rowson and the sentimental to a subordinate position as a false start: "For better or for worse, the best-seller was invented in America ... before the serious successful novel" (93). Moreover, by associating with the sentimental those market characteristics usually linked to the gothic—stereotypical plots, best-seller status, female authors and audiences—Fiedler purges the gothic of its negative commercial attributes; by demonizing the sentimental as a popular female genre, Fiedler saves the gothic's respectability and manliness. In Fiedler's hands, then, American literature becomes a "literature of horror for boys"—a gothic literature written by, for, and about men (29).

In Fiedler's reworking of the gothic, we see what Eugenia DeLamotte describes as the masculinization of the gothic canon. DeLamotte argues that criticism on the gothic has a "tendency to see the 'high' form of Gothic as written by men and ... to see [the] Gothic in its fullest development as centering on a male rather than a female protagonist" (12). Fiedler creates a gender distinction both within the gothic itself—Monk Lewis replaces Anne Radcliffe as the progenitor of the gothic tradition—and between the gothic and the sentimental: the "serious" gothic is written by men whereas the "sub-literary" and popular sentimental is written by women. Given the studies showing the connections between the sentimental and the gothic, Fiedler's insistence that a "profound split" exists between the two genres seems an attempt to divest the gothic from its female and commercial attributes (93).[3] Fiedler's obsessive use of Hawthorne's term "scribbling women" exposes what is at stake: Fiedler must demonize the female writer and her commercially profitable work lest she gain too much cultural capital in the newly "open" canon of American literature. In Fiedler's canon, therefore, gender also signifies class status. His flight from female authors is an attempt not only to solidify a male canon of American literature but also to base that canon on cultural rather than commercial capital.

Instead of fleeing the abject woman (both as fictional character and female author), this chapter locates her at the center of the gothic. Moreover, it argues that the sentimental and the gothic are interdependent, not essentially different. Both are female and commercial genres; both are constructed by, yet manipulate, the marketplace. These genres function like the dark/light pairings of women who populate gothic literature: the gothic enacts the maneuvers of a commodity culture that the sentimental strategically veils. Through theatrical, staged settings, mysterious identities, and the unveiling of the disjunction between appearance and reality, the gothic foregrounds the fluid world of commodity culture and shows how it is performatively constructed. Conversely, by articulating a sincere world populated by stable selves, the sentimental masks the market, creating a separate domestic realm of innate worth. If the gothic reveals that everything is already commercialized, the sentimental mystifies cultural capital, locating it in a separate sphere. The gothic, then, shows how the representation of women is an effect of economics; in making that effect invisible, the sentimental manipulates the market and accrues capital. Like the abject woman, usually killed in favor of her sentimental sister, the gothic's unveilings of the marketplace are often masked and remystified by the sentimental in order to make money.

The commercial exchange between these two genres—how each presents a particular economic model and how these models are interdependent—is central to my examination of Nathaniel Hawthorne's and Louisa May Alcott's work. Both authors had to negotiate the newly commercialized literary marketplace, and both turned to the gothic and the sentimental as strategies by which to work out the commercial investments of their literary enterprises. Whereas Hawthorne remains ambivalent about his commercialization, Alcott manipulates the market masterfully. By examining the links between Hawthorne's and Alcott's careers as well as their deployment of the gothic and the sentimental, this chapter articulates the interconnections of gender, genre, and economics. Race is not foregrounded, but it informs the argument: when commodity culture is read in terms of the slave economy, the author's and the lady's enthrallment to the marketplace is more fully legible.

Veiled Ladies

> Yet what is most interesting about the Veiled Lady is that this personification of woman domestically defined is in no sense domestic.
> —Richard Brodhead, "Veiled Ladies"

In mid-nineteenth-century America, the veiled lady functioned as a dominant image of womanhood. The popularity of the mesmerized soul displayed onstage behind a veil, statues of veiled women such as Chauncey Ives's *Undine* on view in public exhibitions, and model artist shows that had women pose as classical statues behind veils on the theatrical stage all attest to this image's cultural importance. The motionless woman behind the veil represented the dual position of the Victorian woman in America: she both embodied the marketplace and made it disappear. The veil marked her paradoxical position, signifying what it also concealed. By imprisoning the lady in a separate, inviolate sphere, the veil symbolized her disappearance from the marketplace; behind her veil of private purity, the lady took the "true" woman's proper position in the spiritual sphere that transcended the economic one. Yet by signaling her performative nature, the veil uncovered the lady's connections to commercial culture: as the spectral object on display in the public sphere, she embodied the market transactions at the heart of "true womanhood." The veiled lady, then, both tamed and represented the monsters of the marketplace. Whether acting as domesticator or demon, she was located in, responding to, and helping constitute the marketplace.

Indeed, as Alice Kessler-Harris argues, the creation of a domestic ideology in nineteenth-century America was a direct result of economic forces. Returned to the private sphere after the 1837 panic and subsequent depression, women's wage-earning power was replaced by domestic power (46); the rise of domestic ideology corresponded directly to the de-skilling of women's work (51). Deprived of commercial capital, women were compensated with cultural capital. Armed with the spiritual values lacking in the marketplace, the middle-class woman, in the role of angel, was expected to domesticate the market's demons. However, this exorcism itself became a commercialized phenomenon as women's private powers were increasingly displayed in public; the illusion of women's freedom from the marketplace was harder to sustain. The veiled lady, then, represented the "true woman's" double bind: she was produced by the market yet had to veil her connection to it.

The rise of spiritualism in the 1840s and 1850s, along with its more sensational manifestations—mesmerism and mediumship—shows how the veiled lady served to both represent and mask the marketplace. As an extradomestic institution, spiritualism extended women's private powers into the public sphere.[4] On stage, the medium acted out women's private position in antebellum America: covered in white from head to toe, a disembodied spirit imprisoned in her own impenetrable sphere, the veiled lady acted the role of the angel in the house. Mediums exemplified the "true" woman's typical attributes and proper position. They were usually young women who after a lengthy illness found themselves acutely sensitive to the spiritual world; entranced often in an unconscious state, mediums served as the mouthpieces through which voices from the spiritual world spoke.[5] By insisting on their own passivity—relegating their selection as mediums to the spirits and claiming the role of passive instruments—and by making the typical feminine characteristics of sensitivity, suffering, and sympathy the hallmarks of their trade, mediums conformed to the ideal of true womanhood. The mesmerized medium publicly staged her compliance with the ideology of women's domestic powers.

The mesmerized lady also reveals how the private sphere was created in and by the public sphere. The fact that the "essential passivity of women was asserted in a public arena, displayed before thousands of witnesses" marks the lady's central contradiction: she was both private woman and public performer (Braude 85). The medium represented the ideal of femininity as well as its corruption. Her inviolate yet visually penetrated body became the site of social disorder as well as social regulation. In transgressing the boundaries of her proper sphere by going public as a performer, the medium became vulnerable to the male monsters of the market. Mediums were taken over by spirits and male mesmerists and voyeuristically consumed by their audience. Their commercial connections were depicted in sexual terms: since they relinquished their bodies for pay, mediums were viewed as promiscuous and likened to prostitutes (Braude 124). In her guise as the material body on display, the medium symbolized the marketplace: her commodified body was exchanged between men; moreover, her psychic enslavement to the mesmerist suggests her alliance to another market economy, slavery.

The veiled lady's dual role as the soul transcending the market economy and the slave imprisoned in it is evident in the most famous statue of the period: Hiram Powers's *The Greek Slave* (see figure). Sculpted by Powers in several versions between 1844 and 1869 and placed in traveling exhibitions, the statue was seen by over one hundred thousand people in America during the late 1840s and 1850s. Like the veiled ladies on stage, the sculpture embodies the contradictory roles of the "true" woman. Unveiled, with her drapery by her side on the pedestal, she represents the woman in the marketplace; she is a commodity for sale in the American as well as the Turkish

1. Hiram Powers, *The Greek Slave*
Yale University Art Gallery Purchase
Olive Louise Dann Fund

market. But as the woman veiled in Christian modesty, humility, and resignation, her head looking downward, her locket and cross by her side, she symbolizes the "true" woman who can escape the shackles of the marketplace and entrance her viewers. The *Courier and Enquirer* (August 31, 1847) describes the effect of the statue: "Its presence is a magic circle within whose precincts all are held spell-bound and almost speechless. The grey-headed man, the youth, the matron, and the maid alike yield themselves to the magic of its power, and gaze upon it in silent and reverential admiration, and so pure an atmosphere breathes around it, that the eye of man beams only with reverent delight" (qtd. in Hyman 220).[6] Read in the context of the sentimental narratives surrounding it—including the accompanying description of the statue that, as Joy Kasson argues, directs the viewer away from her body to her face and emotions (1992:178–79)—*The Greek Slave* accrues power from her ability to veil, as if by magic, the very thing she so starkly reveals: her nudity and her place as market object for sale both as a statue and as a slave. Surrounded by her veil of purity, the statue turns her spectators' potentially sexual inquisitive glances into reverential admiration. Her veil, as Reverend Orville Dewey argues in an article featured in the statue's accompanying booklet, consists of sentiment: "The Greek Slave is clothed all over with sentiment; sheltered, protected by it from every profane eye. Brocade, cloth of gold, could not be a more complete protection than the vesture of the holiness in which she stands" (qtd. in Kasson 1992:179). The statue's sentimental pose, along with the sentimental narratives that instruct her audience's reading, provides viewers a way to deny her presence in the marketplace as well as their own. As a white body, the Greek slave represents the veil of femininity, but when refigured as a black body in "The Virginian Slave" (see figure), she explicitly symbolizes the market that buys and sells female flesh. As Joseph Roach shows in his reading of the multiple spectacles of the tragic octoroon in the mid-nineteenth century, race functions as a symbolic substitute for gender. Race and gender are both commodities, he argues, but it is "the scarcely visible presence of black blood that provides the signifier of commodification" (219). *The Greek Slave* may in its marble whiteness appear to be above the marketplace, but its signs of bondage mark it as a commodity.[7]

The veil, however, could reveal as much as it concealed. This is apparent in two statues of Undine: Chauncey Ives's *Undine Receiving Her Soul* (1855) (see figure) and Joseph Mozier's *Undine* (1867) (see figure). Demonic water sprite and domestic maiden, the woman who kills her husband and mourns faithfully at his grave, Undine represents the period's dual image of wom-

2. Anonymous, "The Virginian Slave. Intended As a Companion to Powers' 'Greek Slave.'"
Illustration from *Punch* 20 (1851): 236.

anhood.[8] In both Ives's and Mozier's representations, she is shown veiled, the veil both covering her body and drawing attention to it. The undulating folds of the Ives statue draw the viewer's eye upward and the veil forms a shadow that highlights the face. Both emphasize Undine's spiritual qualities receiving her soul; the body, which has yet to move upward under that veil, continues to symbolize the abject nature of her watery state: her clothing adheres to her body and outlines the voluptuous female form. Poised above her face, the veil has yet to come down and fully cover her body. In Mozier's statue a similar disjunction exists between Undine's modestly posed face and her seductively draped figure. Moreover, Undine is pictured as a woman contained within a veil—its circling swathes constrain her—as well as a woman manipulating the veil—she resembles a harem dancer. These two statues, then, offer a contradictory reading: Undine may be the dutiful wife cloaked in mourning, or the mysterious water sprite manipulating the veil of seductive femininity.

The statues' living counterparts also reveal the multiple operations of the veil. The model artist shows of the late 1840s and 1850s, in which "women clad only in close-fitting tights or leotards stood motionless in imitation of classical statuary," manipulated the veil in order to earn audience interest (Dudden 116).[9] Cashing in on the fascination with *The Greek Slave*, theater managers created sexualized spectacles; a veil of gauze was sometimes placed between the audience and the woman to enhance her naked appearance. Unlike in *The Greek Slave*, the veil did not hide the woman's relation to the market but made it more visible. Without the veil, she could not be imagined as naked; however, constructed by it as in a separate sphere, she appeared unattainable. Once the veil was violated, her nakedness would disappear: the veil constructed the very desire it denied.

The veil's ability to cover its own constructions is also evident in the private theatricals of the period: genteel parlor performances. As Karen Halttunen argues, the middle-class parlor became the stage on which the "true" woman performed her "natural" role. Asked to exemplify sincere self-expression, the middle-class woman had to disavow the theatricality of her own performance. As Halttunen writes, these women were asked by etiquette books to "obey the sentimental injunction that there be 'no *stage effect*'" (101). In her sentimental pose, the middle-class woman manipulated the veil even as she denied the effort that created its effects. Her fashionable clothes, transparent signs of her inner state that also hid her body, were veils that carried traces of the market: costumes as well as advertisements of a consumer culture. Parlor theatricals of the 1850s and 1860s,

3. Chauncey B. Ives, *Undine Receiving Her Soul* Yale University Art Gallery; Gift of Alice A. Allen in memory of her father, Simon Sterne

4. Joseph Mozier, *Undine*
Courtesy of The University of Dayton

which often took the form of tableaux vivants, further showed how the illusions of the marketplace operated in the domestic realm. The middle-class mistress of sentimentality might attempt to deny the market's effects through skillful performance, but her theatricality exposed the economic investments of her domestic sphere.

Hawthorne's and Alcott's theatricalized narratives participate in their culture's veiling and unveiling of the marketplace. Pictured as a classical statue scantily clad and stripped by Coverdale's inquisitive stare, Zenobia in *The Blithedale Romance* both attracts Coverdale and threatens to subsume him. She is the veiled lady who threatens to unveil and reveal herself a monster of the marketplace. Alcott's actresses, who perform on the public stage as well as in the parlor, symbolize the performative value of the "true" woman.[10] The cultural ambivalence of the veiled lady is reenacted within both Hawthorne's and Alcott's works and their authorial careers. The veiled lady provides the symbol through which to explore their market investments. The difference in these authors' manipulation of this figure reflects their different economic interests and reveals the market to be not only an unstable but a gendered space.

Zenobia's Ghost Story

A veil may be needful, but never a mask.
—Nathaniel Hawthorne, *The American Notebooks*

Hawthorne's *The Blithedale Romance* (1852) exemplifies how the market is mediated through the veiled lady. While Coverdale claims at the opening of the novel that this lady has "little do to with the present narrative," she lies both literally and figuratively at the center of the story: not only does Zenobia's legend of the veiled lady occur halfway through the novel, but the veiled lady also serves as the novel's central symbol of market relations (6). Following *The House of the Seven Gables* (1851), a novel that anxiously polices the market's intrusion into the domestic sphere of middle-class culture, *The Blithedale Romance* collapses the boundaries between public and private. Whereas in *The House of the Seven Gables*, Phoebe's "homely magic" is able to cleanse the house of market intrusion, *The Blithedale Romance* shows that intrusion to be complete and irreversible.[11] In this novel the veiled lady, not a domestic sprite but a commodified object on public display, manipulates the marketplace.

Throughout *The Blithedale Romance*, the market is depicted through the gothic metaphor of mesmerism. Replete with magicians and magnetism and centered on the veiled lady, mesmerism exposes market identity and relationships as superficial spectacles through theatrical stage effects. As Coverdale's description shows, the mesmerizing magician, Westervelt, exemplifies this identity:

> In the excess of his delight, he opened his mouth wide, and disclosed a gold band around the upper part of his teeth; thereby making it apparent that every one of his brilliant grinders and incisors was a sham. This discovery affected me very oddly. I felt as if the whole man were a moral and physical humbug; his wonderful beauty of face, for aught I knew, might be removable like a mask; and, tall and comely as his figure looked, he was perhaps but a wizened little elf, gray and decrepit, with nothing genuine about him, save the wicked expression of his grin. (88–89)

With his "spectral character," symbolized by the gold band that reveals the falseness of his "brilliant grinders and incisors," Westervelt is the figure of a fluid, insubstantial self. His excessive laughter, like his excessive dress, shows his self-presentation to be a costume, not an indicator of what is inside: he may really be a wizened little elf and his beautiful face just a mask. In fact, far from having any correlation to inner identity, Westervelt's displayed self reveals the lack of a stable core: for instance, by putting on a pair of spectacles he alters his face so much that Coverdale hardly knows him (96). His character, as Coverdale later remarks, is all "artifice" (199).

The alliance between Westervelt's artificial character and the market is achieved through the gothic. As Eve Sedgwick argues, the gothic's concern with surface reveals identity to be superficial, not interior; social, not innate. With mistaken identities, doubles, and disguises, the gothic shows identity to be imposed from the outside, "social and relational rather than original and private" (Sedgwick 1981:256). Andrea Henderson takes Sedgwick's argument a step further by linking the gothic's concern with superficial identity to a fluid market identity. The early British gothic novel, Henderson argues, reflects the market-based model of identity gaining ground at the end of the eighteenth century by making character a matter of "surface, display and 'consumption' by others" (226). As both mesmerist and machine, Westervelt represents the market man in the guise of gothic villain. His "gold" teeth, like his "coal-black" hair and "metallic laugh," signal his relationship to the material objects of commodity culture (92). Moreover, his "cold and dead materialism," which issues from him as if "out of a sepulchral vault" and brings "the smell of corruption along with it," is constantly depicted in gothic terms (200): his body is a "mechanical contrivance, in which a demon walked about" (188). Like Hollingsworth, whose competitive self-interest and lack of sympathy cause Zenobia to describe him as "a monster! A cold, heartless, self-beginning and self-ending piece of mechanism," Westervelt is changed by his market desires into a hollow machine hiding a monster (218).

Westervelt's use of magnetism demonstrates the market exigencies of shadowy transactions and grand illusion. If the mesmerist's theatricality shows identity to be a masquerade, his ability to control other people's characters reveals the self to be purely public. Since human character is "but soft wax in his hands," the mesmerist can alter it with the impress of his powerful will, making a maiden turn away from her lover's kiss or a mother reject her babe (198). By turning people into slaves, magnetism reveals that everything and everyone is subject to commodification: Zenobia is willing to sell Priscilla for Hollingsworth's love, just as Hollingsworth sacrifices his friendship with Coverdale when Coverdale refuses to invest in his scheme. Indeed, the blackness associated with descriptions of the two master magnetists of the novel, Westervelt and Hollingsworth, suggests the market economy's relationship to another economy that turns people into property—slavery. Mesmerism's scenes of horrifying exchange and spectral consumption figure it as a gothic marketplace that replicates the dynamics of the slave economy.[12]

The market realm is portrayed not only by the male mesmerist but also by his slave. The veiled lady, displayed on the public stage and sold by the mesmerist to the gaze of others, also embodies the market self: she is a "shadowy phenomenon" who seems to have "no more reality than the candlelight image of one's self" (108). Daughter of the economic man, Old Moodie, and lover/bond slave to the market magician, Westervelt, the veiled lady is bound to the indeterminate and fluctuating value of commodities.[13] Containing no "single and unchangeable set of features beneath the veil," she is the superficial self whose identity and worth are constructed by the viewer. Shrouded and enigmatic, she is pure exchange value: her relationship to the mesmerist is all contractual, and her "silvery" veil marks her relationship to money. Like money, the veil as a "spell" or "powerful enchantment" works only if it is accepted as a sign for what lies behind it. Without belief in their symbolism, the powers of the veil and the market would both fail. Moreover, by protecting her mystery, the veil increases the lady's interest. Fear that her veil might hide a corpse, the head of a skeleton, or Medusa herself reveals the veiled lady's horrifying embodiment of the market economy (109–10).

While the veiled lady is the riddle that fuels the novel's mystery and the reader's interest, everyone in the novel is implicated in the world of commodities. Far from being a utopian experiment, Blithedale is a theatrical world where identity is hidden and pigs go to market.[14] Even Silas, the novel's representative of common sense and material reality, appears as a specter: "The steam arose from his soaked garments, so that the stout yeoman looked vaporous and spectre-like" (18). The only person who seems exempt from this realm's control is Coverdale. As the representative of the private sphere—constantly figured in domestic spaces or private enclosures—he claims to remain an outsider in Blithedale. Asserting an inviolate identity, Coverdale is the novel's spokesperson for the stable self. He constantly flees a fluid society that threatens to destroy his individuality: fearing the world has turned into an "unsubstantial bubble," Coverdale leaves for the city to take an "exterior view" of things (140). He fears being absorbed by a public realm symbolized by mesmerism. Whether on his sickbed with Zenobia or in the climactic scene with Hollingsworth, Coverdale must fight against each magnetist's "irresistible force" in order to retain his own perspective: "Had I but touched his extended hand, Hollingsworth's magnetism would perhaps have penetrated me with his own conception of all these matters," Coverdale claims (134). In both instances, Coverdale becomes the medium threatened by intrusion from without: "Zenobia's sphere, I imagine, impressed itself powerfully on mine, and transformed me . . . into something like a mesmerical clairvoyant" (46–47). Throughout the novel, Coverdale crosses genders by claiming the position of the inviolate woman who refuses the seductions of the marketplace.

Coverdale's belief in the veiled lady's impenetrability marks his refusal of commercial horrors. Recoiling in "horror and disgust" from readings of the veiled lady as hollow and material, he chooses to "religiously" believe in her "virgin reserve and sanctity of soul"; he would perish sooner than believe that "the individual soul was virtually annihilated" (198, 203, 198). Coverdale responds to the gothic horror of the marketplace with a sentimental belief in interiority and integrity. Indeed, throughout the novel, he reads market signs in sentimental terms. Not only does he want to turn the pigs into pets, but he also reads the lady's veil as a sign of her innocence rather than of her relationship to money: "It was white, with somewhat of a subdued silver sheen, like the sunny side of a cloud" (6). Coverdale's sentimental speculations, however, highlight his investment in veiling the marketplace. Fearful of being subsumed into the gothic market where "true" value only accrues through exchange, Coverdale cloaks the market economy in his sentimental fictions.

Although the novel exposes Coverdale's sentimental constructions at every turn, Zenobia most fully reveals his readings as illusory. She refuses Coverdale's attempt to turn Priscilla into a "domestic sprite" by pointing out the physical marks of her marketplace labor (35); in her drawing room, she unmasks Coverdale's claims to sympathy and duty as prurient self-interest (170). While Zenobia constantly challenges Coverdale's accountings of things, her own gothic tale, which lies at the heart of Coverdale's sentimental story, most fully exposes his attempt to veil the marketplace.

Zenobia's tale breaks into two parts. The first is about a gentleman, Theodore, lured into a market transaction he does not understand. This part discusses the veiled lady's relation to the market economy as sentimental. Theodore, the "young gentleman" who serves as the central character in this section of the tale, sees the world in sentimental terms (109); he thinks that there are characters still to defend and that his senses do not "play [him] false" (109). Armed with his common sense and his "sturdy perception of realities," Theodore aims to dispel the spectral illusion of the veiled lady (111). However, instead of discovering proof of the veiled woman's "true" identity, he witnesses her disappearance. Expecting a world where private identity is openly displayed, he discovers that even in the private space of the lady's dressing room her identity remains hidden. Instead of finding a sentimental world where value appears self-evident, Theodore is plunged into a gothic realm of secret selves where even the private is public, a market world of risk and chance. The veiled lady might promise Theodore "in all maiden modesty" that if "thou shalt be mine" there will be "never more a veil between us," but she also notes that "so much may a maiden say behind the veil" (113). The sentimental can promise a world without mystery only once its representations are believed. Ironically, only investing in the veil's performative qualities can make the veil disappear.

Theodore, however, is unwilling to take this leap of faith. His fear that the veil might disguise "the lips of a dead girl, or the jaws of a skeleton, or the grinning cavity of a monster's mouth" shows his apprehension about how the veil functions (113). Its role is precisely what he fears: to hide the gothic horrors of the market. When Theodore does not have the "heart" to recognize the veiled woman or the "holy faith" to believe in her, he has a failure of sentiment (113). Instead of investing in the veil, Theodore tries to retreat from the marketplace altogether. Falling back on an aristocratic discourse of insult and injury, Theodore rejects the veiled lady's contract and acts out of privilege: " 'Excuse me, fair lady,' said Theodore—and I think he nearly burst into a laugh—'if I prefer to lift the veil first; and for this affair of the kiss, we may decide upon it, afterwards' " (113). His laughter disguises the bare contractual negotiation taking place. In contrast, the sad, sweet-voiced maiden understands the "contemptuous interpretation" he has made: stripped of sentiment, she becomes a mere commodity (114). Theodore may believe that he operates in an economy where power is relatively stable and gentlemen's pledges are not subject to the vagaries of the marketplace, but in his unwillingness to kiss a woman when the "odds were ten to one that her teeth were defective," he shows himself subject to the risks of trade (113). "Concealed" behind a screen, he may think that he can discover the lady's mysteries without showing himself, yet by exposing her without first investing faith in her veil, he loses everything (111). Theodore's punishment is to "pine, forever and ever, for another sight of that dim, mournful face—which might have been his life-long, household, fireside joy" (114). By lifting the veil he enters the economy of unending desire; and by failing to invest in the maiden's sentiment, he loses the woman who could domesticate those desires.

Here ends what could be read as merely a tale of misguided sentiment. However, Zenobia offers a second, supplemental part that rereads the narrative: "Hearken, my sweet friends—and hearken, dear Priscilla—and you shall learn the little more that Zenobia can tell you!" (114). The "little more" comes in the form of a gothic tale that unveils sentiment's investments in the marketplace, exposing the economic relations that the sentimental tries to disguise. Indeed, Zenobia's gothic tale reveals her sentimental narrative to be just another market strategy.

In the supplement, itself another tale, the veiled lady reappears amid a "knot of visionary people," infiltrating the Utopian experiment with her economic presence (114). A terrible magician engages the aid of another woman to capture and reimprison the veiled lady under a silvery veil. The Magician represents an economy built on exchange: his bartered soul gains him her services for seven years while his manipulations of the veil makes her his bond-slave forever. The Magician understands that the marketplace is both a type of hell, where one must barter one's soul in order to make a profit, *and* a place of grand illusion. Unlike Theodore, who wants to lift the veil and discover the secrets behind it, the Magician wants to drop it. In his hands, the veil's airy substance becomes imbued with significance; he not only creates an illusion but also successfully lures others to invest in it. Setting the veiled lady in competition with the maiden who is her "deadliest enemy" in love and fortune, the magician employs the maiden to do his bidding (115). By appropriating this woman's power as well as the veiled lady's, he makes a good profit. Investing not in the veil's representation of reality but in its performative power, the Magician accrues capital.

Zenobia's enactment of her tale marks her alliance with the magician. She too understands the mesmerizing power of performance: "Arriving at the catastrophe, and uttering the fatal words, she flung the gauze over Priscilla's head; and, for an instant, her auditors held their breath" (116). As the mesmerist who looks into Priscilla's eyes for inspiration to tell her tale, Zenobia infuses performance with value. Throwing the veil over Priscilla at the end allows her to translate familiar realities into illusions, removing her audience to an imaginary space that her own tale-telling exploits. Her tale's success depends on her commitment to the gothic marketplace of illusion: she is not concerned with what is behind the veil, but with the unending process of manipulating it. Asking "have you never thought how remarkable it was, that this marvellous creature should vanish, all at once, while her renown was on the increase, before the public had grown weary of her, and when the enigma of her character, instead of being solved, presented itself more mystically at every exhibition?" Zenobia shows her understanding of supply and demand: she too must tantalize her audience with a mystery she never fully solves (108). Indeed, her tale, told "wildly and rapidly, hesitating at no extravagance, and dashing at absurdities," is a gothic one of excess where, as with the veiled lady, "there is more in [the] story than can well be accounted for" (107, 109). This is precisely how Zenobia's tale accrues value. Like the veiled lady, Zenobia gains interest in the constant circulation of tales by and about her. Infinitely consumable, her performance becomes her marketable product.

Hence, even when Zenobia claims to tell a "simple little tale" she is enacting another strategic performance (108). Her sentimental tale, like its gothic supplement, is acted out for an audience; the two tales are part of the same story. When Zenobia asks Priscilla at the end of the performance, "'How do you find yourself, my love?' . . . lifting a corner of the gauze, and peeping beneath it, with a mischievous smile," she reenacts the part of Theodore—but with a knowledge that saves her from his fate: her smile belies her sincerity and points to her understanding that sentiment is merely another layer of illusion (116). Unlike Theodore, Zenobia uses sentiment to cover her market transactions. Her concern about Priscilla's well-being—"Ah, the dear little soul! . . . Pray bring a glass of water!"—distracts her audience from the fact that she has sold Priscilla to Westervelt (116). In refusing her tale's effect only after its ghastly conclusion, Zenobia shows her lack of interest in what or who lies behind the veil; her sentimental sympathy, itself another mask, is part of her play. Zenobia, then, is a grand magician in the guise of a sentimental woman writer. She is Hawthorne's scribbling woman, who exploits sentiment in order to manipulate the literary marketplace.

Able to capitalize on the sentimental without losing sight of its performative nature, Zenobia scorns those who, like Coverdale, invest in the "reality" of its illusion. Throughout the novel, Coverdale operates very much like Theodore. With his bachelor apartment, his "morning lounge at the reading-room or picture-gallery" and his nightly dinner at the Albion, Coverdale lives in a world of leisured privilege (40). Like Theodore, he wants to lift the veil and solve its mystery, to "account" for everything. For instance, by taking a back view of the boarding house, Coverdale desires to lift the front's artificial concealment; yet, as Zenobia emphasizes when she drops the curtain after looking back at Coverdale with her powerful eyes, there are no perspectives without veils or investments. Operating from behind a screen, Coverdale, like Theodore, enters the market even as he claims a safe distance from it.

However, unlike Theodore, Coverdale is in the end willing to suspend his skepticism and invest in sentiment. Both his reading of Zenobia's death and his revelation of his love for Priscilla are sentimentalized versions of what has been transacted. Coverdale converts Zenobia's death into a conventional sentimental story about a woman with a broken heart, complete with a transcendental moral: "It is because the spirit is inestimable, that the lifeless body is so little valued," he concludes (244). Yet this moral is itself marked in economic terms. Coverdale might also tell us in his conclusion that Hollingsworth is morally ruined, but his vengeful comment about Hollingsworth's failure to build an edifice for the reformation of criminals belies Hollingsworth's other ruin, which is economic. Coverdale's sentimental stories constantly reveal their market interests. His confession, an attempt to gain himself some "credit" since he has made such a "poor" figure in his own narrative by establishing "no separate interest," ends up doing just that—earning his story credit: he goes from having "nothing, nothing, nothing" to tell to the biggest revelation of them all (225). Coverdale's final declaration—"I—I myself—was in love—with—PRISCILLA!"—claims to lift the veil and clear up the story's mysteries (247); however, it turns out to be just another veil hiding yet one more story. What claims to be the truth is another tease; Coverdale is more like Zenobia than he imagines. In asking the reader to suppose him blushing and turning away his face as he discloses his secret, Coverdale hides his market manipulation with a sentimental stance. Moreover, his confession, the sentimental supplement to his own story, explains nothing. This solution, however, gives closure and therefore credit to his story. By turning the business transaction that begins the novel into a love story, he can take his tale to market without ever having to explain the novel's market economy or acknowledge his own investments. Unlike Zenobia's supplement, which seeks to unveil the fraud at the heart of the sentimental story even as it invests in sentiment's performative powers, Coverdale's supplement denies the role of sentiment in veiling the marketplace.

By investing in sentiment but refusing knowledge of its illusion, Coverdale is able to evade Theodore's fate and Zenobia's revelation that all stories are driven by the marketplace. He wants to be like Zenobia, whose stories go everywhere, without having to circulate in the marketplace himself. Coverdale's statement that he has given up poetry hides his true position: "I have given it up, notwithstanding that Doctor Griswold—as the reader, of course, knows—has placed me at a fair elevation among our minor minstrelsy, on the strength of my pretty little volume, published ten years ago" (246). His claim is contradictory: he may have given up poetry, yet his reputation as a poet, as the literate reader is expected to know, continues to be circulated in the cultural marketplace through Griswold's literary canonization. Coverdale's poetry might not be profitable commercially, but it has cachet in cultural circles. By taking himself out of circulation—stopping writing poetry and going to Europe—Coverdale manages to retreat to a realm of cultural capital where the vagaries of financial capital do not seem to matter. However, as Coverdale's own confession reveals in its anxiety to establish a "separate" interest from the narrative that preceded it, there are no spheres free and clear of the market.

Like Coverdale, Hawthorne is anxious about his cultural capital becoming commercial, particularly in a literary marketplace where women writers were accruing more money and notoriety than men. Hawthorne reveals his fear of a marketplace outside his masculine and economic control: writing from England to his publisher William Ticknor in 1855, Hawthorne explains that he plans to stay abroad for two more years "for I have not seen half enough of England, and there is the germ of a new Romance in my mind, which will be all the better for ripening slowly. Besides, America is now wholly given over to a d——d mob of scribbling women, and I should have no chance of success while the public taste is occupied with their trash—and should be ashamed of myself if I did succeed" (*Letters, 1853–1856*, 304). In choosing to depict the "scribbling women" as a "mob," Hawthorne uses gender and class hierarchies to demonize women writers' market success: the literary marketplace is not only populated by women rather than men, but also run by a mob rather than an elite ruling class. By staying in England with his romance "ripening slowly," Hawthorne defensively rejects this model of market success. Arguing that economic failure is the sign of cultural superiority, Hawthorne repositions himself, in his wife Sophia's terms, as a "Crowned King in the realm of Letters & Genius" (*Letters, 1843–1853*, 511). Choosing, like many other male authors during this period, to separate culture and commerce, Hawthorne can claim success in the more highly valued realm of the cultural.[15]

Hawthorne's letters to his publishers William Ticknor and James T. Fields, however, reveal the connections between his cultural capital and his commercial success. They are filled not only with concerns about his literary reputation but also with requests for money. Rejecting Fields's wish to republish his early works, particularly *Fanshawe*, Hawthorne writes, "I earnestly recommend you not to brush away the dust that may have settled over them. Whatever might do me credit, you may be pretty sure that I should be ready enough to bring forward. Anything else, it is our mutual interest to conceal" (*Letters, 1843–1853*, 383). Hawthorne's commercial credit was based on his cultural capital, as Richard Brodhead shows in *The School of Hawthorne*; hence, it was in Hawthorne's and his publisher's mutual interest not to reveal his immature productions. Having created a market for fine literature and used the promotional tactics of the mass marketplace to turn Hawthorne into a "classic" writer, Fields relied upon the author's cultural capital to make money.[16] As Brodhead writes, "if Fields's publishing machinery helped make Hawthorne's reputation, it is no less true that Hawthorne's highly visible and exclusive association with Fields helped confer luster on Fields's firm, his magazine, and his salon—prestige those institutions could then distribute onto other authors, in turn" (58). Signing autographs and posing for photographs, Hawthorne was complicit in the commercial process (Brodhead 71). In a letter to Fields about *The Scarlet Letter*, Hawthorne makes his commercial manipulations clear: "If 'The Scarlet Letter' is to be the title, would it not be well to print it on the title-page in red ink? I am not quite sure about the good taste of so doing; but it would certainly be piquant and appropriate—and, I think, attractive to the great gull whom we are endeavoring to circumvent" (*Letters, 1843–53*, 308). Hawthorne is willing to sacrifice "good taste" to dupe readers into buying his book. However, even in this proposal Hawthorne distinguishes his work from the mass marketplace: his novel needs a commercially appealing title page precisely because the gloom of its story will not appeal to popular tastes. As Hawthorne also writes about *The Scarlet Letter*, "my writings do not, nor ever will, appeal to the broadest class of sympathies, and therefore will not attain a very wide popularity" (Ibid. 311). While Hawthorne's literary reputation reflects the interdependence of commercial and cultural capital, his self-construction as a writer too "good" for the mass marketplace allows him to retain the image of a literary gentleman rather than be unmasked as a market magician. With finely bound leather books printed on good paper and stamped with the imprint of the press, the publishing house of Ticknor and Fields enabled Hawthorne to enter the literary marketplace under the pretense of gaining cultural prestige.

Hawthorne's association of the female writer with the commercial market and his own status as male author with a cultural capital exempt from commodification allows him to veil his position. Acting as a gentleman of letters even as he exploits the commercialization of the literary marketplace, Hawthorne desires the privileges of his profession without its liabilities. Like Coverdale, he wants to hide his entrance into the marketplace so that he can retain his cultural capital, since to follow women there would signal a switch in class status. Hawthorne needed to manipulate the market in order to be commercially successful enough to support his family and create his reputation, yet he had to appear to retain his distance from the market in order to protect the myth that his cultural capital was not commercial.[17]

The issue of how to participate in the marketplace and remain untainted by it haunts Hawthorne's romances. Beginning with *The Blithedale Romance*'s supplemental opening preface, the issue of genre is inflected with economic terms. Like the preface to *The House of the Seven Gables*, the term *romance* is defined through an economic discourse of rights and privileges. Hawthorne's claims for the romance reveal his desire to create a genre that is exempt from the exigencies of a market economy. He argues for the "conventional privilege . . . awarded to the romancer" of the "old countries," which allows an author "license with regard to every-day Probability" (2).

In other words, Hawthorne wants the right to make "free" with his experience at Brook Farm (2). In mining this "rich" theme, Hawthorne plans to use his experience as a resource for his fiction without having to pay for it (3). Refusing to comment upon the political and economic project of the Socialist community and claiming, as Coverdale did of the veiled lady, that it is "incidental" to his tale, Hawthorne turns Brook Farm into a theater "a little removed" from the "actual events of real lives" (1). The romance obscures its engagement with reality and in so doing denies its accountability to a market economy. Hawthorne's romances, according to Walter Benn Michaels, claim a "clear and unobstructed title" (157).

However, unlike Coverdale, Hawthorne cannot easily absolve himself of his market investments. He might, like Coverdale, present his organizing version of the novel as supplemental—his opening preface balances Coverdale's closing confession—and claim that he is neither invested nor trapped in the economies that the novel exposes; however, his inclusion of Zenobia's tale, which reveals that nothing is ever supplemental and that all tales operate in the marketplace, undercuts this position. His alliance with Coverdale only serves as a "cover"; the startling revelation of the narrative is not that Coverdale loves Priscilla but that Hawthorne resembles Zenobia. They are both in the business of dropping the veil. Hawthorne is not separate from the mob, but another scribbler like those women, whose art accrues value through performance.[18] Indeed, as several critics have pointed out, his attempt to veil his gloomy productions with sentimental endings was only one way he tried to gain commercial capital.[19]

Having written himself into the disclosure of his own market manipulations, Hawthorne cannot replace the mask; unable to invest in the artifice of his illusions, he can no longer drop the veil. Richard Brodhead describes the problem of Hawthorne's final phase as a recognition that fiction is not a vehicle of truth but a "cheap trick" (1976:114).[20] Indeed, *The Blithedale Romance*, like *The Marble Faun* (1860) and the fragmented gothic romances Hawthorne wrote in his later years, are full of narrative disjunctures that unveil Hawthorne's artifice, the "paint and pasteboard" of his composition (2). Yet *The Blithedale Romance*'s cheap tricks display not only the artifice of Hawthorne's fiction but also its connection to the market. The novel unmasks Hawthorne's illusions as market driven and in so doing reveals him to be a market magician. Instead of showing the author to be free and clear of any debt, *The Blithedale Romance* exposes his subjugation to the marketplace: the male author, like the veiled lady, is a market commodity.

Masking the Marketplace: Louisa May Alcott's Gothic Tales

Speaking of *Little Women* I said:
"The story is so natural and lifelike that it shows your true style of writing,— the pure and gentle type . . ."
"Not exactly that," she replied. "I think my natural ambition is for the lurid style. I indulge in gorgeous fancies and wish that I dared inscribe them upon my pages and set them before the public."

—L. C. Pickett, *Across My Path*

When Hawthorne writes in his journal that "a veil may be needful but never a mask," he reveals his squeamishness about manipulating the marketplace (*American Notebooks*, 23). He may appear to believe in his own fictional illusions, but once he recognizes his investments in the marketplace he cannot actually do so. As the dysfunction of his late period reflects, Hawthorne retreated from the marketplace after he completed *The Blithedale Romance*. Alcott, on the other hand, who followed her early gothic revelations with sentimental productions, masterfully conceals her marketplace manipulations. Whereas Hawthorne's later works "fail" because he cannot sustain his fiction once he discovers it to be fraud, Alcott's are resounding successes since she invests in the performance of sentiment.

Alcott's response to LaSalle Corbell Pickett's comment about *Little Women* (1868) reveals how Alcott constructed her writing to suit the marketplace (107). Her response not only argues that her sentimental style is not "true" but artificial—a mask donned for economic rewards and social respectability—but also suggests that the only thing "natural" about Alcott's writing was her ambition. Her gothic tales, written during the 1860s and published under the pseudonym A. M. Barnard, were, like her sentimental stories and everything else she wrote, written to make money. Unlike Hawthorne, who tried to hide the market investments of his writing, Alcott explicitly articulates her financial interests: "I do it because it pays well," she states (*Selected Letters*, 232). Moreover, she claims that necessity, not inspiration, motivates her: "people mustn't talk about genius—for I drove that idea away years ago. . . . The inspiration of necessity is all I've had, & it is a safer help than any other" (Stern 1985:335). She values commercial, not cultural capital: "Had a fresh feather in my cap; for Mr. Hawthorne showed Fields 'Thoreau's Flute,' and he desired it for the 'Atlantic.' Of course I didn't say no. It was printed, copied, praised, and glorified; also *paid for*, and being a mercenary creature, I liked the $10 nearly as well as the honor of being 'a new star' and 'a literary celebrity'" (Cheney 151). Like so many of her female counterparts, Alcott became a writer to make money. After her father's withdrawal from commerce under the noble cover of transcendental principles, Alcott became the main breadwinner in her family. Unlike Hawthorne, she did not foster any illusions of living in a privileged sphere separate from the marketplace; from her childhood at Fruitlands through her adult life, Alcott was aware of economic necessity. However, like many female writers of the period, she had to disguise her mercenary motives under the pretense of disseminating the feminine values of the private sphere. Even as she skillfully negotiated the market, she had to appear to be above commercial concerns.[21] Hence, while she could publish her domestic fiction under her own name, her gothic tales, which often reveal the "true" woman to be a fraud and which more openly expose her manipulations of the market, had to circulate masked.

Both her sentimental and her gothic fictions were "necessity" stories, as Alcott's private diary entries and letters show. *Little Women*, Alcott writes, was "very hastily written to order" to "supply the need" for "lively, simple books" for girls (*Selected Letters*, 118; Cheney 199); her "blood and thunder tales," she states, are "easy to 'compoze' and are better paid than moral and elaborate works of Shakespeare" (Stern 1979:vii). Alcott seemed willing to write whatever would sell: "Anything to suit customers" (Cheney 196). Savvy about how to sell her tales, she would rewrite stories according to the market's demands: not only did she marry off Jo to please her publisher and her readers, but she also rewrote the ending of *Moods* to make it more sentimental.[22] Stating that "a spunky new one would make the old ones go," Alcott was constantly repackaging her stories in order to get as much mileage as possible out of each of them (Stern 1985:381). Too sensational to be printed in 1866, *A Modern Mephistopheles* was reprinted in the "No Name Series" in 1877; her story "The Steel Bracelet; or, The Skeleton in the Closet" (1859) was later republished as "The Skeleton in the Closet" (1867).

Her movement from gothic tales in the 1860s to sentimental stories after the success of *Little Women* was less a discovery of her "true" art than a smart marketing choice. Jo in *Little Women* begins writing lurid stories for the tabloid press and then goes "to the other extreme" when she takes up moral writing, a style in which her "lively fancy" feels as "ill at ease" as she would "have done masquerading in the stiff and cumbrous costume of the last century"; Alcott also changes modes like costumes (323). Her mode becomes a mask in which to manipulate the marketplace. As Sarah Elbert points out, when Alcott became editor of *Merry's Museum* she left behind "A. M. Barnard" to "disappear under her new aliases, 'Aunt Wee' and 'Cousin Tribulation'" (141).[23] Unlike Hawthorne, Alcott makes extensive use of the sentimental's performative powers. Like Zenobia, she becomes the grand magician masquerading as the sentimental writer, exploiting the market for profit even as she participates in veiling its illusions. Her sentimental writings, then, do not occupy a separate sphere from her gothic tales; instead, they participate in a shared market economy.[24]

The gothic's role in revealing what the sentimental veils is apparent not only over the course of Alcott's career—her earlier gothic tales force us to reread her later sentimental writings—but within her fictions as well. As in Hawthorne's works, the gothic comes to signify the magical world of the marketplace in Alcott's writings. For instance, when Jo goes to sell her stories at the offices of "The Weekly Volcano" she enters a gothic realm where "clothes possess an influence more powerful over many than the worth of character or the magic of manners" and where one can get on "capitally" as long as one doesn't care for right or wrong (313). As Susan Bernstein argues, Jo's trip to the office is a journey into "the world of the unknown, a journey into smoke and darkness" (31): Jo "bravely climbed two pair of dark and dirty stairs to find herself in a disorderly room, a cloud of cigar smoke and the presence of three gentlemen sitting with their heels rather higher than their hats" (313). The seductions of this shadowy realm of men and money are set against the morals of the domestic sphere: "'I've gone blindly on; hurting myself and other people for the sake of money,' Jo thinks. 'I know it's so, for I can't read this stuff in sober earnest without being horribly ashamed of it; and what should I do if they were seen at home, or Mr. Bhaer got hold of them" (322). Internally policed by her family and her future husband, Jo burns her stories and turns to moral writing. When this does not sell, her mother counsels her to write something for her family. Predictably, Jo becomes successful by forgetting about the marketplace: "You have found your style at last. You wrote with no thought of fame or money, and put your heart into it, my daughter," her father explains, "you have had your bitter, now comes the sweet. Do your best, and grow as happy as we are in your success" (394). Her father, like Professor Bhaer, feeds her sentimental sugarplums: by retreating from the marketplace into the bosom of her family and by giving up her sensational tales in favor of the "truth," Jo becomes a moral and financial success. Indeed, the market is transformed from the gothic realm of business into a comforting realm of charity and filial duty: "Jo wrote her little stories and sent them away to make friends for themselves and her, finding it a very charitable world to such humble wanderers; for they were kindly welcomed and sent home comfortable tokens to their mother, like dutiful children whom good fortune overtakes" (394). In a charitable world that works by gifts and duty rather than contracts and debts, market relations are transformed into family affairs. Such sentiment promises women that if they invest in domesticity they will transform and conquer the marketplace.

Given that her father's transcendental project at Fruitlands was sustained by her mother's labor, Alcott understood whom sentiment's fictions served.[25] While she would later invest in these fictions to finance her own career, her gothic tales expose the poison at the heart of the sentimental sugarplum: that the domestic realm is already the site of the market. One of her later stories, "How I Went Out to Service" (1874), a semiautobiographical account of her time as a housemaid, exemplifies the gothic's role in unveiling this fact. Having hated teaching, found sewing too tiresome and writing poorly compensated, and relinquished her desire to go upon the stage because of her relatives' horror, Louisa decides to go "out to service." The perfect job presents itself in the form of a ministerial gentleman, Josephus, looking for a companion for his sister. Described in sinister terms—"tall, thin and cadaverous" (355) with "a pair of large hands, encased in black kid gloves" (350)—this gentleman depicts his home as a "heaven on earth" (351) and the job as consisting of "light tasks" (355). Promoting the job as providing society instead of service, the gentleman refuses to discuss wages, choosing instead to treat his prospective servant as "one of the family" who will gain an inheritance when his old father dies (351). Veiling the contractual nature of these domestic arrangements, the gentleman advertises the job in sentimental terms: as a valued member of the family in his happy home, Louisa need never feel that she has left the private sphere to sell her service.

The imposture of Josephus's story seems to be revealed in the letters he writes to Louisa to acquaint her with the family before she begins work. These letters are full of gothic intrigue: he describes his house as a "stately mansion, fast falling to decay," his sister as a half-wit, and his servant as an evil witch (353). Instead of being put off by this new twist, Louisa casts herself as the heroine in a gothic drama: "Now this was altogether romantic and sensational, and I felt as if about to enter one of those delightfully dangerous houses we read of in novels, where perils, mysteries, and sins freely disport themselves, till the newcomer sets all to rights, after unheard of trials and escapes" (354). Going out to service, like going on the stage, seems a dangerous yet exciting business for a young heroine.

However, the real twist of the story is that nothing happens: the evil servant turns out to be a "motherly old soul," the house is merely dusty, and the gothic villain's fraternal interest turns out to hide not a sexual, but a sentimental agenda (358). Instead of playing a damsel in distress, Louisa is forced to act the part of the little woman, cleaning the domestic sphere and then decorating it with her presence: "I like that graceful cap, that housewifely apron, and I beg you to wear them often; for it refreshes my eye to see something tasteful, young, and womanly about me," Josephus tells Louisa (357). Feeble instead of monstrous, the villain terrorizes Louisa by reading her Hegel and haunts her not for kisses but for sympathy: "I was to serve his needs, soothe his sufferings, and sympathize with all his sorrows—be a galley slave, in fact," she complains (358). The sign of slavery unveils her spiritual occupations as materially motivated and marks the little woman as a laborer. After a month of backbreaking work, she finally leaves "the dull old house, no longer either mysterious or romantic in [her] disenchanted eyes" (362).

With this end, Alcott seems to deflate her gothic tale. Gothic terror, however, does lurk under the sentimental façade in the form of domestic reality. The real horror of the story is that the domestic sphere is neither heaven nor hell but a workplace where women are expected to give their labor for free. Louisa actually loses money in the transaction: she begins her "experiment" with five dollars and is only paid four dollars for her seven weeks of service (352). Going out to service may appear a threatening enterprise, but it is hardly different from staying at home to work—except in how the job is veiled. As Louisa says, "I do housework at home for love; why not do it abroad for money?" (352). Her relatives might approve of the jobs she performs under the guise of domestic seclusion (teaching, sewing, and writing) and disapprove of those jobs linked to the public sphere (service and the stage), but the distinction is false. The true terror of the story is that "going out" is just another version of "going in." Without the veil of sentiment, the domestic sphere is revealed to be the site of wage-labor, not leisured bliss, and the happy soul turns out to be a slave.[26]

The story's moral emphasizes sentiment's role in veiling the marketplace transactions of the domestic sphere. Louisa concludes that the most useful lesson she has learned "has been the power of successfully making a companion, not a servant, of those whose aid I need, and helping to gild their honest wages with the sympathy and justice which can sweeten the humblest and lighten the hardest task" (363). With this moral, Louisa turns servants into companions and wages into sympathy; she also manages to turn herself from servant into master: she is now the one dispensing the work orders, however benevolently. The ending, which turns the market revelations of her story into a sentimental moral, also shows how Alcott gilds her own tales with sentiment to gain mastery over the market. Having gone from writing stories that earn five dollars to stories that earn a hundred, Alcott need no longer go out to service. When she writes at the end of the tale, "over that harrowing scene I drop a veil, for my feeble pen refuses to depict the emotions of my outraged family," she emphasizes her own performative powers as a successful writer even as she denies them with claims of impotence (363). Sentiment becomes the veil that Alcott throws over her market powers in order to secure her investments.

Despite its genteel appearance, writing is another form of service—even slavery—for Alcott, as she writes after the success of *Little Women*: "I wish you'd write an article on the rights of authors, and try to make the public see that the books belong to them but not the peace, time, comfort and lives of the writers. It is a new kind of slavery" (*Selected Letters*, xxxii). Alcott's use of the slavery metaphor to signify the captivity of celebrity marks her authorial bondage to the marketplace. As Michael Newbury shows in his article on slavery and celebrity in antebellum America, many authors discussed their growing commodification in the mass marketplace metaphorically this way. In occupying "the increasingly conspicuous cultural stage" and becoming "corporally consumable workers, laborers whose bodies rather than labor or production were available for consumption," antebellum authors imagined themselves in terms of an economics of slavery (Newbury 161). For Alcott the famous author, as well as for the women who populate her tales, slavery is the sign of commodification. Writing, like housework, is labor; the author, like the little woman, acts on the public stage.

Alcott's early novella, "Behind a Mask" (1866), shows through the main character, a veiled lady, Jean Muir, that everyone operates in the marketplace. Like Louisa, Jean goes out to service under a genteel cloak when she joins the Coventry family as governess. However, unlike Louisa, who merely discovers the demonic side of the domestic sphere, Jean represents the market demons that penetrate it. Like so many of Alcott's femmes fatales, Jean signifies the public image of hidden identity and constant speculation. Arriving as a "little black-robed figure," she appears to be a girl of nineteen, "meek, modest, faithful, and invariably sweet-tempered" (5, 25);

however, she is actually a divorced ex-actress of thirty who is skilled in the art of impersonation. Alone in her attic room, Jean reveals her sentimental self to be a painted mask:

> "Come, the curtain is down, so I may be myself for a few hours, if actresses ever are themselves."
>
> Still sitting on the floor she unbound and removed the long abundant braids from her head, wiped the pink from her face, took out several pearly teeth, and slipping off her dress appeared herself indeed, a haggard, worn and moody woman of thirty at least. The metamorphosis was wonderful, but the disguise was more in the expression she assumed than in any art of costume or false adornment. Now she was alone, and her mobile features settled into their natural expression, weary, hard, bitter. (11–12)

Instead of the stable, sentimental self she projects, Jean is a fluid persona and can change according to circumstances or the viewer. Created through costume and displayed for all to see, her identity is a stage effect; Jean is the veiled lady, the economic witch behind the sentimental woman. Moreover, the tension in this passage between an artificial public self—her mobile features—and a stable private self—her "natural" expression—suggests that Alcott commits to both versions of womanhood. While she constantly points out the constructed nature of the "true" woman in this story—even Jean's natural, "weary, hard, bitter" expression has been created from economic circumstances—Alcott reinvests in a sentimental view of womanhood. This contradiction, which could be seen as ambivalent, might better be read as strategic: Alcott invests capital in both versions of the veiled lady.

In her disguise as a little woman, Jean infiltrates the aristocratic Coventry household, which operates by the laws of sentiment, with her marketplace illusions. Like Alcott's other actresses, she is both foreign (Scottish) and from the lower classes. And like her class, she operates by the laws of the market: as one character says of all actresses in Alcott's short story "La Jeune" (1868), "they are all alike, mercenary, treacherous, and shallow" (*Freaks of Genius*, 194). A "cold, calm machine," Jean pursues her prize, a wealthy husband, in a calculating manner (45). Love, for her, is a business transaction: she chooses Gerald over Ned because he is the elder, and hence richer, son; and despite her attraction to Gerald she hedges her bets by also courting his uncle, Lord Coventry. Sympathy and sentiment are charms, tools she employs to negotiate the transaction. A "perfect mistress of her art," Jean captivates Gerald with "the indescribable spell of womanhood" (6,

53). She performs "little task[s] with a skill and grace that made it pleasant to watch her" (8); she makes "a charming picture of all that is most womanly and winning; a picture which few men's eyes would not have liked to rest upon" (71). Under her direction, the house becomes a stage where she is both stage manager and stage effect: "The arrival of Miss Muir seemed to produce a change in everyone, though no one could have explained how or why" (25). "Eager to profit by each moment," Jean manipulates sentiment to achieve her desired effect: by the end of the tale, she joins the aristocratic household as Lady Coventry (79).

Jean's magical effects appear to threaten both the sentimental and the aristocratic economies. As a lower-class woman, she taints the purity of the aristocratic line when she marries into the family; as the "capital little woman," she reveals the sentimental female's market connections (19). However, Jean's threat is illusory: her profit depends on upholding these economies instead of destroying them. Like the veiled lady, Jean denies her stage effects and her role in the market even as she exploits them. Jean may appear as a medium nursing Gerald back to health, but she is actually a mesmerist, electrifying him with the spectacle of her "true womanhood": "she sat down behind the curtain and remained as mute and motionless as a statue.... Soon a subtle warmth seemed to settle from the soft palms that enclosed his own, his heart beat quicker, his breath grew unequal, and a thousand fancies danced through his brain. He sighed, and said dreamily, as he turned his face toward her, 'I like this' " (40). While Jean dramatizes the fear that the private woman is actually a public performer, she domesticates that fear by veiling her act. She is content to remain a statue behind a veil if it brings her power, and uses her theatricality to deny her commerciality.

The ending of the tale, however, contains Jean's threat when it reveals not that the little woman hides a market monster, but that the veiled lady is imprisoned in the role of sentimental woman. Even when Jean's fraud is uncovered, she refuses to abandon her role. Mrs. Coventry might seek patriarchal protection from Jean and her influence on the family, especially her daughter Bella, but there is no need; Jean, who has just married Sir John, intends to use her magic to join, not destroy, the family: " 'Send for Sir John! I am mortally afraid of this creature. Take her away; do something to her. My poor Bella, what a companion for you! Send for Sir John at once!' cried Mrs. Coventry incoherently, and clasped her daughter in her arms, as if Jean Muir would burst in to annihilate the whole family" (102). By getting the family patriarch to invest in her sentimental fictions, Jean is able to turn her fraud into a few "faults and follies," her calculating duplicity into innocent offenses (103). Transforming herself from a "capital little woman" into "little Lady Coventry," Jean takes cover behind the sentimental veil (83); she promises to repay Mrs. Coventry's kindness and devote her life to Lord Coventry's happiness. "We are going away for a little while," Sir John says, "and when we return let the old life return again, unchanged, except that Jean makes sunshine for me as well as for you" (103). Becoming the producer of sunlight and sentiment, Jean will wrap the whole household in her magic to gain economic rewards and social respectability. Dropping the veil instead of lifting it, her last scene is indeed better than her first, for instead of signaling her exit from the stage, it marks her entrance into the family through stagecraft.

The conclusion of "Behind a Mask" is typical of many of Alcott's gothic tales. The theatrical woman returns to her proper place and the reader, like Jean, is asked to "Come home, love, and forget all this" (104). Despite their sentimental re-veilings, Alcott's gothic tales expose the mercenary woman at the heart of the household. The tale's terror may be denied, but only after the happy household has complied with its threat: not only does Jean become the head of the household by marrying its enfeebled patriarch, but Bella, the innocent daughter whom Mrs. Coventry would protect from Jean's influence, is described as a "capital girl" (17). The sentimental world is already a stage operating by the laws of the market: Jean produces sunshine as her new effect and has a debt of kindness to repay; Gerald and Ned stage a duel in order to compete for Jean's affections; in the market for a husband, Lucia casts weak spells. Jean's entry into the household at the end, then, is less a penetration from without than a manifestation of what already lies within. By betraying the stage effects involved in the sentimental performance even as they reenact it, Alcott's gothic tales unveil the "little woman" and her sentimental fictions as a masquerade, a put-on for profit. While this revelation poses as the horrifying secret of Alcott's gothic tales, the tales' recognition that even the most expert market magician must remain imprisoned behind the veil of sentiment is perhaps more terrifying.

If "Behind the Mask" re-veils even as it reveals the sentimental process, "V.V.: or, Plots and Counterplots" (1865) explains the need for this duplicity: women are punished for manipulating the marketplace. Unlike Jean Muir, who manages to get a powerful man to invest in her before the Coventrys discover her manipulations and try to "take her away" or "do something to her," Virginie Varens does not so easily escape society's condemnation (102). Whereas "Behind a Mask" displays the prizes to be won through the proper manipulation of sentiment, "V.V." reveals the price to be paid if men discover women's deceptions.

The final scene of "V.V.," where all of Virginie's plots are detected, shows men's fear of women's success in, and their need to control women's access to, the marketplace. Another tale about a veiled lady, "V.V." records the same scenario as "Behind a Mask." Like Jean, Virginie is the market woman who uses her acting skills to reincarnate herself as a "little woman" and win a husband. With her golden hair as a "shining veil" and her "silvery laughter," Virginie negotiates Lady Lennox's household by screening her monetary motives with sincerity (53, 68). Disguising her role as a commodity even as she exploits it, Virginie manipulates the market to her advantage. While Diana, her rival, wears diamonds in her hair as if to advertise her wealth and her status as property, Virginie claims that she wears only one jewel, her noble name; moreover, her beauty can magically transform the ugly bracelet she wears to hide a tattoo, the sign of her enslavement: "The beauty of the arm would render any fetter an ornament," the Earl says (59). While Virginie is as expert as Jean in manipulating the role of "little woman," she is more dangerous because she threatens to destroy, not uphold, the sentimental economy. In the process of trying to win her prize, Virginie operates like a ghost, manipulating the sentimental woman, chaste Diana, into madness and then suicide. The chapter heading—"Treason"—suggests the danger of Virginie's duplicity: it is one thing to manipulate sentiment for sentimental ends and quite another to kill off sentiment altogether. Whereas Jean settles into the domestic sphere, Virginie refuses to give up the stage. Explaining to Victor why she is in the city in costume, she states: "At my aunt's in the country... The rooms there were dull; no one came, and at last I ran away. Once here, the old mania returned; I was mad for the gay life I love, and while I waited, I played at carnival" (101). As the theatrical woman, Virginie plans to continue circulating even after the game is won: she promises her companion, Victor, her love once she wins the Earl's money. Unlike Jean, who can be integrated into the domestic sphere through marriage and her sentimental productions, Virginie must be exorcised from society since she refuses to invest in one man or in her sentimental role.

As the story's climax shows, Virginie must be punished precisely because she threatens to undermine the value of sentiment. Indeed, her role in the death of the story's sentimental woman initiates the manhunt to discover her "true" identity and to punish her market manipulations. The conclusion of the story is cast as a competition between female art and male detection.

Claiming that the "masculine eye could not fathom the artifices of costume, cosmetics, and consummate acting," the men who pursue her—the Earl and his friend, the detective figure Duprès—resolve to "oppose craft to craft, treachery to treachery" (125). Their difficulty in discovering Virginie's identity marks her power: "so potent [is] the fascination of her presence" that she can seemingly change her appearance and identity at will (105). Virginie, the veiled lady, is a "lovely devil" who mesmerizes men (104):

> Duprès fixed a searching glance upon her. His keen eyes ran over her from head to foot, and nothing seemed to escape his scrutiny. Her figure was concealed by a great mantle of black velvet; her hair waved plainly away under her bonnet; the heavy folds of her dress flowed over her feet; and her delicately gloved hands lay half buried in the deep lace of her handkerchief. She was very pale, her eyes were languid, her lips sad even in smiling, and her voice had lost its lightsome ring. (103)

Her ability to mask herself is so expert that she thwarts male detection: "She baffles me somewhat, I confess, with her woman's art in dress," Duprès says. "But I shall discover her yet" (108).

The scene of Virginie's unveiling reveals the extent of female power and the extremes to which men will go to police it. Here, Virginie once again performs the role of veiled lady. Drugged and unconscious, she is examined by the men at midnight in her bedroom:

> For a moment a mysterious and striking picture might have been seen in that quiet room. Under the crimson canopy lay the fair figure of the sleeping woman, her face half hidden by the golden shadow of her hair, her white arm laid out on the warm-hued coverlet, and bending over it, the two masked men, one holding the lamp nearer, the other pointing to something just above the delicate wrist, now freed from the bracelet, which lay open beside it. Two distinctly traced letters were seen, V.V., and underneath a tiny true-lover's knot, in the same dark lines. (117)

This spectacle of male voyeurism emphasizes Virginie's power: the men can only see through her dazzling disguise as she lies perfectly passive before their gaze. Only as the mesmerized object can Virginie be penetrated by the masked men. The identity they discover, however, is not personal but public. Under the crimson canopy and her golden hair, Virginie exemplifies the market identity of the veiled lady. As a spectacle, she is discovered by the male gaze to be property; the identifying mark under her bracelet/fetter is less a lover's knot than the sign of Virginie's enslavement to Victor. Virginie is not a devil or an angel, she is simply a piece of property to be marked by or exchanged between men. The scene, then, not only restores the proper power balance between the sexes by allowing the men to act as magnetists but also, in doing so, unveils the process by which men turn women into commodities and then punish them for operating as free agents in the marketplace.

The Earl's punishment for Virginie signifies her threat to male control of the market: she will be imprisoned "far away in Scotland" in a "gray old tower" and live "cut off from all the world" (128). Virginie will pay for her manipulations of the market by being imprisoned in the private sphere. She is punished for her failure of sentiment: "She was *not* innocent—for she lured that generous boy to marry her, because she coveted his rank and fortune, not his heart" (121). Men might marry for money—the Earl, for instance asks "Has she fortune?" (55)—but women must at least appear to marry for love. When Virginie competes in the marketplace without a sentimental veil, the men close ranks to expel her from the market altogether. Victor, once faithful, turns against her at the end of the story and provides the ammunition the Earl needs to discover her guilt: "I have a feeling that I never shall possess you, even if my long service ends this year. You are so cold, so treacherous, I have no faith in you, though I adore you, and shall until I die.... It would be death to me to find that after all I have suffered, done, and desired for you, there was no reward but falsehood and base ingratitude" (101–2). Virginie might once have represented an ideal image to which Victor would have allowed himself to be enslaved; however, her coldness and treachery break the sentimental contract. Instead of rewarding Victor's adoration, she uses it to betray him.

Turning Virginie into a scapegoat, the men deny their own market manipulations. Victor jealously murdered the Earl's cousin, Virginie's first love, and made Virginie his slave, but his crimes are transformed into acts of devotion: "Virginie, I can never forgive him my cousin's death, but for his faithful, long-suffering devotion to you, I honor him, sinner though he was," the Earl proclaims (122). Under the Earl's revisionary tale-telling, Victor is turned from Virginie's evil master into her faithful servant; painted as the passive victim, Victor is forgiven his role in making Virginie a mercenary creature. By pooling their resources, the men cut Virginie out of the market without owning up to their own machinations. Virginie learns in the last scene, as she did in the first when her chosen husband was killed, that she is not free to negotiate the market for herself.

Virginie's loss of power is marked by the unveiling of her plots. Calling the Earl a magician, she takes on the role of mesmerized object: in the "bewilderment of seeing plot after plot unfolded before her, she [looked] up and listened with dilated eyes, lips apart, and both hands holding back the locks that could no longer hide her from his piercing glance" (126). Seemingly unable to manipulate the market any longer—she is warned by the Earl not to try to bribe or deceive her guard, for "escape is impossible"— Virginie counters with her last plot: saving one secret, she drinks some deadly poison from her ring and utters her last words, "I have escaped" (129). In death, she becomes the image of the perfectly veiled woman: "nothing of the fair, false Virginie remained," the last line tells us, "but a beautiful, pale image of repose" (129). Staging the ultimate spectacle, Virginie transforms herself in her final performance from a piece of property into a transcendent image, a sentimental sign. This formulaic escape into death, however, shows the limited room Virginie—and Alcott—have to negotiate their plots. Becoming a "beautiful, pale image of repose" is the only escape for Virginie. Likewise, Alcott must kill off her dark women, re-veiling them through a sentimental conversion, to escape accusations of treason. Alcott's endings, in which sentimental veils magically resolve the stories' conflicts, show her ability to replace the mask. The sentimental counterplots diffuse her gothic plots and allow her to continue operating in the marketplace. However, as Virginie's death signifies, this sentimental maneuver can also be imprisoning.

The endings of Alcott's gothic tales prefigure the trajectory of her career. After *Little Women*, Alcott never returned to her lurid style since she found her masquerade as a domestic novelist more lucrative: "I yet hope to write a few of the novels," she writes toward the end of her career, "which have been simmering in my brain while necessity and unexpected success have confined me to juvenile literature" (Stern 1985:357). Imprisoned by the sentimental conventions that made her rich, Alcott understood how the writer could become enthralled by the marketplace. She also knew that she must maintain the mask of sentiment in order to succeed commercially. If Hawthorne tried to imagine his cultural capital as separate from and uncontaminated by the market, Alcott recognized that she had to invest in her cultural capital as feminine representative of the domestic sphere to earn money and secure her position in the market.

The figure of the veiled lady, then, emerges in Alcott's and Hawthorne's gothic works as a demon of the marketplace, only to be occluded: the lady must remain veiled in order for the market to operate smoothly. Both Hawthorne and Alcott understood that to maintain their cultural capital—whether literary in the case of Hawthorne or domestic in the case of Alcott—they had to keep their investments in commercial capital under cover. Ironically, both became imprisoned in their own success: under the weight of his own cultural capital, Hawthorne could only write fragments; in the formula that earned her social respectability and monetary security, Alcott remained fixed. Like their veiled ladies, both authors were bound by the market even as they manipulated it. The veil, which simultaneously masks and emphasizes the market economy, is the sign of their mastery and of their slavery.

6

Haunting Back: Harriet Jacobs, African-American Narrative, and the Gothic

> Early American writers, Henry James and Nathaniel Hawthorne, complained bitterly about the bleakness and flatness of the American scene. But I think that if they were alive, they'd feel at home in modern America. True, we have no great church in America; our national traditions are still of such a sort that we are not wont to brag of them ... we have no rich symbols, no colorful rituals. But we do have in the Negro the embodiment of a past tragic enough to appease the spiritual hunger of even a James; and we do have in the oppression of the Negro a shadow athwart our national life dense and heavy enough to satisfy even the gloomy broodings of a Hawthorne. And if Poe were alive, he would not have to invent horror; horror would invent him.
> —Richard Wright, "How 'Bigger' was Born," *Native Son*

In this ending to the introduction to *Native Son*, Richard Wright makes a powerful connection between the African-American experience and the gothic.[1] The horror that Poe or Hawthorne had to invent, Wright argues, is already embodied in African-American history—in the haunting legacy of slavery and in the heavy shadow of oppression. For Wright, African-American history is not only material for the gothic writer, but is also itself coded in gothic terms.[2] As Wright's novel, *Native Son*, shows, the African-American experience, written as a realist text, resembles a gothic narrative. Arguing that the gothic, as exemplified by an author like Poe, does not invent horror but is invented by it, Wright unveils the gothic as a complex historical mode: history invents the gothic, and in turn the gothic reinvents history.

By exploring Wright's connection between historical horror and the gothic, this chapter uses the African-American gothic to revise readings of the American gothic that have positioned the genre—and, more broadly, the American literary canon—as exempt from the forces of history. A focus on slavery, America's most glaring cultural contradiction, shows how it produced gothic narratives during the antebellum period and how these narratives reproduced the scene of slavery.[3] The chapter examines two strategies by which the gothic represents the unspeakable event of slavery. First, by signifying the event of slavery through narrative effects, the gothic both registers actual events and turns them into fiction. Its conventions can both rematerialize and dematerialize history: some gothic narratives insist upon the actuality of slavery by refusing to collapse the referent of the narrative with its effects; others displace the event of slavery into fictional form in order to contain its horrors. However, as this book has shown, even in the act of displacement, traces of the material remain to be read by those invested in remembering the horrors of history. African-American writers—particularly Harriet Jacobs, who works within and against an antebellum discourse that gothicizes slavery—recognize the uses and dangers of the gothic as a mode that can remember and combat, but can also erase, the horrors of a racial history. In looking at how particular gothic fictions are produced in relation to the historical institution of slavery and how the gothic mode represents slavery's unspeakable history, this chapter explores the extent to which the gothic is able to rematerialize the ghosts of America's racial history and enable African-American writers to haunt back.

With this final chapter, then, *Gothic America* comes full circle, returning to its founding image: the caged slave in Crèvecoeur's *Letters from an American Farmer*. Instead of focusing on Farmer James, who is struck mute by this encounter, or on the stylistic evasions Crèvecoeur's text performs to contain and silence this horror, this chapter focuses on the voices that emanate from within stereotypes of the gothic and on how to begin articulating the horror. No longer simply the metaphor for dread, the "conveniently bound and violently silenced" black bodies of the gothic return in this chapter to reclaim and revise the gothic mode (Morrison 1992:38). By locating the strategies involved in unveiling slavery's horrors, this chapter listens to how the unspeakable is spoken.

Spectacles of Horror: The Scene of Slavery

> Negro writing has instinctively adopted the Gothic tradition of American literature and given its more supernatural and surrealistic characteristics a realistic basis, founded on actual lives often lived in the Gothic manner, that is indeed terrifying: the nightmare world of Poe or Hawthorne has become the Monday morning of the Negro author....
>
> —Theodore Gross, *The Heroic Ideal in American Literature*

The scene of slavery was often represented as gothic during the antebellum period in America. From newspaper accounts of Nat Turner's insurrection and antislavery writings to slave narratives and literary works such as Lydia Maria Child's "Stand from Under!" (1829) and Melville's *Benito Cereno* (1855), the horrible reality of slavery was depicted through gothic images and a romantic rhetoric. Theodore Weld exemplifies how slavery was easily read as a sensationalized spectacle during the antebellum period when he states, "facts and testimony as to the actual condition of the Slaves" would "thrill the land with Horror" (Barnes and Dumond 2:717). The gothic's focus on the terror of possession, the iconography of imprisonment, the fear of retribution, and the weight of sin provided a useful vocabulary and register of images by which to represent the scene of America's greatest guilt: slavery. According to Kari Winter, the gothic's structural alliance with slavery is not coincidental.[4] Many of the eighteenth-century British male gothicists—such as Monk Lewis and William Beckford—were either slaveowners or proslavery; moreover, the rise of the gothic novel in England at the end of the eighteenth century occurred during the heightened debate about abolition, a debate in which William Godwin and Mary Wollstonecraft, both authors of gothic novels, actively participated (Winter 3). Like revolution—as Ronald Paulson has shown in his study of the gothic and the French Revolution—and the new capitalistic structures that emerged in the eighteenth century—as Andrea Henderson argues—slavery was a significant part of the historical context that produced the gothic and against which it responded.[5]

For instance, slave uprisings in St. Domingue at the end of the eighteenth century and in America during the antebellum period, as epitomized by the figure of Nat Turner, were turned into tales of gothic terror.[6] Nat Turner and his band were demonized by *The Richmond Enquirer* (August 30, 1831) as "banditti" and "horrible ... monsters" (Tragle 43).[7] Turning the event into an ominous warning, *The Liberator* (September 3,

1831) states, "for ourselves, we are horror-struck at the late tidings" and argues that "what was poetry—imagination—in January, is now a bloody reality" (Tragle 64, 63). Turner's insurrection actualized the imagined terror of slave rebellion: its bloody reality both fulfilled and generated a gothic narrative of dread and retribution.

Recounting Turner's reign of terror, *The Constitutional Whig* (September 26, 1831) demonstrates how the historical event of Turner's uprising was represented through gothic conventions:

> In retracing on Tuesday morning the route pursued by the banditti, consisting of a distance of 20 miles, my imagination was struck with more horror, than the most dreadful carnage in a field of battle could have produced. The massacre before me, being principally of helpless women and children.... In future years, the bloody road, will give rise to many a sorrowful legend; and the trampling of hoofs, in fancy, visit many an excited imagination.   (Tragle 96–97)

The bloody scene produces a gothic effect when it strikes the viewer's imagination; the event "gives rise to" a narrative of terror and horror. However, the event is also reinterpreted by that gothic narrative. As symbolized by the bloody road, it will be turned into a legend: Nat Turner will haunt the imagination of future travelers much like the Headless Horseman of Washington Irving's "The Legend of Sleepy Hollow." Translating the event into a gothic symbol, turning it into a legend, the passage reveals how the gothic can dematerialize and displace the source of its effect even while representing it. The present event is constructed as both more "real" and "unreal" as it is imaginatively experienced: the narrator's imagination is struck by the full horror of the scene even as the scene is displaced into the future and translated into a legend to excite the future viewer's fancy. The gothic's conventions, then, gave whites responding to Turner's rebellion a discourse to symbolize and contain their terror. Once subsumed into symbols, imagined instead of experienced, the event could be read as an effect rather than as a reality.

This displacement of event by effect also tends to relocate the horror of slavery from the slave's experience to the white viewer's response. Antislavery and proslavery sympathizers alike deployed the gothicized scene of slavery, the event, as the conduit for a particular effect. In *American Slavery as It Is* (1839), Theodore Weld uses the gothic conventions of clanking chains and swooning maidens to emphasize the horror of slavery. "We repeat it, every man knows that slavery is a curse," he writes. "Whoever denies this, his lips libel his heart. Try him; clank the chains in his ears, and tell him they are for *him*. . . . then look at his pale lips and trembling knees, and you have *nature's* testimony against slavery" (7). Asking the viewer to imagine himself enslaved, responding to this imagined scene, Weld turns slavery into an effect. The clanking chains sound the warning of retribution more than they symbolize actual imprisonment. Nature's testimony against slavery is not the scene itself but the white viewer's response to it: pale lips and trembling knees. Paradoxically, the gothic effect subsumes the gothic event even as it testifies to its horrors.

Sarah Grimké's account of her departure from the South and slavery underscores the way white abolitionists used the gothic's narrative power to subordinate the slave's horror to the white viewer's response:

> As I left my native state on account of slavery, and deserted the home of my fathers to escape the sound of the lash and the shrieks of tortured victims, I would gladly bury in oblivion the recollection of those scenes with which I have been familiar; but this may not, cannot be; they come over my memory like gory spectres, and implore me with resistless power, in the name of a God of mercy, in the name of a crucified Savior, in the name of humanity; for the sake of the slaveholder, as well as the slave, to bear witness to the horrors of the southern prison house.   (Weld 22)

Grimké depicts herself as the innocent maiden fleeing the scene of horror. She, not the slave, is the tortured victim of the slavery system, a displaced wanderer, haunted by bloody specters. In identifying herself as the victim, Grimké abstracts and co-opts the slave's horror.[8] By equating witnessing these scenes with experiencing them, Grimké makes the effect coextensive with the event, thereby establishing her authority. The gory scenes implore her to speak; the shrieks of the tortured victims are articulated through her. Bearing witness to the horrors of the southern prison house in the name of all its victims, slaveholders as well as slaves, Grimké generalizes the horror to everyone involved.

In the hands of antebellum white writers, then, the gothic often enabled the representation of slavery only to departicularize it. As Eric Sundquist argues, "the antislavery imagination, no less than the proslavery, tended to collapse history into timeless images of terror and damnation" (1993:147). The gothic might offer useful metaphors for depicting the historical event of slavery, but its narrative construction could also empty slavery of history by turning it into a gothic trope. Harriet Beecher Stowe's preface to *Dred* (1856) articulates how easily literary discourse could fictionalize the historical reality of slavery. Explaining why she has chosen as a subject "the scenes and incidents of the slaveholding states," Stowe writes:

> in a merely artistic point of view, there is no ground, ancient or modern, whose vivid lights, gloomy shadows and grotesque groupings, afford to the novelist so wide a scope for the exercise of his powers. In the near vicinity of modern civilization of the most matter-of-fact kind, exist institutions which carry us back to the twilight of the feudal ages, with all their exciting possibilities of incident. (29)

Stowe locates slavery as a feudal institution, displaced in time and space and hence offering the romance writer wider scope for her fictional powers. For Stowe, who can see it from a merely artistic point of view, slavery is already a fictionalized scene, full of "exciting possibilities of incident." Its actuality is once again imaginatively subsumed by gothic conventions.

The problem of how literary narrative could displace historical reality was especially troubling for the author of the slave narrative. While slave narratives use many fictional forms to structure their events, the difficulty of negotiating the line between fact and fiction is especially apparent in their use of the gothic.[9] The slave narrative's generic conventions seem to be in direct opposition to the gothic's: its documentary form and adherence to veracity announce a refusal of any imaginative rendering. Although the slave narrative might not incorporate the gothic's typical supernatural elements, it does, however, contain—even in its factual form—many gothic characteristics. With descriptions of slavery as a feudal institution, horrifying scenes of torture and entrapment, lascivious masters and innocent slave girls, and curses on many generations, the slave narrative reads like a gothic romance with a single, crucial difference: the scenery is not staged but real. The slave narrative's representations have historical referents that embody horror; however, though recording a horror beyond the pale of most gothic romances, the slave narrative could be read within the gothic's fictional conventions. As Massachusetts Senator Charles Sumner stated of slave narratives, "Romance has no stories of more thrilling interest than theirs" (qtd. in *The Liberator* [October 22, 1852], 169). Or, as Angelina Grimké wrote in a letter to Theodore Weld in 1838, "Many and many a tale of romantic horror can the slaves tell" (Barnes and Dumond 2:523). The realization that their factual narratives could read like fiction caused many authors to insist on the veracity of their tales. In *My Bondage and My Freedom* (1855), Frederick Douglass writes, "The reader is, therefore, assured, with all due promptitude, that his attention is not invited to a work of ART, but to a work of FACTS—Facts, terrible and almost incredible, it may be—yet

FACTS, nevertheless" (3).[10] In her "authentic narrative describing the Horrors of slavery," Harriet Jacobs, for example, feels compelled to assure her readers that her narrative is not fiction: "I am aware that some of my adventures may seem incredible," she writes, "but they are, nevertheless, strictly true" (1).[11] Jacobs's opening disclaimer marks the complex relationship between the romance and the real in her text. Paradoxically, the horrifying facts seem, as Lydia Maria Child states, "more romantic than fiction" (3); overflowing the boundaries of the real, Jacobs's factual narrative can read like a gothic fiction. It is important to note the slave narrative's double bind: the difficulty of representing a gothic history through gothic conventions without collapsing the distinctions between fact and fiction, event and effect. The slave narrative must rewrite the conventions of gothic fiction for its own factual ends.

Frederick Douglass's gothic scene of slavery in his *Narrative of the Life of Frederick Douglass* (1845), Aunt Hester's whipping, is one example of this rewriting. Placed at the end of the *Narrative*'s first chapter, the gothic scene serves as both the reader's and Douglass's entrance through the "blood-stained gate" of slavery (51). Douglass gives northern antebellum readers a familiar scene: the southern gothic spectacle of slavery.[12] With its gothic villain, the slavemaster, and its innocent maiden, his Aunt Hester, who "stood fair for his infernal purpose," the scene plays up but also resists its gothic effects (52). It offers the reader the villain and the maiden but transposes their conventional associations: the black villain is white and the virginal, innocent maiden is a black slave. As the viewer of, rather than a participant in, this infernal scene, Douglass signifies against white narratives of gothic spectatorship. Framing the scene with his response to it, Douglass both plays to northern readers' sympathy and critiques their voyeurism. Situated in Douglass's position as witness to this scene of brutality, the reader is asked to identify with Douglass's horror and against the iron-hearted slavemaster. Douglass hopes that the scene will strike the reader with the same "awful force" as it struck him (51). By drawing a parallel between the way the scene "strikes" the viewer and the blows Aunt Hester experiences from the slavemaster, the narrative suggests the power of the gothic scene to relay the experience of horror. However, in identifying the viewer with the victim and in depicting the viewer as a passive and safely distant observer (the young Douglass hiding in the closet), the scene also reveals how the gothic spectacle can enable identification without initiating a corresponding action. The scene exposes not only the victimization inherent in the white reader's relationship to slavery but also the voyeurism. Like the young boy peeping out of the closet to witness the sexualized spectacle of slavery, the white reader is both repulsed and fascinated with its horrors. In this way, Douglass also identifies the viewer with the slavemaster and his "great pleasure" (51). The scene, then, offers a typical gothic scenario only to critique the white reader's role in viewing it.

The scene further exposes the slave narrative's use and revision of the gothic by employing the gothic to rematerialize history while resisting its possible dematerializing effects. Following a general description of his Aunt Hester's whippings, Douglass pauses to reflect upon the scene before he describes the first time he witnessed this event: "I was quite a child, but I well remember it. I never shall forget it whilst I remember any thing. . . . It was the blood-stained gate, the entrance to the hell of slavery, through which I was about to pass. It was a most terrible spectacle. I wish I could commit to paper the feelings with which I beheld it" (51). Here, Douglass captures the difficulty of speaking the unspeakable: slavery is at once unforgettable and indescribable. The performative quality of Douglass's simultaneous insistence that he cannot capture his response to the scene and attempts to do so shows that the gothic provides tropes by which the unspoken can be represented, if not fully spoken. In its pseudodocumentary and excessively mediated form (a manuscript that has been translated and passed to the narrator through a number of sources), the gothic claims historical veracity even as it points to the limits of historical representation. Similarly, Douglass recounts the scene of Aunt Hester's whipping while insisting that the scene of slavery is ultimately unrepresentable. Douglass repeats it two times, first as a general occurrence and then as a particular event, the first time he witnessed it. His twice-told tale, however, like his performative gesture, signals the unrepresentability of the scene: its excessiveness implies that it cannot be fully captured. By insisting on the gothic's resistance to representation, Douglass negotiates the uneasy relationship between his gothic tale and his gothic history: he both represents his history and insists that it defies narrative reconstruction.

Douglass's resistance to turning the event of slavery into a narrative effect is also evident in the way he represents Aunt Hester's whipping. The focus in the scene is as much on the "it," the spectacle of the whipping, as on the "I," the narrator who responds to it. Douglass's insistence that he cannot commit his feelings to paper is as much an articulation of slavery's unrepresentability as a refusal to focus more on the response to the event than on the event itself. Douglass uses the gothic to translate Aunt Hester's whippings into a symbol of slavery—"a terrible spectacle"—but he also refuses to abstract the horror by turning it into a timeless trope of terror. Not only does he generalize his account of the whipping between two versions, but he also goes to great lengths in the second recounting to particularize the scene, giving the context of the whipping and describing it in a matter-of-fact tone. The frame, more than the narrative, sensationalizes the scene. This tension between the depiction of the actual event and the gothicized effect of its narrative frame is also evident in Douglass's first description: "I have often been awakened at the dawn of day by the most heart-rending shrieks of an own aunt of mine, whom he [the slavemaster] used to tie up to a joist, and whip upon her naked back till she was literally covered with blood" (51). In this statement, Douglass deploys the gothic with a twist: instead of waking *from* the nightmare, he wakes *to* it. Unveiling reality as the nightmare and emphasizing that Aunt Hester is "literally" covered with blood, Douglass rewrites the gothic as actual horror instead of stage effect. Moreover, by describing the event as occurring in the continuous present—"I have often been awakened"—he re-experiences the scene in the act of reimagining it, making the event hauntingly present. When he ends, "I had therefore been, until *now*, out of the way of the bloody scenes that often occurred on the plantation," he suggests that the reader, like himself, is awake to the nightmare of slavery: the gothic effect does not dematerialize the event but makes it ever-present (52, emphasis added). By redeploying the gothic, Douglass is able to materialize the scene and resist its representation as mere effect.

Douglass's use of the gothic, then, acknowledges that the scene of slavery is conventionally constructed but rewrites those conventions to his own ends. By making the reader enter his narrative of slavery through the conventions of the gothic, Douglass discloses how the spectacle of slavery is mediated and structured generically. The event is accessible only as a narrated scene, constructed for the viewer.[13] However, in using gothic conventions, Douglass marks the differences as well as the similarities between gothic narrative and gothic history. Gothic conventions might usefully reproduce the scene of slavery, but they also might dematerialize it. By allying the gothic with reality and yet insisting that its effects cannot fully capture the event, Douglass utilizes the gothic's narrative power to represent slavery and to create a strong effect while insisting on the difference between event and effect. Like other African-American authors who employ the gothic mode, Douglass must negotiate between its power and its danger.

Douglass's redeployment of the gothic exposes it as a mode intimately connected to history.[14] The gothic's typical association with the "unreal" and the sensational, however, has created a resistance to examining African-American narratives in relation to the gothic. Alice Walker, for instance, dislikes the categorization of her work as gothic since it "conjures up the supernatural" and since she "feels what she writes has 'something to do with real life' " (263). Similarly, Toni Morrison is reluctant to have her writing described as gothic. She dislikes the term *black magic* used in conjunction with her work since the "implication [is] that there [is] no intelligence there" (C. Davis 145).[15] The gothic's apparent lack of connection to reality and intellectual purpose has made it troubling to use in conjunction with African-American writers.[16] However, instead of accepting traditional readings of the gothic as unrealistic and frivolous, thereby excluding African-American narratives from this genre, we should use the African-American gothic to revise our understanding of the gothic as an historical mode. Re-viewing the gothic through the lens of African-American transpositions and recognizing that the gothic itself is a dynamic and contradictory mode whose tropes and conventions can be used for a variety of ends makes visible the American gothic's relationship to history.

In order to examine how the African-American gothic revises standard notions of the American gothic tradition, I now examine the dialogue that occurs between two texts: Harriet Beecher Stowe's *Uncle Tom's Cabin* (1852) and Harriet Jacobs's *Incidents in the Life of a Slave Girl* (1861). The relationship of influence and resistance between these texts reveals how the African-American gothic is working within and against a broader American gothic tradition. My aim is not to subsume African-American narratives under some reified concept of the American tradition, but rather to show how the African-American gothic highlights the historicity of the American gothic.[17]

Loopholes of Influence: Harriet Beecher Stowe and Harriet Jacobs

Signifyin(g) functions as a metaphor for formal revision, or intertextuality, within the Afro-American literary tradition.
—Henry Louis Gates, Jr., *The Signifying Monkey*

Incidents in the Life of a Slave Girl exemplifies the slave narrative's connection to the gothic romance through its use of fictional conventions. As late as the 1970s, *Incidents*'s authenticity remained in doubt because of its perceived similarity to the novel of seduction. In *The Slave Community*, for instance, John Blassingame discusses *Incidents* as a fictional story, arguing that Jacobs's tale was too melodramatic to be considered an authentic slave narrative. The debate over whether *Incidents* was fact or fiction was not fully resolved until Jean Fagan Yellin verified the narrative's authenticity in 1981.[18] However, it is precisely Jacobs's use of fictional tropes to represent authentic fact that fueled this confusion. On the one hand she claims, "Reader, be assured this narrative is no fiction"; on the other hand, in the act of claiming her narrative's authenticity she uses a trope from the novel (1). While *Incidents*'s relationship to the conventions of the sentimental novel has been extensively explored, it has rarely been discussed in terms of the gothic.[19] Whether this is because the gothic continues to be viewed as opposed to the realist conventions of the slave narrative or because the sentimental has become canonized as *the* nineteenth-century woman's genre is hard to say; however, Jacobs's refashioning of the gothic mode calls for further examination.

The history of Jacobs's relationship to Harriet Beecher Stowe foregrounds *Incidents*'s connection to the conventions of the gothic. Instead of writing her own story, Jacobs initially planned to dictate her narrative to Stowe, who wanted to use it for her *Key to Uncle Tom's Cabin* (1853). Outraged by Stowe's subsequent treatment of her and her daughter, Jacobs decided to write her story herself, claiming that "it needed no romance" (Yellin 1985:266).[20] Despite Jacobs's claim, her story was the perfect factual source for Stowe's gothic romance. Jacobs's factual account of her seven-year imprisonment in her grandmother's garret, written almost a decade after *Key*, echoes Stowe's fictional tale about Cassy haunting Legree's attic. This uncanny connection—fact mirroring fiction—exemplifies the complex intersection between the romance and the real in both texts. If Stowe desired Jacobs's factual history to authenticate her fictional tale, Jacobs also revised Stowe's fictional story in her own factual account. Since Jacobs refers in her penultimate chapter to Stowe's treatment of the Fugitive Slave Law in *Uncle Tom's Cabin*, it is evident that Jacobs was familiar with Stowe's novel (194). Moreover, Jacobs's borrowing of Cassy's "loophole in the garret" to name her own "loophole of retreat" suggests connections between the two stories that have yet to be fully explored (Stowe 597; Jacobs 114).[21] In both instances, the gothic is the fictional mode by which the factual horrors of slavery can be represented. However, understanding how Jacobs revises Stowe's loophole along with other gothic conventions makes apparent the power and the limitations of the gothic mode for African-American authors.

Harriet Beecher Stowe's *Uncle Tom's Cabin* is a fiction that claims the status of fact. Her subtitle to *The Key to Uncle Tom's Cabin* argues that her fictional effects are grounded in actual events: "Presenting the Original

Facts and Documents Upon Which the Story is Founded. Together with Corroborative Statements Verifying the Truth of the Work." Moreover, Stowe claims that the novel "more, perhaps, than any other work of fiction that ever was written, has been a collection and arrangement of real incidents, of actions really performed, of words and expressions really uttered, grouped together with reference to a general result" (1). However, in defending *Uncle Tom's Cabin* as a true story, Stowe reveals a complicated relationship between fictional effect and factual event. Events may authenticate her effects, but they remain subordinate. *Uncle Tom's Cabin* achieves its realist status primarily through its impression on the reader and only secondarily through its factual authentication. Stowe writes, "the book had a purpose entirely transcending the artistic one, and accordingly encounters at the hands of the public demands not usually made on fictitious works. It is *treated* as a reality—sifted, tried and tested, as a reality; and therefore as a reality it may be proper that it should be defended" (1). Once treated as reality, the novel can then be defended as such. The narrative effect not only claims the status of event but supersedes it. However, even as Stowe subsumes fact into fiction, she recognizes the difference between the two:

> The writer acknowledges that the book is a very inadequate representation of slavery; and it is so, necessarily, for this reason—that slavery, in some of its workings, is too dreadful for the purposes of art. A work which should represent it strictly as it is would be a work which could not be read; and all works which ever mean to give pleasure must draw a veil somewhere, or they cannot succeed. (*Key*, 1)

The scene of slavery exceeds the representation of art. By passing over what is too dreadful, fiction makes the unreadable readable, paradoxically unveiling slavery yet concealing its worst aspects. It is precisely this paradox—the need for narrative to represent historical reality yet the danger that fiction will be equated with fact—that troubles Jacobs's narrative. Stowe, who has different goals, negotiates this paradox more easily. For her, narrative effects can both be grounded in reality and evade it.

Stowe's use of the gothic in *Uncle Tom's Cabin* exemplifies this complicated relationship between the event of slavery and its narrative effects. Stowe employs the gothic to represent the southern spectacle of slavery.[22] In the last third of the novel, as Tom travels down the blood-red river to Legree's decaying mansion in a chapter titled "The Middle Passage," the gothic intrudes into the sentimental in order to register the full horror of slavery: Legree's ruined plantation unveils what lies just behind the seemingly enlightened edifice of St. Clare's home. On another level, Stowe's description shows just how easily slavery is transcribed into gothic terms. Hell and the Inquisition serve as apt metaphors for the horror chamber of slavery where one can be "burned alive . . . scalded, cut into inch-pieces, set up for the dogs to tear, or hung up and whipped to death" (512). Indeed, as Cassy tells Tom, slavery's everyday occurrences make a fine gothic tale: "I could make any one's hair rise, and their teeth chatter, if I should only tell what I've seen and been knowing to, here" (512). This section of the novel shows how the event of slavery is structured in gothic terms, and also demonstrates how gothic stories are produced by history. The scene of actual terror—a female slave imprisoned in the garret and beaten to death—is turned into a ghost story that then terrifies Legree: "it was said that oaths and cursings, and the sound of violent blows, used to ring through that old garret, and mingle with wailings and groans of despair" (565). As the transformation of event into legend makes clear, gothic devices terrify because of their relation to actuality. Legree's superstition is not illusory; his fright is grounded in reality.

The inclusion of Cassy's gothic tale within the novel's already gothicized plot shows the gothic operating on yet another level: it allows the objects of torture and terror to haunt back. In order to escape the horrors of Legree's house, Cassy directs her own ghost story, reviving the legend of the garret to enable her escape. Adding some special effects—she inserts the neck of an old bottle into the garret window to ensure the proper shrieks, leaves ghost stories around for Legree to read, and finally turns herself into a ghost with the requisite white sheet—Cassy uses the gothic's terror effects to free herself from the imprisoning plot of slavery. The author of her own "Authentic Ghost Story," as Stowe's chapter heading informs us, Cassy appropriates the place of terror and imprisonment, the "weird and ghostly" garret—and turns it into a safe haven and the site of her liberation (564). As the haunter, Cassy may first roam the house freely and then escape it altogether. The gothic serves as a means of resistance in Cassy's hands: by turning the horror of her own history into the source of her power, Cassy finds liberation in the very terror that has imprisoned her.

However, although Cassy's ghost story shows that gothic effects are grounded in historical events, Stowe's narrative tends to dematerialize those effects. Not only does her gothic tale demonize Cassy, turning her into a stock character, partly insane, with a supernatural laugh, but it also reminds the reader that the horror is not true, only a play. "At the time when all was matured for action," the narrator interrupts, "our readers may, perhaps, like to look behind the scenes, and see the final *coup d'etat*" (571). By introducing Cassy's machinations with this address to the reader, the narrative unveils itself as a fiction. We are not asked to identify with Legree and read Cassy's effects as true; rather, we are shown behind the scenes to see the effect as merely that—an effect. Instead of being frightened by the ghost, we are made privy to Cassy's plan to "play ghost for them" (574). Whereas Legree is terrified by Cassy's effects, the reader is amused. By parodying the gothic, Stowe's narrative undercuts its relation to actual incidents: "Authorities were somewhat divided," Stowe writes at the beginning of chapter XLII, "as to the outward form of the spirit, owing to a custom quite prevalent among negroes, —and, for aught we know, among whites, too,—of invariably shutting the eyes, and covering up heads under blankets, petticoats, or whatever else might come in use for a shelter, on these occasions" (594). Here, Stowe spoofs the gothic to play the scene for laughs rather than fear. Blacks, and perhaps whites, are made to appear stupidly superstitious, a position the reader is implicitly instructed to avoid. Asked not to take the white sheet too seriously, the reader is exempted from the horrors of history. Cassy's effects have power over Legree, who sees them as true, but not over the reader, who is reminded that they are a fiction.

Stowe's deployment of the gothic in *Uncle Tom's Cabin* demonstrates how the gothic can resurrect or dematerialize history by turning it into a fiction; the gothic might allow the objects of terror to haunt back, but it also offers its viewer an avenue of escape. This double-edged nature of the gothic is precisely what Jacobs negotiates in *Incidents in the Life of a Slave Girl*. At the outset of her narrative, Jacobs articulates the problem of writing her life story: it is at once incredible and indescribable.

> I am aware that some of my adventures may seem incredible; but they are, nevertheless, strictly true. I have not exaggerated the wrongs inflicted by Slavery; on the contrary, my descriptions fall far short of the facts. I have concealed the names of places, and given persons fictitious names. I had no motive for secrecy on my own account, but I deemed it kind and considerate towards others to pursue this course. (1)

This opening address to the reader signals the intricate connections between fact and fiction in Jacobs's narrative. The facts of Jacobs's history are unspeakable, but once represented, even partially, they resemble fiction. Paradoxically, her narrative of slavery appears to be an effect even as it falls short of capturing slavery's grim reality. Caught between exaggerated effect and unspeakable fact, Jacobs's narrative must negotiate the two poles without collapsing them; her history must not be subsumed by the fictional conventions she uses to represent it. The canny revelation that she concealed the true names of places and people in her narrative suggests the narrative's dual function: like the author's pseudonym, Linda Brent, her narrative veils her history while appearing to unveil it. By highlighting her narrative's fictionality and inadequacy as well as its truth, Jacobs signals the way it both reveals and conceals her unspeakable history.[23]

Lydia Maria Child seemingly disregards the difficulty of Jacobs's narrative position when she writes: "This peculiar phase of Slavery has generally been kept veiled; but the public ought to be made acquainted with its monstrous features, and I willingly take the responsibility of presenting them with the veil withdrawn. I do this for the sake of my sisters in bondage, who are suffering wrongs so foul, that our ears are too delicate to listen to them" (4). Child assumes not only that withdrawing the veil is her responsibility but also that it is simple, however indelicate. Yet her metaphor of slavery as a monster reveals the veil to be multilayered. Beneath it is another veil: a metaphor of slavery rather than slavery itself. Even uncovered, the event is transcribed as another effect. In arguing that slavery's wrongs are too foul for listeners' delicate ears, Child echoes Stowe's sentiments that slavery in all its dreadfulness is unreadable, or in this case unhearable. Child's paradoxical point—that slavery's horrors must be unveiled, yet once unveiled they might be too foul to be heard—suggests the difficult space within which Jacobs had to negotiate her narrative.

Incidents, then, has to perform a play of veils. Jacobs's manipulation of the gothic's conventions is central to this performance. Like Stowe and Douglass, Jacobs understands and exploits the gothic's conventionalized relationship to the scene of slavery in the antebellum period; she gothicizes slavery from the outset of her narrative by describing it as a "deep, and dark, and foul . . . pit of abominations" peopled by "fiends who bear the shape of men" (2, 27). However, like Douglass, she also resists the gothic's romantic effects. In chapter 9, "Sketches of Neighboring Slaveholders," Jacobs recounts a series of horrifying punishments to reveal the "abominations of slavery": slaves are bludgeoned, flogged, and burned to death (52). Like Stowe, she suggests how these actual events produce gothic narratives. The slavemaster's fear of retribution prompts his belief in ghosts: "Murder was so common on his plantation that he feared to be alone after nightfall," she says of Mr. Litch. "He might have believed in ghosts" (47). However, Jacobs insists, unlike Stowe, that the gothic's effects are real: the bloodhounds "literally tore the flesh from his bones," she states of one slave (47). The compilation of narratives in this chapter, which resembles the narrative techniques of antislavery tracts like Theodore Weld's *American Slavery as It Is*, produces a factual basis for these incredible horrors. Piling narrative upon narrative, Jacobs marshals a multitude of cases as evidence of slavery's real terrors, proving the punishments to be a "general rule" rather than an exaggerated exception (50). Repetition rather than progression marks her narrative mode in this chapter, and indeed, her entire narrative. For instance, in comparing her easy fate in slavery to that of others, she writes:

> I was never cruelly over-worked; I was never lacerated with the whip from head to foot; I was never so beaten and bruised that I could not turn from one side to the other; I never had my heel-strings cut to prevent my running away; I was never chained to a log and forced to drag it about, while I toiled in the fields from morning till night; I was never branded with hot iron, or torn by bloodhounds. (115)

The parallel construction of her sentences as well as the proliferation of examples marks the way repetition functions to substantiate a single fact: slavery's torture.

However, Jacobs's use of repetition also points to the inadequacy of narrative in reconstructing reality. No matter how many examples she recounts, she says, "I could tell of more slaveholders as cruel as those I have described" (49). Moreover, at the end of her list of examples Jacobs writes, "No pen can give an adequate description of the all-pervading corruption produced by slavery" (51). Claiming the factual nature of slavery's gothic horror even as she argues that an excess of examples still falls short of the fact, Jacobs at once narratively constructs the gothic event as actual and insists that it exceeds such representation. The narrative excess that the gothic event produces (in this case, the repetition) allows it to remain uncontained. While Child edits the chapter in order to contain its horrors and shield its reader—"I put the savage cruelties into one chapter, entitled 'Neighboring Planters,' in order that those who shrink from 'supping upon horrors' might omit them, without interrupting the thread of the story" (qtd. in Yellin 1987:xxii)—Jacobs refuses to quarantine the gothic to this chapter or to the South. Her use of repetition not only weaves this thread of her story throughout her narrative but also refuses her reader any escape from history's horrors. Stowe allows readers to separate themselves from the frightening effects of the gothic by showing them behind the scenes, but Jacobs blocks the avenues of escape for her northern reader. From the title-page epigraph indicting the North for lack of effort in overthrowing slavery and her imaginative projection of the northern reader as a negro trader at the end of chapter 9, to her conditional freedom at the end of the narrative,

Jacobs implicates the North in the horrors that she presents and curtails her readers' ability to read her history as a romantic tale.

Although Jacobs licenses her reader to view her narrative within certain gothic conventions—she recounts a typical female gothic plot when she portrays herself as an innocent maiden pursued by a lascivious villain, the "vile monster" Doctor Flint (27)—she also rewrites them, especially the gothic's demonization and victimization of blacks.[24] She might use Dr. Flint's persecutions to emphasize her extreme vulnerability, but she also refuses to be imprisoned in the role of victim: "My master met me at every turn, reminding me that I belonged to him, and swearing by heaven and earth that he would compel me to submit to him. If I went out for a breath of fresh air, after a day of unwearied toil, his footsteps dogged me. If I knelt by my mother's grave, his dark shadow fell on me even there" (28). By locating the gothic's evil blackness in Dr. Flint's dark shadow, Jacobs both emphasizes her persecution and reverses the gothic's usual demonization: the master, not the black slave, is the source of horror and dread. Unlike Stowe's Cassy, who embodies the demons of slavery—she tells Legree, "I've got the devil in me" (525)—Jacobs refuses to become a projection of the slavemaster's villainy. By presenting herself as the innocent maiden attempting to flee the corruptions of slavery, Jacobs both gains the sympathy of her reader and resists being demonized.

While Jacobs exploits her position as the victim of a gothic plot, she also insists on her ability to haunt back. She portrays herself as both the victim of Dr. Flint's deceptions and his competitor in cunning: "Being surrounded by mysteries, deceptions, and dangers," Jacobs writes, slaves "early learn to be suspicious and watchful, and prematurely cautious and cunning" (155). Jacobs might represent herself as the unsuspecting maiden who, when Dr. Flint begins to people her "young mind with unclean images," lets his signs "pass, as if [she] did not understand what he meant," but she is actually out-manipulating him (27, 31). Refusing to react to his words, she evades the actual terror in which those verbal deceptions are meant to result—rape. By cloaking her strong reading of events as a seeming nonreading, Jacobs plays both helpless heroine and active combatant.[25]

By emphasizing her role as the victim of slavery's imprisoning gothic plot even as she manipulates that plot, Jacobs appeals to and resists her readers' conventional view of the slave as victim of monstrous evils. For instance, when she describes Dr. Flint's plan to give her a home of her own and "make a lady" of her, she rewrites his sentimental story as a gothic plot: she "shudders" as she listens to his plan, realizing that the "secluded place" would imprison her in a "dreaded fate," a "living death" (53). By revealing the gothic terror behind Dr. Flint's sentimental smoke screen, Jacobs justifies her sexual fall. Her gothic scene not only underscores her role as helpless victim but also sets the stage for her resistance: "I was determined that the master . . . should not . . . succeed at last in trampling his victim under his feet. I would do any thing, every thing, for the sake of defeating him," she writes (53). As the innocent maiden unwillingly initiated into evil, the victim "struggling alone in the powerful grasp of the demon Slavery," Jacobs mounts her defense (54). If the gothic monster has her in his grasp, then her manipulations of slavery's evil plots are justified. Asking the reader to pity her and pardon her for taking Mr. Sands as a lover, she argues that she saw no other "way of escaping the doom [she] so much dreaded" (55).

Jacobs's ultimate escape plan highlights her revision of and resistance to the gothic's conventions. Over the "living death" that awaits her in Dr. Flint's secluded cottage, she chooses her own place of live burial when she imprisons herself in her grandmother's garret (53). She describes her garret in gothic terms: it is a "dungeon," a torture chamber, a prison, a grave (127). Indeed, her "dismal hole" resembles the "deep, and dark, and foul" pit of slavery (113, 2). Jacobs's description symbolizes slavery's extreme entrapment: "The garret was only nine feet long and seven wide. The highest part was three feet high, and sloped down abruptly to the loose board floor. There was no admission for either light or air" (114). Jacobs's refusal to sensationalize her garret—she describes it in a factual tone—reflects her general resistance to the gothic's dematerializing effects. She might exploit gothic metaphors (for instance, she describes herself as a "poor captive in her dungeon" [133]), but she insists that they be taken as truth.

Her address to the reader about her seven years of imprisonment in the garret emphasizes the truthfulness of her tale:

> I hardly expect that the reader will credit me, when I affirm that I lived in that little dismal hole, almost deprived of light and air, and with no space to move my limbs, for nearly seven years. But it is a fact; and to me a sad one, even now; for my body still suffers from the effects of that long imprisonment, to say nothing of my soul. Members of my family, now living in New York and Boston, can testify to the truth of what I say. (148)

The incredibleness of her revelation makes her assume her reader's disbelief, so Jacobs authenticates her description of the extreme physical and psychological conditions of her imprisonment with the continued effects on her body and soul, to which her family can bear witness. By presenting herself and her family as factual evidence, Jacobs asserts her own materiality: she asks the reader to credit her story by crediting her as a person rather than as a character. Moreover, in insisting that her staged death is not a performance from which she can walk away unscathed, Jacobs points to the costs of her conjuring. Cassy says to Tom, "I know no way but through the grave," but Jacobs signifies against Stowe by actualizing that escape (562).

Thus, Jacobs refuses to dematerialize the gothic event of slavery. Unlike Cassy, who can walk away from slavery dressed in a white sheet, Jacobs reminds the reader of the physical costs of her disappearing act. After her first live burial under the floorboards, she remarks, "the fright I had undergone, the constrained posture, and the dampness of the ground, made me ill for several days" (110); later, in her garret, she describes being tortured by dripping turpentine, excessive temperatures, and insects until her body becomes so crippled that it makes escape impossible. Jacobs also argues that the gothic's ghostly effects are the result of actual events. When she reappears in the realm of the living, her friend Fanny declares, "Linda, can this be *you*? or is it your ghost?" (156). Figured as a specter returned from the dead, she resembles a gothic effect. However, as Jacobs's earlier discussion of her brother's figure suggests, a ghostly appearance is one of the physical effects of slavery: "long confinement had made his face too pale, his form too thin"; he looks "like a ghost" (23, 24). In Fanny and Brent's exchange of their tales of terror and suffering, Jacobs underscores the events behind all gothic effects. When her son imagines her as the victim in a gothic story, "O mother! you ain't dead, are you? They didn't cut off your head at the plantation, did they," Jacobs demonstrates how the supernatural is based in institutionalized threats of power (88). Benny has not made up this terrifying story but has learned it from his master's threats: Dr. Flint says to him, "Get out of the way, you little damned rascal! If you don't, I'll cut off your head" (116).

Jacobs refuses to spoof the gothic or undermine the reality behind its effects, and thus she mounts an implicit critique of Stowe's gothic episode. Her garret stands in marked contrast to Cassy's "great, desolate space" (564). Cassy's attic serves as a new home, not a prison (she can roam the house at night and walk around the attic during the day, and she also reclaims the role of "true womanhood" there, becoming mother to Emmeline and making a home for them), but Jacobs's garret is both a safe haven and a grave. Cassy is in "no danger" and can make any noise that she pleases since "it will only add to the effect," but Jacobs states that she had to remain still and quiet for fear of being caught (576). Jacobs might depict herself as using her gothic location to combat slavery's terrors—with "spying eyes and ventriloquist voice" she is able to out-manipulate Dr. Flint by disappearing and by projecting herself, through her letter-writing, up North—but she constantly reminds the reader what this costs her (Andrews 1986:259). She remains the object of terror and torture even as she haunts back.

Jacobs's refusal to exploit Stowe's story overtly in this scene emphasizes her resistance to the gothic's fictionalizing conventions. Jacobs authenticates her own incredible imprisonment with a narrative of horrifying fact rather than a fictional tale. Her description of her garret directly echoes her previous tale of a runaway slave who is punished by being whipped and then screwed into a cotton gin: "He was then put into the cotton gin, which was screwed down, only allowing him room to turn on his side when he could not lie on his back. . . . When the press was unscrewed, the dead body was found partly eaten by rats and vermin" (49). The cotton gin is like Jacobs's dark hole, where she can only sleep on one side and has to endure rats and mice running over her bed; both the gin and Jacobs's grave represent the torture chamber of slavery.[26] Indeed, Jacobs's use of repetition places her garret in a long line of imprisoning places—the cotton gin, the attic storeroom in her friend's house, the shallow grave under the floorboards in her friend's kitchen, the Snaky Swamp—enabling her to verify and generalize her scene of suffering. The garret is not an exceptional example of slavery's horror but its typical representative. As Deborah Garfield argues, instead of letting Stowe narrow Jacobs's experience to a single romantic event in *Key*, Jacobs insists on a broader context for the gothic horrors of slavery (284).

Just as Jacobs refuses to restrict the gothic horrors of slavery to a single event or a single chapter (as Child would do), so too does she argue that they exceed the borders of the South. Through repetition, Jacobs demonstrates that her life in the North replicates her imprisonment and persecution in the gothic South.[27] Instead of being a place of freedom, the North "aped the customs of slavery" (163).[28] She describes it as a place of reimprisonment and persecution: not only is she pursued by her "Old Enemy Again" but she portrays herself as entrapped in another "reign of terror," this time in the form of the Fugitive Slave Law (191). Upon arriving in the North, she claims that she barely has time to find a home before Dr. Flint comes looking for her: "Again I was to be torn from a comfortable home, and all my plans for the welfare of my children were to be frustrated by that demon Slavery!" she exclaims (180). Describing herself as constantly moving (she flees her home four times to evade her persecutors) and ever fearful (she never goes out "without trepidation" since Mr. Dodge, Dr. Flint's surrogate, "might at that moment be waiting to pounce upon [her] if [she] ventured out of doors" [195, 196]), Jacobs depicts herself in a reactive position. No matter how many "double veils" and assumed names she takes on, she can never disappear or find a safe space (181). Dr. Flint's renewed power over her is marked as so omnipotent that it not only extends upward from the South but also from beyond the grave. Even after he dies, Jacobs is not free from his curse, for his family, now destitute, is even more eager to regain its "property." Jacobs, then, argues that the daylight world of the North resembles the nightmare world of the South.

Portraying herself as a victim of the terrors of the North, Jacobs exposes the North's complicity in the South's gothic plots. The North obeys southern laws when it buys people their freedom and returns runaways: "when victims make their escape from this wild beast of Slavery, northerners consent to act the part of bloodhounds, and hunt the poor fugitive back into his den" (35–36). Moreover, she specifically indicts northern readers for their voyeuristic pleasure in and appropriation of the slave's suffering. Jacobs might end the book by presenting a portrait of the sympathetic northern reader in the form of Mrs. Bruce, but she begins the book by critiquing the voyeuristic reader in the person of Mrs. Flint, whose "nerves were so strong, that she could sit in her easy chair and see a woman whipped, till the blood trickled from every stroke of the lash" (12). Her opening also insists that reading about gothic horror is different from experiencing it: "Only by experience can any one realize how deep, and dark, and foul is that pit of abominations," she states (2). When at the end of her narrative Jacobs argues that she is only as free from "the power of slaveholders as are the white people of the north," which is "not saying a great deal," she places the northern reader in the position of southern terrorist or imprisoned victim and allows no loophole out of the horrors of the nation's history (201). Returning to New York from England, she writes that "from the distance spectres seemed to rise up on the shores of the United States. It is a sad feeling to be afraid of one's native country" (186). For Jacobs, the gothic shadows of slavery encompass the entire nation.

Although Jacobs continues to be haunted by her "mournful past" in the North, she is able to haunt back by writing her narrative and by speaking the unspeakable about slavery (161). Jacobs describes it as the gothic horror that must be unveiled: "the secrets of slavery are concealed like those of the Inquisition" (35). Throughout her narrative, Jacobs makes evident how a veil of silence supports slavery: it serves as the slavemaster's single most important weapon in the battle of appearances. Jacobs emphasizes this point in chapter 9, "Sketches of Neighboring Slaveholders." The litany of terror and torture she recites here depends on the fact that "Nothing was said" (47); the cruelties pass "without comment" (46). Silence fuels and secures slavery's reign of terror.

Against the master's powerful prohibition, Jacobs insists on speaking the unspeakable. From early on, she realizes the power of exposure.[29] Even as a young girl, she understands that Dr. Flint's hesitancy in whipping her stems from a fear that "the application of the lash might have led to remarks that would have exposed him" (35). Instead of exposing the marks on her flesh, as many ex-slaves did, Jacobs reveals the horrors of slavery through her pen: "Rise up, ye women that are at ease!" the title page announces, "Hear my voice, ye careless daughters! Give ear unto my speech." In doing this, she reverses the position of terror. She is recording a litany of real-life horrors—from scalding drops of fat falling on bare skin and bloodhounds tearing the flesh from runaways, to whipping posts surrounded by pools of blood and slaves going insane—but in writing these horrors, she reclaims them for her own purpose: to haunt back by exposing the difference between slavery's appearance and its reality.

This rending of the veil, however, is not easy. Like most gothic texts, Jacobs's narrative encodes the difficulty inherent in speaking the unspeakable. Her invocation to speech on her title page is balanced in both the preface and the appendix of her text with a desire for silence. Her text begins with her stating that "it would have been more pleasant to me to have been silent about my own history" and ends with Post's description of Jacobs' reluctance to tell her story (1). The narrative frame both exhibits her resistance to exposing her painful history as a sentimental stance and registers the very real difficulty of representing such excessive horror and the pain involved in remembering it.

While the conclusion of Jacobs's narrative appears to veil the horrors she has spent her narrative revealing in the cloak of sentiment, it remains haunted by her history: "it has been painful to me, in many ways, to recall the dreary years I passed in bondage. I would gladly forget them if I could. Yet the retrospection is not altogether without solace; for with those gloomy recollections come tender memories of my good old grandmother, like light, fleecy clouds floating over a dark and troubled sea" (201).[30] The passage registers Jacobs's desire to alleviate the pain of her horrific history with the healing salve of forgetfulness, but it also insists on the futility of this desire. Haunted by the shadows of her past and the continued oppression of her present, Jacobs cannot completely exorcise the demons of slavery; yet in bearing witness to them she haunts back.

Epilogue: Remembering History

> Is gwine ter be ha'nted tel de las' piece er plank is rotted en crumble inter dus'—
>
> —Charles Chesnutt, *The Conjure Woman*

African-American authors' appropriation and revision of gothic conventions shows that the gothic is not a transhistorical, static category but a dynamic mode that undergoes historical change when specific agents adopt and transform its conventions. In the works of African-American writers from Frederick Douglass and Harriet Jacobs to Charles Chesnutt, Pauline Hopkins, Richard Wright, Ann Petry, Ralph Ellison, Gloria Naylor, August Wilson, J. California Cooper, Toni Morrison, and others, the gothic has served as a useful mode in which to resurrect and resist America's racial history. As Ralph Ellison insists in his opening to *Invisible Man*, the gothic must be understood in realistic terms: "I am an invisible man. No, I am not a spook like those who haunted Edgar Allan Poe; nor am I one of your Hollywood-movie ectoplasms. I am a man of substance, of flesh and bone, fiber and liquids—and I might even be said to possess a mind" (3). The invisible man who haunts Ellison's text is not a Halloween trick or a special effect, but the specter of race; not a disembodied ghost, but a person of flesh and blood. By arguing for the material sources and effects of the gothic, Ellison resists dematerializing the ghosts of America's racial history. At the same time, he uses invisibility to insist on the pervasiveness of racism's effects; his novel shows how this hidden history can be made visible through a redeployment of gothic tropes.

Remembering this gothic history, as Harriet Jacobs demonstrates, is not without its costs. Since the African-American gothic's horrors are actual, not fictional—written in the flesh as well as the text—any attempt to resurrect them can be painful and difficult. Toni Morrison's *Beloved*, one of the fullest articulations of the gothic's role in rematerializing African-American history, acknowledges this problem. Locating slavery's horrors and subsequent hauntings in the body—not only in the baby ghost's materialization in Beloved's body, but also in the physical reminders of slavery as exemplified by Beloved's smiling scar and Sethe's chokecherry tree—*Beloved* addresses the difficulty of transforming the debilitating history of slavery into a usable past. Like Jacobs's narrative, which pairs the desire to forget with the need to remember, *Beloved* attempts to remember an unspeakable history by charting a middle course between Sethe's willed forgetfulness and Beloved's greedy memory. The epilogue's chorus—"This is not a story to pass on"—reveals how difficult this balance is to achieve (274). Both prohibiting memory and insisting upon it, the chorus registers the dilemma of the novel. In an interview about *Beloved*, Morrison states, "You are condemned to repeat the mistakes if you do not fully understand them. And that's true for black people as well as whites. In the move toward a life here, we didn't want to dwell on slavery. You can't absorb it; it's too terrible. So you just try your best to put it behind you. It's a perfect dilemma. Forgetting is unacceptable. Remembering is unacceptable" (*U.S. News and World Report*, 75). Beloved becomes the spectral embodiment of this dilemma: she represents a history that can never be completely spoken or silenced, never be fully controlled. "Comes back whether we want it to or not," Sethe says to Paul D, speaking of their time spent in slavery at Sweet Home (14). Suggesting that the past will never be completely purged—Beloved "could be hiding in the trees waiting for another chance"—the novel's ending offers no easy relief from the horrors of history (263).

However, despite the difficulties inherent in resurrecting a gothic history, *Beloved*, like *Incidents*, insists on speaking the unspeakable. As *Beloved* makes clear, silence is an understandable response to the horrors of history, but it is ultimately disempowering and isolating: unable to "say a word" after watching Sethe be milked, Halle goes insane; unable to answer her schoolmate's inquiries about her mother, Denver retreats into a "silence too solid for penetration" (103); unable to marshal her powerful call after Sethe's murder of Beloved, Baby Suggs withdraws to her bed to die. Like Amy, who is at first "struck dumb" by the sight of Sethe's bloodied back but then uses her "dreamwalker's voice" to transform that terror into a tree, Morrison revises the horrifying history of slavery by transforming it into a tale (79). While the gothic, as the site of excess, haunting, and ill health, threatens to resurrect a history that can never be exorcised, it also offers a way to signify against that history. For Morrison as for Jacobs, the gothic serves as a mode of resistance. By writing their own gothic tales, these authors combat the master's version of their history; by breaking the silence, they reclaim their history instead of being controlled by it.

It is this model of history—a history that must be reclaimed, if only partially—on which the African-American gothic insists. Offered no escape route from history's horrors, Morrison's characters must find a way to live with them. When Sethe suggests to Baby Suggs that they move in order to avoid the ghost, Baby Suggs replies, "What'd be the point? . . . Not a house in the country ain't packed to its rafters with some dead Negro's grief" (5). Unable to flee America's racial history, African Americans, Morrison argues, incorporate its terror into their everyday lives: "Black people in general don't annihilate evil. We believe that evil has a natural place in the universe. We try to avoid it or defend ourselves against it but we are not surprised at its existence or horrified or outraged. We may, in fact, live right next door to it, not only in the form of something metaphysical, but also in terms of people" (Parker 253). Terror is part of everyday reality for African Americans of all social classes.

For Morrison, then, looking back to the past in order to make the present coherent is a necessary act; however, it is double-edged. Resurrecting one's history may be crucial to any forward movement, but it can be debilitating as well. There is never any assurance that the horrors of history can be assimilated or transformed. Once recognized, the abject history that Beloved represents may refuse to be exorcised and subsume both the present and the future. The solution the novel offers is the act of community. Sethe must put Paul D's story next to hers; the women must communally exorcise the ghost. Sharing the past makes its burden bearable—communal comfort offers some protection. Refusing to deny history's horrors or the difficulty of speaking them, *Beloved* suggests how to productively face the past: everyone must collectively participate in bearing witness to its horror.

In her recent critical works, "Unspeakable Things Unspoken: The Afro-American Presence in American Literature" and *Playing in the Dark*,

156 *Epilogue*

Morrison also argues that America's racial history must be resurrected and combated: its horrors haunt all of American literature. Her search for "the ghost in the machine"—the haunting black presence that hovers in the absences and silences of America's greatest romances—remembers American literature as the site of racial hauntings and the locus of a racial history (1989:11). By re-envisioning the American literary canon in gothic terms, Morrison calls for critics to be wakeful to the nightmares of history that inform it. American literature, Morrison argues, is both burdened and constituted by its racial history. Slavery and racial oppression are abject presences, the unspeakable things that must be spoken.

The image that haunts the cover of this book—a panel from Jacob Lawrence's *Harriet Tubman* Series (No. 11)—makes visible the terrifying hand of slavery and oppression that hovers over the national landscape (see figure). Lawrence, a prominent African-American artist, is known for his flat, cut-out style, bold color schemes and historical series that document African-American culture. Lawrence's *Harriet Tubman* Series (1939–40) is composed of thirty-one panels, each accompanied by a narrative caption.

5. Jacob Lawrence, *Harriet Tubman* Series, No. 11
Hampton University Museum

The series tells the story of Tubman's life from slavery to escape, from her work in the Underground Railroad and the abolitionist movement to her role as nurse in the Civil War. Panel 11, a night landscape, is one of several panels that depicts Harriet Tubman's original escape from slavery. Under a midnight-blue sky dotted with stars, Tubman takes flight, protected from the searching hand of slavery by the cover of darkness and a canopy of trees. Invisible in this landscape, Tubman appears only in her master's description of her in the accompanying caption. Reiterating the actual reward notice for Tubman's capture, the caption reads:

> $500 Reward! Runaway from subscriber on Thursday night, the 4th inst., from the neighborhood of Cambridge, my negro girl, Harriet, sometimes called Minty. Is dark chestnut color, rather stout build, but bright and handsome. Speaks rather deep and has a scar over the left temple. She wore a brown plaid shawl. I will give the above reward captured outside the county, and $300 if captured inside the county, in either case to be lodged in the Cambridge, Maryland, jail.
>
> (Signed) George Carter
> Broadacres, near Cambridge, Maryland,
> September 24th, 1849. (Wheat 91)

Reducing Tubman's human characteristics to signs that mark her as chattel, the reward notice paradoxically paints a picture of Tubman only to turn her into property. Her invisibility in the picture, then, serves as her protection. The hand of slavery, the only anthropomorphic object in the picture, is emblematic of the terrors she flees as well as of the bondage and oppression that seek to recapture her.

Within the context of the series, the Caucasian flesh-colored arm and long-fingered hand are associated with the slavemaster. From the similarly colored arm and hand of the enraged overseer who strikes Tubman over the head with an iron bar (No. 5) to the clawlike fingers and arms with eyes in them that represent the intensifying search (No. 18), the arm and hand symbolize the terrifying power and reach of slavery. The metonymic substitution of snake, chain, whip, and arm/hand throughout the series further links the Caucasian flesh-toned hand to the evil, bondage, and torture of slavery. Taken by itself, this hand could be read as an abstract form, a comet's trail, or even a hand pointing toward the potential of freedom symbolized by the stars; however, as the panel's caption and connective images make clear, the hand represents the pursuing and oppressive arm of slavery.[1]

The opposing images of Tubman's black arm and hand throughout the series signify Tubman's ability to haunt back against her oppressive pursuer. Her hands are shown as not only strong (No. 7), but also protective. Her outstretched arm, with a cape draped over it, hides two runaways from a group of slavemasters (No. 19); her hands comfort and heal a Union soldier in a panel that recounts her career as a nurse in the Civil War (No. 29). In both panels, her arm and hand echo the image of the slavemaster's outstretched hand: her arm is horizontal; her hand has long, spread-out fingers. Moreover, throughout the series Tubman is depicted as haunting back against the slavemaster's terrifying power. In one caption (No. 19) she is the "terror" that the slaveholder fears (99); in another (No. 24) her raids are characterized as "mysterious" (104). In No. 17 she is not only described in the caption as a "half-crazed sybilline creature" who "began to haunt the slave masters, stealing down in the night to lead a stricken people to freedom," but pictured in the panel as a phantom who harnesses the supernatural powers of the lightning that strikes her heart (97). Once again, her hands are large and powerful, like the slavemaster's. In her subsequent journeys to the South to liberate other slaves, Tubman resists and relocates the slavemaster's terrifying power: she now haunts the landscape; her hand protects and frees other slaves. While the reward notice is confident of its descriptive power and its sufficient economic reward, the context of the series marks its inadequacy in the face—and hands—of Tubman's counternarrative: her history of freeing other slaves through the Underground Railroad.

Lawrence's series not only depicts the phases of Tubman's personal history but also symbolizes the history of the nation. The picture that shows Tubman's flight from the oppressive hand of slavery resembles an American flag. With horizontal stripes of color, a dark-blue background dotted with five-point stars, and no human representation, the image is national rather than personal. The hand that reaches over this national landscape both constitutes and defamiliarizes the national image it projects. The sinuous fingers of the horizontal hand help to create the stripe imagery of the picture as well as the movement of a flag wavering in the wind; however, the hand also disrupts the night, cutting into the fabric of the blue sky, distorting the stars closest to it. With the tentacles of slavery reaching out over the landscape, the nation, the picture suggests, exists under an oppressive cloud.

Lawrence's emblematic image of the nation points to the gothic's social engagement. The horrifying hand has a specific social referent, as the caption underscores. Moreover, the gothic, while associated with the South, does not remain safely quarantined there. Like the fingers stretching out into the night, the horrors of slavery are woven into the fabric of the nation. As later panels in the series show, the North is not the land of freedom. When Tubman must lead her escaped slaves into Canada (No. 20), she flees the United States, not the South; the hand reaches beyond regional boundaries. Finally, the last image of the series (No. 31)—a barren landscape of twiglike trees with a moon and stars partially obscured—suggests that while slavery might have ended with the Civil War, its horrors will continue to haunt the nation. A streak of lighter paint in the blue sky, positioned in the same spot as the hand in the night sky of panel 11, shows that although the arm of oppression is gone, its trace remains. Morrison argues that these traces of the nation's racial history require attention, for the costs of the unspeakable unspoken are greater than the dangers and difficulty of articulation. Through its excessive effects, its displacements, its hauntings, the gothic encodes these traces and is a route toward that articulation.

Notes

Introduction

1. See chapter 5, "The Ghost of Race: Edgar Allan Poe and the Southern Gothic," for a fuller critique of the identification of the gothic with the South.
2. The American gothic's challenge to the truisms of American identity as well as to the coherence of gothic conventions explains its critical neglect. Only three book-length studies have been published on the American gothic since Leslie Fiedler's groundbreaking work, *Love and Death in the American Novel* (1960): Irving Malin's *New American Gothic* (1962), a psychological reading of twentieth-century American gothic; Donald Ringe's *American Gothic: Imagination and Reason in Nineteenth-Century Fiction* (1982), a literary history of the gothic in America from Brown to Hawthorne; and Louis Gross's *From* Wieland *to* The Day of the Dead: *Redefining the American Gothic* (1989), a critical reassessment of the American gothic as an alternative vision of America. When the American gothic is discussed within general works on the gothic (which occurs infrequently), it is either examined as a derivative of the British gothic or segregated from the tradition altogether. For instance, David Punter writes that the "American Gothic seems to be a refraction of English Gothic in that it can only *attempt* to transplant the English themes into American soil" (*The Literature of*

Terror, 212). Even Eugenia DeLamotte, who does a fine job of examining the American gothic in relation to the broader gothic tradition (*Perils of the Night*), finds it necessary to distinguish the American gothic from the gothic's classic models by invoking a notion of primary, secondary, and tertiary gothic. Whether the American gothic is subsumed into the British, excised from the tradition, or relegated to a subsidiary role, the British paradigm remains securely in place. By marginalizing the American gothic, both American and gothic studies limit its challenge to critical consensus.

3. Other general works that catalogue the conventions and trace the development of the British gothic include E. Railo's *The Haunted Castle: A Study of the Elements of English Romanticism*, Mario Praz's *The Romantic Agony*, Montague Summer's *The Gothic Quest: A History of the Gothic Novel*, Devendra Varma's *The Gothic Flame*, Elizabeth MacAndrew's *The Gothic Tradition in Fiction*, and William Patrick Day's *In the Circles of Fear and Desire: A Study of Gothic Fantasy*.
4. See also Jay Clayton's "Pure Poetry/Impure Fiction" in *Romantic Vision and the Novel* for a discussion of the "genre's theoretical preoccupation with impurity" (51).
5. This is Francis Hart's term; see his "Limits of the Gothic: The Scottish Example" and Frederick Garber's "Meaning and Mode in Gothic Fiction" for excellent discussions of how the gothic gets defined in essentialist terms. Both argue that the gothic, like all genres, needs to be historicized and its diversity recognized. In *Kinds of Literature*, Alastair Fowler argues that all genres, not just the gothic, become transmuted; hence, instead of creating essentialized definitions of genres, we should historically situate them. In "On the Dangers of Defining 'Gothic'," (*Art of Darkness*, 12–24), Anne Williams suggests that the definition of the gothic is so troubling precisely because it "challenges almost everything we thought we knew about genre as a critical concept" (15).
6. As Morris Dickstein writes, "gothic novels ... are among the bastard children of literature" ("Popular Fiction and Critical Values," 60). Eve Sedgwick also points to the "unrespectable" nature of studying the gothic when she argues that she wants to "make it easier for the reader of 'respectable' nineteenth-century novels to write 'Gothic' in the margin next to certain especially interesting passages" (*The Coherence of Gothic Conventions*, 4). David Reynolds's use of gothic metaphors to demonize the popular ("the monster of popular culture" [567]) in his study *Beneath the American Renaissance* reveals how the gothic and the popular are often conflated.
7. See Robert Hume, "Gothic versus Romantic," and James Keech, "The Survival of the Gothic Response," for further examples of the critical preoccupation with differentiating the romantic from the gothic. Anne Williams counters the

critical premise that the two forms are distinct, arguing that " 'Gothic' and 'Romantic' are not two but one" (*Art of Darkness*, 1).
8. For example, *Harper's* magazine (July 1857) uses the term "romance" to describe the novels of Mrs. Radcliffe (Baym 1984:437). See Baym's "Concepts of the Romance in Hawthorne's America" for a critique of Chase's deployment of the term "romance." See also John McWilliams's "The Rationale for 'The American Romance' " for an overview of the romance's reign in American critical discourse.
9. The replacement of *gothic* with the broader term *dark* also occurs more generally in studies on the gothic. Note, for instance, G. R. Thompson's collection, *The Gothic Imagination: Essays in Dark Romanticism*.
10. David Punter was one of the first critics to call for the gothic to be historicized. Others who argue that the gothic should be read in social terms include Noël Carroll, *The Philosophy of Horror*; William Patrick Day, *In the Circles of Fear and Desire*; Eugenia DeLamotte, *Perils of the Night*; Joseph Grixti, *Terrors of Uncertainty*; Rosemary Jackson, *Fantasy: The Literature of Subversion*; Ronald Paulson, "Gothic Fiction and the French Revolution"; and Martin Tropp, *Images of Fear*. Many of these studies outline the gothic's historical dimensions in broad strokes, but localized and sustained readings of the gothic's cultural engagements are still needed.
11. See also Martha Banta's "The Ghostly Gothic of Wharton's Everyday World" for a reading of Wharton's ghost stories within the cultural context of ethnography.
12. My understanding of the abject has been informed by Julia Kristeva's discussion in *Powers of Horror*. While Kristeva's concept of the abject stresses the psychosymbolic economy, a "horror of being," it is also useful for a sociohistorical understanding of horror.
13. As I was completing this project, two studies appeared that complement my reading of the gothic in relation to national narratives: Priscilla Wald's *Constituting Americans* (1995) and Russ Castronovo's *Fathering the Nation* (1995). Both works discuss how the national narrative is unsettled by "untold stories" (Wald 4) or "bastard histories" (Castronovo 4); both focus on narrative disruptions and incoherence as well as on how race and slavery serve as crucial contradictions in the nation's official narratives.

1. Haunted by History: Crèvecoeur's National Narrative and the Gothic

1. *Letters* has a complicated textual history. It was first published in England in 1782. An expanded and heavily rewritten two-volume edition was published in France in 1784; the second edition of the French version appeared in three volumes in 1787. *Letters* was published in the United States in 1793 and not reprinted until 1904. In 1925, a number of letters not originally published in the English edition were collected and arranged by Henri Bourdin et al. under

the title *Sketches of Eighteenth Century America*. More recently, Dennis Moore has edited *More Letters from an American Farmer* (1995), which contains all of the essays that Crèvecoeur wrote in English but did not include in *Letters* and restores the original manuscript's arrangement of the letters. I am working from Albert Stone's edition of *Letters*, which is based on the second English edition (1783). For more on the textual history of *Letters*, see Chevignard, "St. John de Crèvecoeur in the Looking Glass"; Plotkin, "Saint-John de Crèvecoeur Rediscovered"; Plumstead, "Hector St. John de Crèvecoeur"; Philbrick, *St. John de Crèvecoeur*; and Putz, "Dramatic Elements and the Problem of Literary Mediation."

2. Rowland Berthoff discusses the importance of the yeoman identity in "Independence and Attachment, Virtue and Interest." Claiming that this self-concept was fanciful to begin with and quickly became obsolete, Berthoff argues that "the farther the classical ideal receded from the dynamic reality of the nineteenth-century American economy, the more Americans liked to think of themselves in its terms" (106). Edmund Morgan also shows how the concept of the yeoman "sustained the government of the many by the few, even while it elevated and glorified the many" (*Inventing the People*, 173). For another instance of the use of the yeoman persona, see John Dickinson's *Letter from a Farmer in Pennsylvania* (1768).

3. John Adams, for instance, claims in a letter to Congress in 1780 that language had the power to change the social order: "It is not to be disputed that the form of government has an influence upon language, and language in its turn influences not only the form of government, but the temper, the sentiments, and the manners of people" (7:249). As Robert Ferguson writes, the founding fathers "believe[d] that knowledge expressed in the language of reason leads to virtue and then harmony" and they trusted that "anything [was] possible with the proper word" ("'We Hold These Truths'," 13, 3).

4. Hugh Blair's *Lectures on Rhetoric and Belles Lettres* (1782, first published in America in 1784), which became the grammar for the nation's colleges, states the plain style's aims as follows: "to explode false ornament, to direct attention more towards substance than show, to recommend good sense as the foundation of all good composition, and simplicity as essential to all true ornament" (2).

5. For other discussions of the crucial role print culture and the "word" played in the nation's self-invention, see Bernard Bailyn, *The Ideological Origins of the American Revolution*; Sacvan Bercovitch, *The American Jeremiad*; Cathy Davidson, *Revolution and the Word*; Robert Ferguson, "'We Hold These Truths'" and *The American Enlightenment*; Christopher Looby, *Voicing America*; and Michael Warner, *The Letters of the Republic*. For a specific reading of how Crèvecoeur and his text intersect with republican print ideology, see Grantland Rice, "Crèvecoeur and the Politics of Authorship in Republican America."

1. *Haunted by History*   165

6. I am relying here on Roland Barthes's understanding of myth as a mode that "abolishes the complexity of human acts" by giving them "the simplicity of essences," and that establishes "a blissful clarity" where "things appear to mean something by themselves" (*Mythologies*, 143). He argues that myth is experienced as innocent speech (131).
7. For biographical information on Crèvecoeur, see Allen and Asselineau, *St. John de Crèvecoeur*; Julia Mitchell, *St. Jean de Crèvecoeur*; and Philbrick, *St. John de Crèvecoeur*; for a specific study of Crèvecoeur's politics, see Jehlen, "J. Hector St. John Crèvecoeur."
8. See Doreen Alvarez Saar, "Crèvecoeur's 'Thoughts on Slavery'," for a discussion of the specific political meanings slavery had in the eighteenth century and slavery's relationship to the corruption of the body politic.
9. This scene has received much critical attention; however, while critics remark upon the horror of the scene, they rarely discuss it as gothic. For example, Robert Lawson-Peebles uses the terminology of the gothic to describe the scene, but does not label it as gothic; he states that the landscape "opens out into a vista of terror" (*Landscape and Written Expression in Revolutionary America*, 103) and that the scene is described in "horrific detail" (105). Thomas Philbrick calls it a "nightmarish little vignette" (*St. John de Crèvecoeur*, 47) and a "hell-scene" (81). Critics also tend to discuss this scene, and the final letter of the book, as "dark." Pamela Regis writes, "In this letter, critics usually detect a darkening and shift in the book" (*Describing Early America*, 117); "Letter IX is dark" (118). Once again, *darkness* is a signifier for and displacer of the gothic. Marius Bewley was the first to read the gothic symbolism of this scene: "In the sense the passage gives of an eighteenth century filled with neatly plotted categories, and socially with conceptions of regulation and caste, the cage suddenly becomes a symbol of metaphysical nightmare, and the negro himself a symbol of the terrible cost of merely man-made order" (*Eccentric Design*, 105). Since he is concerned with how Crèvecoeur imaginatively enhances his factual observations, Bewley is interested not in the historical foundations of this gothic scene but rather in its symbolic effect. Martha Banta sets the scene within the literary tradition of the gothic and sees the gothic as being concerned with actual events: "the James who emerges from this particular gothic tale of horror has met a black man, just as Goodman Brown encounters the Black Man; but James's black man is not the Devil, rather the victim of the whites' demonic ruthlessness in the name of self-preservation, that law of life which James will have to acknowledge as lord by the final chapter" ("American Apocalypses," 9).
10. There are numerous echoes of the crucifixion in this passage, mainly in the form of sacrificial imagery.
11. The issue of slavery is raised as early as Letter 2, where James compares his lot as an American farmer to that of "a Russian boor or an Hungarian peasant"

"condemned to a slavery worse than that of our Negroes" (51, 52). Grantland Rice suggests that the issue of slavery is also embedded in the book's dedication to the Abbé Raynal, "whose 1770 *Histoire des deux Indes* declared that the scarcely born liberty in Europe was buried in American cruelty, slaughter, and despotic slavery." *Letters*, Rice argues, "constitutes a *study* of the American scene within the matrix of Raynal's theories on slavery and degeneracy" ("Crèvecoeur and the Politics of Authorship," 94).

12. Elayne Rapping argues that "this entire interlude, is, in fact, Crèvecoeur's device for rebuilding his model of America at that point in the narrative when James' experience contradicts it most strongly" ("Theory and Experience in Crèvecoeur's America," 713); Thomas Philbrick writes "Letter XI becomes an ominous interlude during which James is silenced, as if he could no longer speak, could no longer sustain the accents and tone that the terms of the correspondence assume" (*St. John de Crèvecoeur*, 84).

13. See Bailyn (*Ideological Origins*, 232–46) for a discussion of the rhetoric of slavery in revolutionary discourse as well as David Brion Davis, *The Problem of Slavery in the Age of Revolution 1770–1823*, and Eric Sundquist, *To Wake the Nations*, part 1, for an extended discussion of how slavery and revolution were bound together in eighteenth- and nineteenth-century American culture.

14. See Mitchell's appendix (*St. Jean de Crèvecoeur*, 346–50) for a list of periodicals that reprinted sections of Crèvecoeur's text. Rice points out that journals "such as *The Gentleman's Magazine* and *The Westminister Magazine, or the Pantheon of Taste*, reproduced only the ninth letter . . . apparently appropriating Crèvecoeur's description of American slavery in a larger invective on the inconsistency of the ideals of the American Revolution with social realities" ("Crèvecoeur and the Politics of Authorship," 109).

15. For instance, Russel Nye argues that *Letters* "is one of those authentic American artifacts which first gave expression to the national consciousness. The book stands, without a doubt, at the beginning of an American literary tradition" ("Michel-Guillaume St. John de Crèvecoeur," 43). Albert Stone also situates *Letters* at the beginning of the American literary tradition: "What makes this work American?" he asks. "Nothing that is unique to Crèvecoeur but rather several qualities that in the test of time have turned out to be characteristic of numerous later writers in this country" (Introduction to *Letters*, 14).

16. See, for example, Mohr, "Calculated Disillusionment"; Nye, "Michel-Guillaume St. John de Crèvecoeur"; Rapping, "Theory and Experience"; and Rucker, "Crèvecoeur's *Letters* and Enlightenment Doctrine."

17. *Letters*'s contending discourses have most often been read as oppositional rather than integrated. For instance, James Mohr argues that the first eight letters become "the dream against which the intensity of later disillusionment is measured" ("Calculated Disillusionment," 355). Myra Jehlen writes that for Crèvecoeur, "America is precisely about one side in an unreconcilable opposi-

tion" (*The Literature of Colonization*, 148). When the discourses are integrated, as in readings of the ending, the gothic tends to be neutralized by the mythic. Robert Winston's reading of the text as ending on a "neutral note" (" 'Strange Order of Things!' " 251) is echoed by other critics. Russel Nye, for example, argues that the book ends in "equivocation" and that the two strands of the book balance each other: "The rural peace of James's farm so movingly described in the early letters is balanced by the rapacity of Charles-Town" ("Michel-Guillaume St. John de Crèvecoeur," 42). Stephen Arch resists this oppositional reading: "*Letters* is not a romance that simply and inconclusively juxtaposes opposing sets of terms (the idyllic and the demonic, idealism and realism, romanticism and skepticism), it is a philosophical work of fiction that comments on the dangers of revolution and on the inadequacies of man's fictions about himself" ("The 'Progressive Steps' of the Narrator," 146).

18. Annette Kolodny argues that the final letters are "inevitable consequences of problems that have been given expression with Letter II" (*The Lay of the Land*, 56); Norman Grabo writes that the letters "are studded with curiously wrong notes" ("Crèvecoeur's American," 168); Nathaniel Philbrick's insightful reading of the Nantucket sequence shows how the middle section of *Letters* "directly challenges the optimistic vision of the book's beginning" ("The Nantucket Sequence," 415). Despite these and other arguments for the interpenetration of the two discourses well before Letter 9, Larzer Ziff still claims that *Letters* "suddenly and violently collapses at its very close into a nightmare that, in formal literary terms, has not been prepared" (*Writing in the New Nation*, 20).

19. For an examination of the differences between *Letters* and *Sketches* see Manfred Putz, who argues that *Sketches* is not only more pessimistic in theme, but also less unified in style: James's authorial voice fades out of *Sketches* as "the whole structure collapses and is dissolved into a cacophonic concert of many dissociated voices bearing witness to the incomprehensible nature of experience" (127). Thomas Philbrick argues that *Sketches* is "less a book than a jumbled compilation of sketches, anecdotes, and descriptive surveys" ("Crèvecoeur as New Yorker," 26). David Robinson claims that *Sketches* highlights the tensions and contradictions inherent in *Letters* ("Community and Utopia in Crèvecoeur's *Sketches*," 18). See also Hales's reading of "Susquehanna" ("The Landscape of Tragedy") and Grabo's "Crèvecoeur's American," for other discussions of *Sketches*.

2. Diseased Discourse: Charles Brockden Brown's Arthur Mervyn

1. Written in response to the 1985 MOVE bombing in Philadelphia, "Fever" is John Edgar Wideman's "historical meditation" on this episode and an earlier moment of the city under siege, the 1793 yellow fever epidemic. Using plague as a metaphor for racism, "Fever" reconstructs the history of racism and its recurrent symptoms.

2. During the 1790s, republicanism was an ideology in transition and contained contradictory discourses. See Gordon Wood, *The Creation of the American Republic*; Bailyn, *Ideological Origins*; and J. G. A. Pocock, *The Machiavellian Moment* for discussions of how American republican ideology was rooted in older ideas of civic humanism. For studies of how the classical notion of republicanism was transformed by the demands of the commercial marketplace see Joyce Appleby, *Capitalism and a New Social Order* and *Liberalism and Republicanism in the Historical Imagination*; Linda Kerber, *Federalists in Dissent* and "Republican Ideology and the Revolutionary Generation"; Isaac Kramnick, "Republican Revisionism Revisited"; Drew McCoy, *The Elusive Republic*; Carroll Smith-Rosenberg, "Domesticating 'Virtue'"; and Steven Watts, *The Republic Reborn*. Watts sums up the movement from classical to commercial republicanism as follows: "The sacrifice of personal advantage to the commonwealth, a long-standing republican ideal, slowly receded before the notion that personal enterprise created productivity and prosperity and thereby *produced* the public good" (*The Romance of Real Life*, 6–7).
3. See Norman Grabo's "Historical Essay" for a full account of the novel's textual history.
4. Benjamin Rush, a prominent Philadelphia physician, made this connection explicit when he medically codified the republican belief that individual and national health were symbiotically related. In *Medical Inquiries* (1812), he set forth an environmental theory of disease, writing that certain "forms of government, have a considerable influence in predisposing [individuals] to derangement" (65). Moreover, in his *Inquiry into the Natural History of Medicine*, presented to the American Philosophical Society in 1774, he "observed that disease, political institutions, and economic organizations were so interrelated that any general social change produced accompanying changes in health" (Rosen, "Political Order and Human Health in Jeffersonian Thought," 33).
5. See Mathew Carey, *A Short Account of the Malignant fever*; Thomas Condie and Richard Fowell, *History of the Pestilence*; and Noah Webster, *A Collection of Papers on the Subject of Bilious Fevers* for contemporary accounts of the yellow fever epidemics in Philadephia. See Martin Pernick, "Politics, Parties and Pestilence"; Norman Grabo, "Historical Essay"; J. H. Powell, *Bring Out Your Dead*; William Hedges, "Benjamin Rush, Charles Brockden Brown and the American Plague Year"; and Robert Ferguson, "Yellow Fever and Charles Brockden Brown" for background on the yellow fever in Philadelphia; see also Shirley Samuels, "Plague and Politics in 1793" and "Infidelity and Contagion," for readings of the cultural and political significance of the plague.
6. Several critics have read *Arthur Mervyn* in terms of the burgeoning market economy. James Justus argues that *Arthur Mervyn* is "a novel about the generative power of money" ("Arthur Mervyn, American," 314) and Daniel Cohen explores the novel in terms of "the conflicting signals of a rapidly changing

culture," especially the movement from a society based on kinship and patronage to a market economy ("Arthur Mervyn and His Elders," 363). For the fullest account of Brown and *Arthur Mervyn*, see Steven Watts's cultural biography, *The Romance of Real Life*, where he situates Brown within the complex web of the emerging market society. Watts and Cohen both emphasize Philadelphia as a commercial as well as a political center for the new republic. Operating as a hub for international trading and for a regional market structure, Philadelphia emblematized the rapid expansion of the market revolution (49–50).
7. See Christophersen (*The Apparition in the Glass*, 104–11) for an extended reading of how blacks operate in the plague scenes. In particular, Christophersen shows how yellow fever and black insurrection are linked in the novel.
8. This confusion is typical of Brown's style. Instead of being read as one of Brown's many plot lapses, it might more usefully be seen as a way to accrue meaning around this single transaction. By having the ship originate from French St. Domingue, the site of slave insurrection, and/or British Jamaica, the novel registers the nation's multiple commercial fears. The novel's burgeoning and often contradictory story lines reflect the way that it accumulates meaning and earns capital not through a single, linear story but by multiple stories and the connections among them. This same overlapping occurs in Welbeck, who is English but who, in his dress and speech, is also associated with the French.
9. America's late-eighteenth-century language-reform movement exemplifies the symbiotic connection between language and society in postrevolutionary America. As Benjamin Franklin's plan for a new alphabet (an effort to make the American language more democratic, with the written word reflecting the spoken, and to provide social cohesion by creating a uniform utterance) and Webster's dictionary (a conservative attempt to codify and standardize the written word in order to slow down social change) show, Americans were convinced that national order and unity could be achieved through linguistic legislation. For more on language reform, see Dennis Baron, *Grammar and Good Taste*; David Simpson, *The Politics of American English*; Looby, "Phonetics and Politics"; and Richard Rollins, "Words as Social Control."
10. In the eighteenth century, moral management gained ascendancy in France with Pinel, who unchained all the mental patients in the Bicêtre, and was continued by Samuel Tuke at the York Retreat in England in 1792. As the basis for modern psychiatry, moral management operated from "the conviction that man naturally possesses an inner light or moral sense, which if properly nourished and treated, would restore happiness and reason to the diseased mind" (David Brion Davis, *Homicide in American Fiction*, 70). Two forms of therapy were used: occupational therapy and exclusion from the social group for nonsocial behavior. By telling Arthur that he will be denied company if he

does not reform and by offering Arthur a new occupation, medicine, Stevens practices this therapy on him. For discussions of mental illness and moral management during the eighteenth century, see Albert Deutsch, *The Mentally Ill in America*; Kathleen Jones, "Moral Management and the Therapeutic Community"; Norman Dain, *Concepts of Insanity in the U.S., 1789–1865*; and David Brion Davis, *Homicide in American Fiction*.

11. The text registers the conflicting views of language at the end of the eighteenth century. On the one hand, fiction was associated with the symptoms of a market economy: novels were seen as polluting agents that undermined the moral fiber of the republican citizen. On the other hand, republican print discourse argued for the efficacy of publication and the circulation of letters as conducive to public virtue. See Michael Warner, *The Letters of the Republic*, for a discussion of these contradictory discourses in the novel. While I agree with Warner that the novel offers these two discourses, we disagree on how it resolves them. Warner sees the republican print position as finally winning out, whereas I argue that the novel, despite its impulses, continues to be haunted by Welbeck's diseased discourse. See Gilmore, *The Literature of the Revolutionary and Early National Periods*, for a recasting of this contradictory discourse in terms of the displacement of oral by print culture at the end of the eighteenth century. Also see Joseph Ellis, *After the Revolution*, for a discussion of the role the arts played in postrevolutionary America.

12. Confidence, as many of Brown's novels show, serves as a defense against the contagion of disease. Stevens, for example, remains free from contagion not only because he takes wholesome measures in his diet and cleanliness, but also because he has faith in their effectiveness: "I had more confidence than others in the vincibility of this disease, and in the success of those measures which we had used for our defence against it" (8). On the other hand, those who allow fear to destroy their faith are easily infected. In *Ormond*, anxiety and panic can make the seeds of disease grow: Baxter's case "may be quoted as an example of the force of imagination," writes the narrator; "he had probably already received, through the medium of the air, or by contact of which he was not conscious, the seeds of this disease. They might perhaps have lain dormant, had not this panic occurred to endow them with activity" (71). Since the mind has the power to repel anxiety or encourage panic, a crisis in confidence can lead to disease.

13. Critical opinion usually falls into one of these camps. James Russo stands at one extreme when he reads with total suspicion: "I maintain, [Arthur] is a conscious liar who uses his pious protestations and innocent good looks as tools in his con man's trade" ("The Chameleon of Convenient Vice," 382). Jane Tompkins (*Sensational Designs*) stands at the other extreme when she gives an optimistic reading of Arthur's reform: for her, Arthur is the epitome of republican virtue. Davidson, who argues against a "totalizing reading that

largely resolves ambiguities and inconsistencies through explanation, judicious evasion, or, more often, by recourse to some overriding ideology that 'makes sense' of difference," offers a compelling argument for refusing either position (*Revolution and the Word*, 248).

14. Norman Grabo remarks that against the "masculine cunning, deceit and sickness" of part 1, part 2 offers "exposure to forces of healing and wholeness" (*The Coincidental Art of Charles Brockden Brown*, 117). Jane Tompkins argues that in part 2 Arthur exorcises Welbeck's ghost and devotes himself to undoing Welbeck's "tangle of lies, forgeries, and seductions"; serving as a "good Samaritan" who spends most of part 2 spreading benevolence, Arthur acts "according to the rules that govern . . . society," supporting the social currency instead of subverting it like Welbeck (*Sensational Designs*, 76, 68). By focusing on the gothic narrative in part 2, my argument shows how the novel criticizes, rather than embraces, the liberal ethos of commercial republicanism; it is allied with Cathy Davidson's reading of the early American gothic, *Revolution and the Word*, which sees the gothic as a critique of the excesses of individualism in the early republic.

15. See Joyce Appleby for a reassessment of commerce in the early republic. While traditional republicanism had been anticommercial, the founders (including Jefferson) accepted that a modern republic gained strength through commerce. The difference between Jeffersonianism and Federalism, Appleby argues, should not be seen as "a conflict between the patrons of agrarian self-sufficiency and the proponents of modern commerce, but rather as a struggle between two different elaborations of capitalistic development in America" (*Liberalism and Republicanism*, 258).

16. In "Arthur Mervyn's Revolutions," Robert Levine sees *Arthur Mervyn* as a novel specifically about revolutionary disruption. Moreover, he argues that in part 2, Arthur Mervyn is a "revolutionary agent unaware of his disruptive potential" (153).

17. Because of its lack of wholeness, critics have usually claimed that part 2 is little more than an afterthought to part 1. Even Norman Grabo, a champion of Brown's formal experiments, argues that the "Second Part is an afterthought, more interesting for its incidental perceptions than for its structural and emotional integrity" ("Historical Essay," 462).

18. Witherington argues the exact opposite: "the removal of the frame constitutes a denial of indirection, and of art" ("Benevolence and the 'Utmost Stretch'," 188). He sees the change between parts 1 and 2 as a movement toward a simpler, less ironic story. Grabo also reads Arthur's act of coalescing all tales "into one sweeping view (his own)" as a confident act of closure, lending coherence to his entire tale (*Coincidental Art*, 129). Hedges, however, argues that in using borrowed identities, Arthur moves toward a "highly self-conscious 'literary' style" ("Charles Brockden Brown and the Culture of Contradictions," 129).

172   *2. Diseased Discourse*

Michael Davitt Bell states that this move is typical of Brown's work as a whole: "[Brown] turns . . . to the forms which pretend to authenticity and immediacy—letters, memoirs, confessions. And yet the paradoxical effect of this immediacy is to *subvert* authenticity, to bring narration into the action and thereby to raise questions about the novel's overt sincerity" (" 'The Double-Tongue Deceiver'," 159). George Spangler also sees *Arthur Mervyn* as a "writerly text" ("C. B. Brown's *Arthur Mervyn*," 592). I argue that in the guise of being simplified, the novel becomes more textualized. Part 2 foregrounds the mediated nature of the text by highlighting the written form of the narrative: Colville's letter from prison, Eliza's letter to Arthur, Achsa's song. Arthur's invocation of his muse also signals the narrative's move to a more overtly literary style: "Move on, my quill! wait not for my guidance. Reanimated with thy master's spirit, all-airy light!" (413). This textualization of the novel suggests the way in which language creates reality in *Arthur Mervyn*. Mark Seltzer, "Saying Makes It So"; Mark Patterson, *Authority, Autonomy, and Representation*; and Larzer Ziff, *Writing in the New Nation* all discuss how authority is lodged in language in Brown's novels. As Patterson writes, language does not so much represent events as "invok[e] and authoriz[e] them" (70).

19. See Stephen Fortune's *Merchants and Jews* for a discussion of the Jewish Portuguese involvement in the slave trade in the West Indies.
20. The Sedition Act reads in part as follows:

> That if any person shall write, print, utter or publish, or shall cause or procure to be written, printed, uttered or published, or shall knowingly and willingly assist or aid in writing, printing, uttering or publishing any false, scandalous and malicious writing or writings against the government of the United States . . . with intent to defame the said government . . . or to excite against them . . . the hatred of the good people of the United States or to stir up sedition within the United States . . . then such person . . . shall be punished by a fine not exceeding two thousand dollars, and by imprisonment not exceeding two years."
>
>   (qtd. in James Smith, *Freedom's Fetters*, 442)

The Sedition Act was enforced more rigorously than the Alien Acts; verbal sedition, not imported outsiders, was viewed to be the more dangerous threat to an orderly government. See *Freedom's Fetters* for a history of this act.

21. Steven Watts argues that Brown retreats from his radical social criticism and embraces a bourgeois moralism in the new century (*The Romance of Real Life*, 133). As an advocate of cultural stability and genteel behavior, Brown defended bourgeois values as a mode of social constraint for the liberated individual (155). See the final two chapters of Watts's *The Romance of Real Life* for a discussion of Brown's disengagement from his earlier position.
22. In *Wieland*, Clara says: "My uncle's testimony is peculiarly worthy of credit, because no man's temper is more skeptical" (19). Mr. Cambridge urges Clara

not to purge herself of her passions through writing but to repress them: "A swift succession of new objects, and the exclusion of everything calculated to remind [Clara] of her loss" is his method of cure (235). Against Edgar's talking therapy, Saresfield also opts for repression. Believing Clithero to be incurably ill, Saresfield refuses to sympathize with Clithero's tale or to heal his wounds. "Common ills," he tells Edgar, "are not without a cure less than death, but here, all remedies are vain. Consciousness itself is the malady; the pest; of which he only is cured who ceases to think" (277).

3. Literary Nationalism and the Gothic: John Neal's Logan

1. John Neal was a native of Portland, Maine. The son of Quakers, he took up writing to finance his law studies in Baltimore. While studying for the bar and beginning his literary career, he also served as an editor for *The Portico*, indexed *Niles' Weekly Register*, wrote for the Baltimore *Telegraph*, and coauthored Paul Allen's *A History of the American Revolution* (1819). His works include: *Keep Cool* (1817), *Battle of Niagara, a Poem, without Notes; and Goldau, or the Maniac Harper* (1818), *Otho, a Tragedy, in Five Acts* (1819), *Logan* (1822), *Errata* (1823), *Seventy-Six* (1823), *Randolph* (1823), *Brother Jonathan* (1825), *Rachel Dyer* (1828), *Authorship* (1830), *The Down-Easters* (1833), *True Womanhood* (1859), *Great Conflagration in Portland* (1866), *Wandering Recollections* (1869), *Great Mysteries and Little Plagues* (1870), *Portland Illustrated* (1874). He also edited two periodicals briefly (*The Yankee and Boston Literary Gazette* and *Brother Jonathan*) and wrote three dime novels for Beadles. Neal is perhaps best known for being America's first literary critic and for encouraging the careers of Poe, Longfellow, and Whittier. For a full biographical history, see Irving Richards, "The Life and Works of John Neal"; Sears, *John Neal*; Daggett, *A Down-East Yankee from the District of Maine*; and Lease, *That Wild Fellow John Neal and the American Literary Revolution*, as well as Neal's autobiography, *Wandering Recollections*.
2. See John Seydow, "The Sound of Passing Music: John Neal's Battle for American Literary Independence," for an overview of Neal's literary nationalism.
3. See Spencer, *The Quest for Nationality* (81–90) for an extended discussion of the gothic's role in America's literary development.
4. See Pearce, *Savagism and Civilization*, and Sayre, *Thoreau and the American Indians* for a detailed explanation of this theory, which naturalized the Indian's disappearance from the American landscape. See Sheehan, *Seeds of Extinction*, and Dippie, *The Vanishing American* for further discussions of the ideological bases for the myth of the Indian as the "vanishing" American. Dippie argues that the nostalgic and fatalistic rhetoric that described the Indian supported the nation's belief in its progressive destiny.
5. For a full discussion of the Indian's important role in the American literary imagination, see Louise K. Barnett's *The Ignoble Savage*.

6. For a comprehensive reading of how the border romance helped to construct national identity see Dana Nelson's chapter, "Romancing the Border: Bird, Cooper, Simms, and the Frontier Novel," in *The Word in Black and White*.
7. For readings of the conjunction between the frontier and the gothic, see the articles in Mogen, Sanders, and Karpinski, *Frontier Gothic: Terror and Wonder at the Frontier in American Literature*, as well as David Mogen's "Frontier Myth and American Gothic."
8. See Benjamin Lease, "Yankee Poetics"; Harold Martin, "The Colloquial Tradition in the Novel"; and Joseph Jay Rubin, "John Neal's Poetics" for discussions of Neal's stylistic innovations. Neal's own criticism, especially *American Writers, Randolph*, "The Unpublished Preface to the North American Stories," and the prefaces to his novels, remain the best source of his stylistic theories. See also John Engell, "Hawthorne and Two Types of Early American Romance" for a discussion of Neal's use of the term "romance" and Francesca Orestano, "The Old World and the New in the National Landscapes of John Neal" for a reading of the nationalist implications of Neal's style.
9. Neal claims that everything he wrote had been "dashed off, *with a rapidity which has no parallel in the history of literature*":

> "Logan," which re-appeared over sea in four volumes, I wrote in six or eight weeks, ending Nov. 17, 1821; "Randolph," published here in two volumes, I began Nov. 26, 1821, and finished in thirty-six days: "Errata, or Will Adams," in two volumes, was begun Jan. 8, 1822, and finished in thirty-nine days; "Seventy-Six," begun Feb. 16, 1822, and finished March 19, 1822—four days off—in twenty-seven days, republished at London in three volumes: so that between October, 1821 and March, 1822, I wrote and published no less than eight large duodecimos, which in England would have been equal to thirteen volumes, and this, while pursuing my law studies, and writing the "Telegraph" and the "Portico."
> (*Wandering Recollections*, 173)

> Neal's "fatal facility" earned him the nickname Jehu O'Cataract since "he was known to overflow in word or print like a cataract with no more restraint than the biblical Jehu" (*Wandering Recollections*, 174; Sears, *John Neal*, 25). His literary output between 1821 and 1822 nearly equals that of Brown's feverish writing period (1799–1800). Neal writes, "mine was a clear case of spontaneous combustion" (*Wandering Recollections*, 5).

10. Logan's speech is still anthologized today. See Donald McQuade et al., *The Harper American Literature*.
11. Neal also describes *Logan* in *Randolph*:

> The first is no novel. It is a wild, fiery, protracted dream—a tale—not, perhaps "*told by an ideot*," not "signifying" absolutely nothing—but, "*full of sound and fury*." It would seem rather a vehicle for the peculiar and daring opinions of the author, than, any connected, and intentional development, of a preconceived design. It is

a great void, peopled with phantoms. And when the author wants to terrify you; or provoke you, by any startling paradox, or a discharge of sky rockets, he *makes* the occasion, heedless of all consequences. The whole book is full of darkness, repetition, anachronism and extravagance. Nobody can read it through, deliberately, as novels are to be read. You feel fagged and fretted to death, long and long before you forsee the termination. It is not dull—nor common place; but it is too exciting. The author won't let you cool off, for a moment, in your ascent.... The author appears to have written, only, while the fit was upon him; and always to have forgotten, what he had already done; and, finally, to have collected all the loose and flying fragments, and tacked them together, any how—to make a book. To my view, it is rather a great, troubled poem, than a novel—and rather a common place book than either. It is a world in confusion.... It is a torrent, that comes down upon you—thundering through the mountains—stained with subterranean ore; and encumbered with the wreck and ravage of a deluged empire.
(2:223–24)

12. Concerned with Neal's wildness and incoherence, traits, they argued, that were "not well calculated for the novel readers of our day," Carey and Lea refused to publish Neal's works after *Logan* (qtd. in Lease, *That Wild Fellow John Neal*, 40). *Logan* was republished in England in 1840 and 1845.
13. There were some positive contemporary responses. For instance, Whittier writes in 1830 that "critics may talk as they please but for ourselves we *do* like the bold, vigorous and erratic style of Neal. We could fall asleep over the delicately rounded period and the studied and labored paragraph, but the startling language—the original idea standing out in bold relief of all its native magnificence, roused up our blood like a summoning trumpet call" (qtd. in Lang and Lease, *The Genius of John Neal*, xix); and one lady, as Lease states, "is said to have become so infatuated with Neal's pungent style that she lost her taste for all other books and died with a copy of *Seventy-Six* in her hand" (*That Wild Fellow John Neal*, 41). In the twentieth century, Oral Sumner Coad argues for the power of Neal's style: "His stories are the wildest, most incoherent pieces of imagination in American literature.... His style is a perfect medium for his purpose: violent, hysterical, shrieking, it defies all laws of order and lucidity. Perhaps for this reason, Neal's novels are not without melodramatic power. One can hardly fail to respond to their tremendous intensity and their devastating terror" ("The Gothic Element in American Literature Before 1835," 85–86).
14. Even those critics who have done full-length studies of Neal end their discussions of *Logan* shortly after summing up its plot. See Lease, *That Wild Fellow John Neal*; Sears, *John Neal*; Grove, "John Neal, American Romantic"; and Fiorelli, "Literary Nationalism in the Works of John Neal (1793–1876)."
15. The oppositional rhetoric, used to describe the Indian as both brother and demon, capable of being civilized and destined for extinction, marks the Indian's contradictory status: the Indian was at once like and unlike the

American, both familiar and frightening. See Priscilla Wald (*Constituting Americans*, 14–47) for an analysis of how the Indian's uncanny identity was legislated by the courts. See Takaki, *Iron Cages*; Dippie, *The Vanishing American*; Rogin, *Fathers and Children*; Pearce, *Savagism and Civilization*; Maddox, *Removals*; and Slotkin, *Regeneration Through Violence* for discussions of the narratives that enabled the differentiation between the Indian and the white. As Roy Harvey Pearce argues, "the Indian became important for the English mind, not for what he was in and of himself, but rather for what he showed civilized men they were not and must not be" (5). Slotkin terms this "definition by repudiation" (22).

16. See Richard Drinnon, *Facing West*, for an argument about how "Indian-hating" created a rationale for a policy of extermination.

17. As Michael Rogin points out, "American rhetoric filled the white-Indian tie with intimate symbolic meaning. Indians were, every treaty talk insisted, our 'friends and brothers.' 'Our red brethren' were the 'voice of nature' in 'the human family'" (*Fathers and Children*, 5). There were, however, limits to these familial associations. As Virginia congressman Thomas Bouldin states, Indians might be symbolic forefathers, but they were not blood brothers: "Many of our first families and most distinguished patriots are descended from the Indian race. My heart compels me to feel for them for some of my dearest relations (not that I have myself any of their blood) are descended from the Indian race" ("Statement to Congress," 1835; qtd. in Rogin 5).

18. The novel's stylistic maneuvers take on a recognizably gothic form in volume 2. The love letters exchanged by Elvira and Oscar in this volume follow a traditional gothic plot. They also contain illegible writing and broken-off manuscripts, and are written in blood: "Canst thou read this? the characters smoke as I trace them. I tried a pen, but the ink was red and thick. I could not bear it. I then took this pencil—but lo! the characters are clotted—no matter—if we must have miracles—why, the more— —'The paper was torn here" (2:163). The gothic's metaphor of writing in blood allows Neal to capture Oscar's extreme emotional response. *Logan* resembles a "shattered ivory tablet" whose "leaves [are] glued together with blood" (2:52).

19. We are told in volume 2 that Oscar almost succeeds in hatching a plot against the state: "While we were looking upon him, as a growing honour to the nation, he lay, preparing and compounding the elements of a more bloody, and tremendous revolution to his country, than ever before shook its foundations" (2:210).

20. Although the process of civilization had its adherents well into the nineteenth century, the inevitability of Indian extermination and removal was clear from the beginning of the republic. Jefferson, who advocated assimilation, saw the Louisiana Purchase as a possible space for removed Indians; and by the early decades of the nineteenth century, even after the successful civilization of the Cherokees in the 1820s, removal was seen as the only option. The 1830 removal

bill solidified a policy that had been building through the century. See Satz, *American Indian Policy in the Jacksonian Era*, and Prucha, *American Indian Policy in the Formative Years* for a history of the nation's policies toward the Indian.

21. Neal's own self-mythologization helped to deflect attention from his work to his personality: in *Randolph*, he writes that Mr. Neal is "thought to be a downright madman, with an occasional lucid interval" (2:220). He also claims that *Logan* was attributed to "several persons, most of whom are remarkable for nothing but belles-lettres-foppery, and pretension;—and the rest are mad—stark, staring mad: any one of them, I believe is actually under confinement, while I am writing, in the Pennsylvania hospital" (*Seventy-Six*, v).

22. In *Marginalia*, Poe writes that Neal ranks "first, or at all events second, among our men of indisputable *genius*" (May 1849, 185); in an 1845 essay in *Graham's Magazine*, Lowell argues that Neal has "that indescribable something which men have agreed to call *genius*" (qtd. in Sears, *John Neal*, 126); in *The Prose Writers of America*, Griswold proclaims that Neal has the "unquestionable stamp of genius" (315); and *Emerson's United States Magazine* claims that Neal's "genius is everywhere acknowledged, although comparatively few are able to give a reason for their faith therein" (49). In this century, Neal continues to be called a "genius"; note, for instance, Lang and Lease's collection of his writings, *The Genius of John Neal*.

23. Neal and his novels are often depicted as freaks of genius. Cowie argues that "with more art Neal might have rivaled Cooper as a writer of romance or Poe as an exponent of the tale of terror," but without it he is "remembered chiefly as the eccentric and slightly choleric author of a few freakish novels and as a friend of Poe" (*The Rise of the Novel*, 165). Pattee calls Neal's novels "believe it or not" specimens (*The First Century of American Literature*, 282). Neal is also often described as mad. After reading *Logan*, one contemporary reviewer had no doubt that "the poor gentleman is at this time suffering the wholesome restraint of a straw cell and a strait waistcoat" (*Magazine of Foreign Literature* [1823], qtd. in Cairns, *British Criticisms of American Writings*, 208). The obverse of Neal's genius is his madness. For additional readings of Neal's canonization, see Fritz Fleischmann, "'A Likeness, Once Acknowledged'," and Robert Bain, Introduction to *Seventy-Six*.

24. Even when Neal is claimed, as by David Reynolds in *Beneath the American Renaissance*, as a "pioneering" spokesman of subversive fiction, he is relegated to the role of the subordinate savage (203). While Reynolds argues that "because Neal's crucial role in developing a native Subversive idiom has been unrecognized, his importance in the emergence of America's major literature is not adequately accepted," his own paradigm reinforces Neal's secondary role (199). In Reynolds's hierarchy, dark adventure (subversive literature), with its formlessness and excess, represents the savage state of art; moral adventure, with its "success in bringing intelligence and civility to the treatment of wild

subjects," is placed "quite close to the major writings" (184). Great art purges the savage excesses of both forms, for it absorbs "the disturbing stereotypes and ironies unleashed in Dark Adventure . . . but simultaneously retain[s] the reconstructive firmness of Moral Adventure . . . and introduce[s] potent structuring devices of their own" (184). Neal, a writer of dark adventure, therefore is not as "good" as Cooper who "comes up on the side of restraint and moral clarity" (185).

25. Jane Tompkins makes a similar point in her article, " 'Indians': Textualism, Morality, and the Problem of History."

4. The Ghost of Race: Edgar Allan Poe and the Southern Gothic

1. Lewis himself became a slaveholder upon his father's death in 1812. See Lewis's *Journal of a West India Proprietor* (1834) for an account of his life in Jamaica.
2. See Moira Ferguson, *Subject to Others: British Women Writers and Colonial Slavery, 1670–1834*. Ferguson traces the intensification of the antislavery debate in England back to 1791 and the St. Domingue revolution; she locates the end of that debate in the Emancipation Bill of 1833. These dates roughly coincide with the rise of the gothic novel in England.
3. In making this argument for viewing "whiteness" as a racial category, Morrison adds her voice to a growing number of critics who are demanding that "whiteness" be recognized. See Hazel Carby, "The Canon: Civil War and Reconstruction"; bell hooks, "Representing Whiteness in the Black Imagination"; Richard Dyer, "White"; Dana Nelson, *The Word in Black and White*; Ruth Frankenberg, *White Women, Race Matters*; David Roediger, *The Wages of Whiteness*. Shelley Fisher Fishkin gives a comprehensive overview of the scholarship on "whiteness" and "blackness" in her article, "Interrogating 'Whiteness,' Complicating 'Blackness': Remapping American Culture."
4. See, for example, *The Columbia History of the American Novel*, where the connections between romance and race are discussed only in relation to Poe in Joan Dayan's fine essay, "Romance and Race" (89–109).
5. There is some debate about when the South actually became a "problem" for the nation. Most historians, however, agree that during the 1830s the South's problematic status became solidified. During this period there was also an increase in the use of gothic rhetoric, especially by abolitionists, to describe and demonize the South. For examples of this rhetoric, see Ronald Walters, *The Antislavery Appeal*. The most famous spokespeople for the South's oppositional identity are C. Vann Woodward and W. J. Cash. For examinations of the South as an idea rather than a fact, see Richard Gray, *Writing the South*, and Michael O'Brien, *The Idea of the American South*; for various perspectives on the "problem" of the South, see Griffin and Doyle, *The South as an American Problem*.

6. Note, for instance, the ongoing debate about the authorship of an anonymous review published in the *Southern Literary Messenger* in 1836, known as the "Paulding-Drayton Review." The proslavery views of this article have alternately been attributed to Beverly Tucker and to Edgar Allan Poe. In "Poe, Slavery, and the *Southern Literary Messenger*: A Reexamination," Bernard Rosenthal attributes the article to Poe and states: "it is hard to believe that any serious scholar could still doubt that Poe supported the institution of slavery" (29). See Nelson, *The Word in Black and White*, pp. 90–92, for a fuller history of this debate. Given the disproportionate amount of critical energy spent on the relatively few documentary sources that reveal Poe's attitude toward race, I argue that the debate signals a critical desire to pinpoint Poe's views on slavery so that they can then be read into his text. While there is evidence for Hawthorne's conservative position on the question of slavery, critics seem less interested in exploring these views in connection to the "blackness" in his texts. Some notable exceptions include Jay Grossman's "'A' is for Abolition?: Race, Authorship, *The Scarlet Letter*" and Nancy Bentley's "Slaves and Fauns: Hawthorne and the Uses of Primitivism." For a discussion of the critical construction of Hawthorne's politics, see Eric Cheyfitz, "The Irresistibleness of Great Literature: Reconstructing Hawthorne's Politics."
7. Note also Carl Holliday's southernization of Poe: "Perhaps, after all, this sense of the artistic effect of sound, —this seeking for perfection in harmony, is the best evidence of the influence of Poe's Southern environment" (*A History of Southern Literature*, 237).
8. Two critics who have placed Poe within a complex set of interlocking discourses are Dana Nelson and Joan Dayan. Nelson argues in *The Word in Black and White* "that while on one level *Pym* is a racist text, on another the text provides a reading that counters racist colonial ideology and the racialist, scientific knowledge structure" (92). Dayan not only historicizes Poe in terms of race but also discusses how his racial vision intersects with his contradictory discourse on womanhood. She also points to a class-focused reading of Poe. See her "Romance and Race" and "Amorous Bondage: Poe, Ladies and Slaves."

5. (Un)Veiling the Marketplace: Nathaniel Hawthorne, Louisa May Alcott, and the Female Gothic

1. For example, see Carpenter and Kolmar, *Haunting the House of Fiction*; DeLamotte, *Perils of the Night*; Doody, "Deserts, Ruins and Troubled Waters"; Kate Ferguson Ellis, *The Contested Castle*; Kahane, "The Gothic Mirror"; Fleenor, *The Female Gothic*; Gilbert and Gubar, *The Madwoman in the Attic*; Tamar Heller, *Dead Secrets*; Massé, *In the Name of Love*; Modleski, *Loving with a Vengeance*; Moers, *Literary Women*; Mussell, *Women's Gothic and Romantic Fiction*; Restuccia, "Female Gothic Writing"; Showalter, *Sister's Choice*; Wilt,

Ghosts of the Gothic; Winter, *Subjects of Slavery, Agents of Change*; and Wolstenholme, *Gothic (Re)Visions*.

2. Critics have begun to focus on the complex intersection of class and gender in nineteenth-century American culture. See Amy Schrager Lang, "Class and Strategies of Sympathy"; Joel Pfister, *The Production of Personal Life*; and Gillian Brown, *Domestic Individualism* for examinations of how gender often displaces and domesticates class in American culture. In terms of genres, the sentimental presents the female type most often historicized in relation to commodity culture. See, for instance, Susan Coultrap-McQuin's study of American women writers in the marketplace, *Doing Literary Business*; Glenn Hendler's reading of Alcott's sentimental productions, "The Limits of Sympathy"; or Lori Merish's work on Stowe, "Sentimental Consumption."

3. Montague Summers (*The Gothic Quest*, 28–30) uses the category "sentimental-gothic" and David Punter (*The Literature of Terror*, 28–30) examines the sentimental origins of the gothic novel.

4. Spiritualism was one of many extradomestic institutions (others included education and philanthropy) by which women were authorized to move from the private to the public sphere. See Carroll Smith-Rosenberg's essays in *Disorderly Conduct* for examinations of how women used domestic power to gain access to and influence in the public sphere.

5. See Ann Braude's *Radical Spirits* for case studies of nineteenth-century mediums. My debt to Braude's fine study is apparent throughout this section. For other studies on mesmerism, mediums, and spiritualism, see Brodhead, "Veiled Ladies"; Fuller, *Mesmerism and the American Cure of Souls*; Kerr, *Mediums and Spirit-Rappers and Roaring Radicals*, *The Haunted Dusk*, and *The Occult in America*; Moore, *In Search of White Crows*; St. Armand, "Veiled Ladies"; Tatar, *Spellbound*; and Wrobel, *Pseudo-Science and Society in Nineteenth-Century America*.

6. See Kasson, "Narratives of the Female Body," and Hyman, "*The Greek Slave* by Hiram Powers" for further descriptions of viewers' responses to the statue.

7. Art historians continue to debate the extent to which the statue was viewed by its culture in relationship to slavery. Hyman, "*The Greek Slave*," and Green, "Hiram Powers's *Greek Slave*" show how the statue was read within the context of slavery and was used both by antislavery interests as an abolitionist statement (*The Christian Inquirer* argued that the statue was "an impersonation of SLAVERY" [qtd. in Hyman 222]) and by proslavery interests to critique abolitionists who saw the statue in merely aesthetic terms. While the statue's connection to slavery was evident to many observers, Joy Kasson cautions that "much of its audience was apparently oblivious to the ironies of driving past American slave marts to shed tears over the fate of the white marble captive" ("Narratives of the Female Body," 185). Joseph Roach's reading of the spectacles of the slave auction (*Cities of the Dead*, 211–33) offers a broader context

for understanding how antebellum society might have viewed *The Greek Slave*. See, in particular, his discussion (220–21) of John Bell's statue *The Octoroon* (1868); in stating that "the invisible presence of blackness marks her flesh as a commodity even as her whiteness changes its value," Roach suggests how the statue's whiteness could displace or transmute the sign of slavery (232). Interestingly, it was the British magazine *Punch* that published "The Virginian Slave" and parodically made the connection between *The Greek Slave* and American slavery so visible.

8. The statues of Undine were based on Friedrich de La Motte-Fouqué's German romantic tale (1811). For further discussion of the Undine story and how she represented the "interpermeability of the domestic and the demonic" in nineteenth-century America, see Joy Kasson's *Marble Queens and Captives* (169–73) and Wayne Craven's *Sculpture in America* (286–87).

9. See Dudden, *Women in the American Theatre* (116–18) for a fuller description of the live model show and its place in the development of the American theater.

10. See Karen Halttunen, "The Domestic Drama of Louisa May Alcott," for an examination of Alcott's participation in parlor theatricals.

11. See Teresa Goddu, "The Circulation of Women in *The House of the Seven Gables*" and Joel Pfister, "Cleaning House" in *The Production of Personal Life* for readings of how women domesticate the intrusion of the marketplace in Hawthorne.

12. Hawthorne often codes the horrors of the marketplace in terms of blackness and slavery. For instance, in *The House of the Seven Gables*, the voracious consumption of the marketplace is figured through Ned Higgins's devouring of the gingerbread Jim Crow; the tide of humanity that Clifford is magnetically attracted to outside his window is not only exemplified by the monkey who is both slave and performer, but is also described as "black with mystery" (165). The gothic blackness of the market is marked again by the particular historical conditions of slavery. Walter Benn Michaels's reading of *The House of the Seven Gables*, which situates the novel's focus on property in relation to slavery, develops the historical connections between the two economies. See also Michael Newbury, "Eaten Alive," for an articulation of the conjunctions between the economies of mass-culture celebrity and slavery; and Gillian Brown, *Domestic Individualism*, for a reading of how mesmerism exemplifies an economy of consumption in *The Blithedale Romance*.

13. Zenobia and Priscilla are both daughters of Old Moodie, the novel's other figure of the economic man. With his eye patch veiling his shadowy identity and his hair of "perfect silver," Moodie represents the lower-class man who makes his living selling purses in the marketplace (82). Priscilla and Zenobia are also represented as Westervelt's lovers: Zenobia is rumored to have been in a love relationship with him; and Priscilla, as the veiled lady, is penetrated by him every night on stage.

14. The community constantly partakes in theatrical performances ranging from the May-Day celebration to the tableaux vivants and the carnival. On Blithedale's stage, character becomes a function of costume. No character appears without an elaborate description of their clothing and each is identified with a particular prop: Priscilla with her purse, Zenobia with her flower, Moodie with his patch. Identity is implied by external signs. For example, merely by holding a letter from Margaret Fuller, Priscilla can remind Coverdale of her: "I wish people would not fancy such odd things in me! . . . How could I possibly make myself resemble this lady, merely by holding her letter in my hand?" Priscilla exclaims (52).

15. Throughout his letters, Hawthorne makes this same point: cultural and commercial success are at odds. He writes in the continuation of this passage, "What is the mystery of these innumerable editions of the Lamplighter, and other books neither better nor worse?—worse they could not be, and better they need not be, when they sell by the 100.000" (*Letters, 1853–1856*, 304). Of *The House of the Seven Gables*, he states, "Being better (which I insist it is) than the Scarlet Letter, I have never expected it to be so popular" (*Letters, 1843–1853*, 435). As Lawrence Buell shows, this rationalization was typical of many of the male transcendentalist writers of Hawthorne's day. Concerned with the commercialization of letters, "Thoureauvian and Emersonian idealizations of art as prophecy" could be read "as leisure-class rationalizations made possible by the fact (or illusion, in Emerson's case) that one's survival was not contingent on the verdict of the marketplace" (*New England Literary Culture*, 63). See also Michael Gilmore's *American Romanticism and the Marketplace* on how commercialization affected writers and how a split between elite and mass culture was constructed.

16. See Brodhead (*The School of Hawthorne*, 48–66) for an analysis of how Fields created Hawthorne's canonical status. See also Jane Tompkins for a reading of Hawthorne's literary canonization (*Sensational Designs*, 3–39).

17. Hawthorne's need to write for money is evident in the publication of *The Blithedale Romance*. Just as Hawthorne was finishing the novel, he purchased Bronson Alcott's home in Concord. He wrote to Fields: "You have succeeded admirably in regard to the Blithedale Romance, and have got just £150. more than I expected to receive. It will come in good time, too; for my drafts have been pretty heavy of late, in consequence of buying an estate!!! and fitting up my house" (*Letters, 1843–1853*, 550).

18. Hawthorne describes his own writing as "scribbling" and in so doing reveals his alliance with the popular woman writer who sends her productions into a gothicized marketplace. He sends *The Blithedale Romance* to E. P. Whipple with the following letter: "Behold a huge bundle of scribble, which you have thoughtlessly promised to look over! If you find it beyond your powers, hand it over to Ticknor at once, and let him send it to the Devil" (Ibid., 536).

19. See, for example, Michael Gilmore's reading of the ending of *The House of the Seven Gables* in *American Romanticism and the Marketplace* (106–12), which argues that Hawthorne felt uncomfortable with a model of the artist as deceptive con man even as he endeavored to manipulate the literary marketplace by giving his book a cheerful ending. T. Walter Herbert takes Gilmore's argument a step further when he states, "Yet the confidence game in which Hawthorne himself was engaged . . . is more insidious than a market strategy. It engages the substance of the domestic relation, whose 'sunshine' is itself a deception" (*Dearest Beloved*, 106).
20. See also Brodhead's reading of the late Hawthorne in *The School of Hawthorne* (67–80). Brodhead argues that Hawthorne becomes a dysfunctional writer in the face of his own canonical status.
21. For more on the paradoxical place of the woman writer in nineteenth-century America, see Baym, *Woman's Fiction*; Coultrap-McQuin, *Doing Literary Business*; Kelley, *Private Woman, Public Stage*; and Hendler, "The Limits of Sympathy." Alcott's skillful manipulations of the market sphere are evident in her letters to her publishers. See Madeleine Stern's "Louisa May Alcott's Self-Criticism" for a collection of many of these letters.
22. Her explanation for her revision of *Moods* in her preface to the novel reveals Alcott's savviness. She claims that it was to be sentimental all the time and that it was original market forces—namely the publisher—that made her swerve from this aim:

> When "Moods" was first published . . . it was so altered, to suit the taste and convenience of the publisher, that the original purpose of the story was lost sight of, and marriage appeared to be the theme instead of an attempt to show the mistakes of a moody nature, guided by impulse, not principle. Of the former subject a girl of eighteen could know but little, of the latter most girls know a good deal; and they alone among my readers have divined the real purpose of the book in spite of its many faults, and have thanked me for it.
> (Stern, "Louisa May Alcott's Self-Criticism," 349)

Her letters show her attention to how her stories were to be packaged and recycled: "as I am not able to write new stories I want to make the old ones profitable & think a Christmas book might do well if finely gotten up" (367).
23. Indeed, Alcott seemed to like this play of masks. She writes of *A Modern Mephistopheles*: " 'M.M.' appears and causes much guessing. It is praised and criticised, and I enjoy the fun, especially when friends say, 'I know *you* didn't write it, for you can't hide your peculiar style" (Stern, *Critical Essays on Louisa May Alcott*, 12–13).
24. The relationship between Alcott's gothic and sentimental canons has been discussed by several critics. Both David Reynolds (*Beneath the American Renaissance*, 408–9) and Judith Fetterley argue that Alcott changes modes like

184   6. Haunting Back

costumes and remains detached from her literary persona. Fetterley's groundbreaking essay, "Impersonating 'Little Women': The Radicalism of Alcott's *Behind a Mask*," points out that Alcott's sensation story "provides us with a frighteningly prophetic vision of the act she will eventually perform": the heroine adopts the mask of femininity to survive economically (1). Susan Bernstein, "Writing and *Little Women*," Mary Capello, " 'Looking About Me With All My Eyes,' " and Elizabeth Keyser, *Whispers in the Dark* also argue for the interrelationship between Alcott's literary styles. Although some work has been done on how the gothic invades Alcott's domestic literature (for example, see Estes and Lant, "Dismembering the Text"), Alcott's sensational stories have received relatively little critical attention.

25. See Elbert, *A Hunger for Home*, for a discussion of Alcott's childhood at Fruitlands and Bronson's influence.
26. This relationship between the servant and the slave is made more explicit in Alcott's novel *Work*. When Christie goes out to service, she is allied with Hepsey, the black cook and former slave.

6. Haunting Back: Harriet Jacobs, African-American Narrative, and the Gothic

1. Despite his historicizing of the African-American gothic, Wright continues to reinforce an ahistorical reading of Poe. My discussion of *The Narrative of Arthur Gordon Pym*, which places race at the center of Poe's gothicism, shows how Poe dealt with the racial hauntings of his own culture. Contrary to Wright's statement, Poe need not be resurrected to be imagined in terms of race, for its horrors had already invented him.
2. Historical studies such as Trudier Harris's *Exorcising Blackness*, with its accounts of ritualized violence against African Americans, or Neil McMillen's *Dark Journey*, with its description of "Negro Barbeques," reveal the horrors of African-American history. McMillen recounts a public burning where a crowd of a thousand watched while whites tortured their black victims, "chopp[ing] off their fingers and ears, one by one, goug[ing] their eyes until they 'hung by a shred from the socket,' and pulled 'big pieces of raw, quivering flesh' from their bodies with corkscrews" (234); Trudier Harris gives similar accounts of lynching and mob violence. In his introduction to *American Slavery as It Is*, Theodore Weld also records a litany of real-life horrors: "We will prove that the slaves in the United States are treated with barbarous inhumanity . . . that they are frequently flogged with terrible severity, have red pepper rubbed into their lacerated flesh, and hot brine, spirits of turpentine, &c, poured over the gashes to increase the torture; that they are often stripped naked, their backs and limbs cut with knives, bruised and mangled by scores and hundreds of blows with the paddle, and terribly torn by the claws of cats, drawn over them by their tormentors. . . . All these things and more, and worse, we shall *prove*" (9). See Stephen Browne's " 'Like Gory Spectres': Representing Evil in

Theodore Weld's *American Slavery as It Is*" for an analysis of the modes of representation Weld uses to prove these horrors.
3. Indeed, as Edmund Morgan has shown in *American Slavery, American Freedom*, the marriage of slavery and freedom is America's central paradox: the rise of the American republic and its requisite myths depended on the terrifying realities of slavery (4).
4. Other critics have also noted connections between slavery and the gothic. Robert Hemenway argues that slavery is "an extreme form of Gothic entrapment" ("Gothic Sociology," 113) and Joseph Bodziock claims that the slave narrative incorporates "the fundamental forms and values of the European gothic" ("Richard Wright and Afro-American Gothic," 29). In *Haiti, History, and the Gods*, Joan Dayan insists on the integral connection between the gothic and slavery. Reading the Black Codes as a gothic text, Dayan argues that the supernatural fictions of the Americas are rooted in the natural histories of slavery (193).
5. See Paulson's "Gothic Fiction and the French Revolution" and Henderson's "An Embarrassing Subject: Problems of Value and Identity in the Early Gothic Novel."
6. See Sundquist's *To Wake the Nations* (145–47) for a discussion of the gothic discourse used in response to the revolution in St. Domingue.
7. The rhetoric of monstrosity that permeates descriptions of Turner's insurrection exemplifies Joan Dayan's theory that whites externalized images of their own power—the "bodily tortures and incarnate terrors necessary to sustain the institution of slavery"—by projecting them onto their victims (*Haiti, History, and the Gods*, 247).
8. The abolitionist's identification with/as the victim of slavery's horrors is a common trope. See Nudelman for a discussion of the abolitionist's sympathetic identification with the slave and their "tales of suffering witnessed rather than suffering endured" ("Harriet Jacobs and the Sentimental Politics of Female Suffering," 948). In *American Slavery as It Is*, C. C. Robin gives the following testimony after recounting a whipping scene:

> The reader is moved; so am I: my agitated hand refuses to trace the bloody picture, to recount how many times the piercing cry of pain has interrupted my silent occupations; how many times I have shuddered at the faces of those barbarous masters, where I saw inscribed the number of victims sacrificed to their ferocity. (59)

The reader's and writer's pain and horror here subsume the slave's terror, which is further displaced since it is visible only in the face of the master. By rendering the slave as victim, this passage raises a corresponding problem: abolitionist discourse not only appropriated the victim's position but also tended to picture the slave as the victim of the gothic prison of slavery, thereby denying the slave agency or resistance.

9. The slave narrative's fictional characteristics have been examined by a number of critics, most notably William Andrews. No longer seen merely as transparent transcriptions of history, slave narratives have come to be read as sophisticated autobiographical acts. Andrews argues that the genre is a "scene of a complex discursive encounter" (*To Tell a Free Story*, 2); his "The Novelization of Voice in Early African American Narrative" examines the genre's relation to fiction. Carla Peterson also discusses the gradual shift from autobiography to novel in nineteenth-century African-American writing, arguing that the "autobiographical narrative already contained within it subversive fictional techniques" ("Capitalism, Black (Under)Development, and the Production of the African-American Novel in the 1850s," 563). Also see Barbara Foley ("History, Fiction, and the Ground Between" and *Telling the Truth*) for an examination of the representational strategies nineteenth-century African-American authors used to authenticate their writing.
10. In "Letters to His old Master" in the appendix to *My Bondage and My Freedom*, Douglass further emphasizes that the gothic horrors of slavery are not imaginative renderings but actual events:

> The grim horrors of slavery rise in all their ghastly terror before me; the wails of millions pierce my heart and chill my blood. I remember the chain, the gag, the bloody whip; the death-like gloom overshadowing the broken spirit of the fettered bondman; the appalling liability of his being torn away from wife and children, and sold like a beast in the market. Say not that this is a picture of fancy. You well know that I wear stripes on my back, inflicted by your direction.... All this, and more, you remember, and know to be perfectly true, not only of yourself, but of nearly all the slaveholders around you. (269)

I will discuss Douglass's use of gothic conventions while resisting their dematerializing effects at greater length in the body of this chapter, but it is crucial to note here how he refuses to reduce the gothic horrors of slavery to fancy.
11. This need to argue that the incredible facts of slavery are true also occurs in Weld's *American Slavery as It Is*. Weld presents his documentary evidence in order to disprove the objection that "such cruelties are INCREDIBLE" (121). Arguing that the evidence is not the "exaggerations of fiction," the text constantly reiterates that its statements, "incredible as [they] may seem" fall "short, very short of the truth" (61).
12. As many critics have noted, Douglass presents the reader with another common trope of slavery in this opening episode: the sexualized scene of whipping. Ronald Walters's "The Erotic South" and *The Antislavery Appeal* argue that the antebellum discourse that gothicized slavery also eroticized it. Abolitionist discourse, he claims, pictured the evils of slavery in terms of corrupted femininity and the corrosive effects of unrestrained sexuality (*The Antislavery Appeal*, 111). Karen Halttunen takes this argument a step further

by showing how the whipping scene eroticizes pain by turning the dreadful into the obscene, the sympathetic spectator into a sadistic voyeur ("Humanitarianism and the Pornography of Pain in Anglo-American Culture"). The sexual sensationalism of this scene has been criticized by several feminist critics including Franchot, "The Punishment of Esther"; McDowell, "In the First Place"; and Foster, "'In Respect to Females.'"

13. Hortense Spillers argues that slavery is marked by its narrativity: slavery "remains one of the most textualized and discursive fields of practice that we could posit as a structure for attention" ("Changing the Letter," 29).

14. As Gladys-Marie Fry shows in her study *Night Riders in Black Folk History*, the gothic has long been allied with reality in African-American history. During slavery and Reconstruction, the supernatural was used by whites as a form of psychological control of African Americans. Whether it was a master designating haunted places or the Ku Klux Klan riding as ghosts through the night, the supernatural kept African Americans literally and figuratively in their place. African-American fear of the supernatural was based less on a belief in the master's stage effects than on the institutionalized power that lay behind them (McWhiney and Simkins, "The Ghostly Legend of the Ku-Klux Klan"). As James Cameron points out in the compelling account of his own near-lynching in his memoir, *A Time of Terror*, African Americans grew up knowing that the hair-raising accounts of terror they heard were not figments of the imagination but daily realities.

15. Many of the reviewers of *Beloved* also seem uneasy affiliating Toni Morrison with the gothic: "To outline this story is to invite the very resistance I felt on first reading it," writes one reviewer. "A specter returned to bedevil the living? A Gothic historical romance from Toni Morrison?" (Clemons, "The Ghosts of Sixty Million and More," 74). Other reviewers use this seeming disjunction between serious writer and melodramatic form to attack Morrison. In his notorious review of the novel, Stanley Crouch uses a gothic metaphor to begin his assault: "the book's beginning clanks out its themes" ("Aunt Medea," 42). Carol Iannone claims Morrison's use of the gothic marks her lack of seriousness: "The graphic descriptions of physical humiliation begin to grow sensationalistic, and the gradual unfolding of secret horror has an unmistakably Gothic dimension which soon comes to seem merely lurid, designed to arouse and entertain" ("Toni Morrison's Career," 63). All of these examples reveal how *gothic* has become a negative, demeaning term. Associated with the sensational, the formulaic, and the popular, the gothic is seen to lack seriousness of purpose and connection to actual experience.

16. This is perhaps the reason for the scant attention given to the African-American gothic within critical discourse. The work that has been done tends to focus on individual authors. For discussions of the African-American gothic, see Joseph Bodziock, "Richard Wright and Afro-American Gothic";

Erik Curren, "Turning the Tables on the White Savage" and "Should Their Eyes Have Been Watching God?"; Louis Gross, *Redefining the American Gothic*; Theodore Gross, *The Heroic Ideal in American Literature*; Michel Fabré, "Black Cat and White Cat"; Robert Hemenway, "Gothic Sociology"; Keith Sandiford, "Gothic Intertextual Constructions in *Linden Hills*"; Mary Sisney, "The Power and Horror of Whiteness"; and Geraldine Smith-Wright, "In Spite of the Klan."

17. Ashraf H. A. Rushdy warns of the dangers inherent in any project that attempts to reconstruct the interplay of black and white literary traditions. Counseling against any "easy resolution" or "short-term *rapprochement*" between the traditions that glosses over the "substantial drama of conflict in intercultural literary engagements," Rushdy argues that "we need to seek out the deeper meanings of conflicts in literary history and not forget that it is the social order of our nation, with its fundamental material inequities, that defines and determines the sites of contestation where those conflicts occur in our national literature" ("Reading Black, White, and Gray in 1968," 63).

18. See Jean Fagan Yellin, "Written by Herself: Harriet Jacobs's Slave Narrative." Yellin explains the confusion over *Incidents*'s literary status as follows: "It is no accident that many critics mistook Jacobs's narrative for fiction. Its confessional account of sexual error and guilt, like the passages in which Linda Brent presents herself to be judged by her reader, link *Incidents* to a popular genre, the seduction novel" (Introduction to *Incidents*, xxix–xxx). The text's relationship to fiction continues to be clarified. Jacqueline Goldsby and P. Gabrielle Foreman have both argued against reading Jacobs's text in a purely factual way. Goldsby states that *Incidents* should be examined in terms of how "it engages and resists the closure implied by historical documentation" (" 'I Disguised My Hand'," 15). Concerned with how the "implicit demands for referentiality" force critics to "interpret the principal script as if [Jacobs] had not loaded it with narrative explosions, with subversive scriptmines, so to speak," Foreman critiques the "politics of transparency" that often informs readings of black women's sentimental writing ("Manifest in Signs," 77).

19. Because of its "novelization of her autobiographical voice," as Claudia Tate describes it, *Incidents* is perhaps the slave narrative most often examined in terms of other literary traditions (*Domestic Allegories of Political Desire*, 26). P. Gabrielle Foreman, for instance, argues that *Incidents* "defies easy generic categorization" and that it "blurs the parameters of fiction and slave narrative" ("The Spoken and the Silenced," 315). *Incidents*, however, is usually discussed only in terms of the sentimental tradition. Views on *Incidents*'s connection to sentimentalism range from early studies like Annette Niemtzow's, which argues that the "domestic novel swallows Linda Brent's voice" ("The Problematic of Self in Autobiography," 105), and Raymond Hedin's, which claims that Jacobs does not act "against the grain of sentimental fiction" ("Strategies of Form in the American Slave Narrative," 28), to more recent

perspectives—Carby, *Reconstructing Womanhood*; Doherty, "Harriet Jacobs' Narrative Strategies"; Doriani, "Black Womanhood in Nineteenth-Century America"; Nelson, *The Word in Black and White*; Nudelman, "Harriet Jacobs"; Sanchez-Eppler, *Touching Liberty*; Valerie Smith, *Self-Discovery and Authority*; Tate, *Domestic Allegories of Political Desire*; Walter, "Surviving in the Garret"; Yellin, Introduction to *Incidents*; and others—that argue that Jacobs appropriates, revises, and elaborates the sentimental tradition. For an extended discussion of the parallels between *Incidents* and the gothic, see Kari Winter's *Subjects of Slavery, Agents of Change*.

20. See Yellin (Introduction to *Incidents*, xviii–xix) and Hedrick (*Harriet Beecher Stowe: A Life*, 248–49) for a fuller account of Jacobs's relationship to Stowe.
21. Jacobs's use of the term "loophole of retreat" has most often been traced to William Cowper's poem "The Task" (see Yellin's note to Jacobs's chapter title in *Incidents*, 277). I suggest that Jacobs is also referencing Stowe in her title. In "Carnival Laughter," Anne Bradford Warner also points to the connections between Stowe's and Jacobs's texts. She argues that Brent's crippling discomfort in her garret "cannot help but comment on the gothic romance and trickery of Cassy's escape episode in *Uncle Tom's Cabin*" (224). Warner develops this connection further in her conference paper "No *Key* to Cassy: Jacobs Revises Stowe." While our arguments intersect in illuminating ways, Warner is concerned more with Jacobs's discomfort with the gothic mode and her resistance to the gothic's eroticization. Also see Phyllis Cole, "Stowe, Jacobs, Wilson," for a more general discussion of how Jacobs rewrites *Uncle Tom's Cabin*.
22. See Karen Halttunen's "Gothic Imagination and Social Reform: The Haunted Houses of Lyman Beecher, Henry Ward Beecher, and Harriet Beecher Stowe" for a study of the Stowe family's use of the gothic in their various social critiques; and Diane Roberts's *The Myth of Aunt Jemima* for a reading of Stowe's use of the gothic in the novel.
23. The dual movement of Jacobs's narrative, what Carla Peterson calls her "double discourse," has been discussed in a variety of ways ("Capitalism, Black (Under)Development," 565). See Braxton, "Harriet Jacobs' *Incidents*"; Burnham, "Loopholes of Resistance"; and Foreman, "The Spoken and the Silenced" for readings of how the text uses concealment and revelation.
24. The narrative follows a typical female gothic plot. Jacobs, like so many earlier gothic and sentimental heroines, traces her initiation into a world of evil to the death of her mother. Only after the loss of this "shield" does she become self-conscious of her position as a slave: "When I was six years old, my mother died; and then, for the first time, I learned, by the talk around me, that I was a slave" (6). Jacobs is left even more vulnerable when at age twelve her mistress, who was "almost like a mother to [her]," also dies, leaving her without any protection from the sexual evils that accompany slavery (7). Jacobs's dual initiation into the trials of slavery and maidenhood is made explicit in her relationship to her new master, Doctor Flint. Imprisoned in a plantation (read castle)

that is cut off from the laws of the outside world, she finds herself at the mercy of a lascivious villain, her "persecutor," Doctor Flint (35). She is saved in part, as she later remarks, by the proximity of the plantation to town and a surrogate protector, her grandmother: "If I had been on a remote plantation . . . I should not be a living woman at this day" (35).

25. See Valerie Smith, *Self-Discovery and Authority in African-American Narrative*, for an extended discussion of the power of passivity in *Incidents*.
26. Mary Titus has a wonderful reading of the cotton gin: "The image encapsulates Jacobs's argument, uniting in a single horrific image the slave, the verminous slaveholder who consumes him, and the central machine of the cotton economy" (" 'This Poisonous System'," 203).
27. The clearest case of repetition is Jacobs's description of her daughter Ellen. Not only does Ellen relive Brent's plight when she has "vile language" poured into her ears by Mr. Thorne, but also, unlike her mother, she is defenseless against these words since she "scarcely knew her letters" (179, 166). Ellen's position emphasizes Brent's own powerlessness in the North. Unlike Stowe's novel, which provides a happy ending for Cassy when she is magically reunited with both of her children, Jacobs's text offers no such conclusion: Brent does not recognize her daughter when they are first reunited precisely because Ellen has deteriorated from neglect. It is through her daughter-double—who is more of a slave in the North, where her mother's protection is ineffectual, than she ever was in the South, under her mother's hidden protection—that Jacobs marks the North as the South's double (165).
28. Jacobs was keenly aware of the North's complicity with slavery since her employer, Mr. Willis, was proslavery. See Yellin (Introduction to *Incidents*, xviii) for a discussion of Jacobs's relationship to the Willises.
29. This is not to say that silence is not an equally powerful weapon. Turning the tables and adapting the slave master's tool, Jacobs, like many former slaves, used silence to protect those who helped her and to keep the master "in the dark." See Valerie Smith, *Self-Discovery and Authority*, and Braxton, "Harriet Jacobs' *Incidents*" for further discussions of the gaps and silences in Jacobs's text.
30. It is important to note that Child sentimentalized Jacobs's ending. As Bruce Mills points out in "Lydia Maria Child and the Endings to Harriet Jacobs's *Incidents in the Life of a Slave Girl*," Jacobs originally planned to end her narrative with a discussion of John Brown, which would have emphasized a gothic narrative of violent retribution. However, Child counseled her to end by focusing on her grandmother instead.

Epilogue: Remembering History

1. For readings of the hand as pointing toward freedom see Wheat, *Jacob Lawrence: The Frederick Douglass and Harriet Tubman Series of 1938–40*, and

Patricia Hills, "Jacob Lawrence as Pictorial Griot." When this hand is read in relation not only to the other images in the series but also to other artistic influences—namely Aaron Douglas's iconography of the clutching hand of slavery and oppression in his mural *Song of the Towers* (1934) and his illustration *Charleston* (1929)—the image accrues a more negative connotation. See Amy Kirschke, *Aaron Douglas*, for readings of Douglas's works.

Works Cited

Adams, John. *The Works of John Adams*. Vol. 7. Edited by Charles Francis Adams. Boston: Little, Brown, 1852.
Alcott, Louisa May. *Little Women*. Boston: Little, Brown, 1968.
———. "V.V.: or, Plots and Counterplots." In *Plots and Counterplots: More Unknown Thrillers of Louisa May Alcott*. Edited by Madeleine Stern. New York: Morrow, 1976.
———. *Work: A Story of Experience*. New York: Arno Press, 1977.
———. "Behind a Mask." In *Behind a Mask: The Unknown Thrillers of Louisa May Alcott*. Edited by Madeleine Stern. Mattituck, N.Y.: Aeonian Press, 1979.
———. *The Selected Letters of Louisa May Alcott*. Edited by Joel Myerson, Daniel Shealy, and Madeleine Stern. Boston: Little, Brown, 1987.
———. *A Double Life: Newly Discovered Thrillers of Louisa May Alcott*. Edited by Madeleine Stern. Boston: Little, Brown, 1988.
———. "How I Went Out to Service." *Alternative Alcott*. Edited by Elaine Showalter. New Brunswick, N.J.: Rutgers University Press, 1988.
———. *Freaks of Genius: Unknown Thrillers of Louisa May Alcott*. Edited by Daniel Shealy. New York: Greenwood Press, 1991.
Alderman, Edwin Anderson and Joel Chandler Harris, eds. *Library of Southern Literature*. Vol. 9. New Orleans: Martin and Hoyt, 1909.

Works Cited

Allen, Gay Wilson and Roger Asselineau. *St. John de Crèvecoeur: The Life of an American Farmer*. New York: Viking Penguin, 1987.

Andrews, William L. *To Tell a Free Story: The First Century of Afro-American Autobiography, 1760–1865*. Urbana: University of Illinois Press, 1986.

———. "The Novelization of Voice in Early African American Narrative." *PMLA* 105 (1990): 23–34.

Appleby, Joyce. *Capitalism and a New Social Order: The Republican Vision of the 1790s*. New York: New York University Press, 1984.

———. *Liberalism and Republicanism in the Historical Imagination*. Cambridge: Harvard University Press, 1992.

Arch, Stephen Carl. "The 'Progressive Steps' of the Narrator in Crèvecoeur's *Letters from an American Farmer*." *Studies in American Fiction* 18 (1990): 145–58.

Bailyn, Bernard. *The Ideological Origins of the American Revolution*. Cambridge: The Belknap Press of Harvard University Press, 1967.

Bain, Robert A. Introduction to *Seventy-Six*, by John Neal. Bainbridge, N.Y.: York Mail-Print, 1971.

Banta, Martha. "American Apocalypses: Excrement and Ennui." *Studies in the Literary Imagination* 7 (1974): 1–30.

———. "The Ghostly Gothic of Wharton's Everyday World." *American Literary Realism* 27 (1994): 1–10.

Barnes, Gilbert H. and Dwight L. Dumond, eds. *Letters of Theodore Dwight Weld, Angelina Grimké Weld, and Sarah Grimké*. Vol. 1, 1822–1844. New York: Appleton-Century, 1934.

Barnett, Louise K. *The Ignoble Savage: American Literary Racism, 1790–1890*. Westport, Conn.: Greenwood Press, 1975.

Baron, Dennis E. *Grammar and Good Taste: Reforming the American Language*. New Haven: Yale University Press, 1982.

Barthes, Roland. *Mythologies*. Translated by Annette Lavers. New York: The Noonday Press, 1972.

Baym, Nina. "Concepts of the Romance in Hawthorne's America." *Nineteenth-Century Fiction* 38 (1984): 426–43.

———. *Woman's Fiction: A Guide to Novels by and About Women in America, 1820–70*. 2nd ed. Urbana: University of Illinois Press, 1993.

Beaver, Harold. Introduction to *The Narrative of Arthur Gordon Pym of Nantucket*, by Edgar Allan Poe. Edited by Harold Beaver. London: Penguin, 1986.

Bell, Michael Davitt. " 'The Double-Tongue Deceiver': Sincerity and Duplicity in the Novels of Charles Brockden Brown." *Early American Literature* 9 (1974): 143–63.

Bentley, Nancy. "Slaves and Fauns: Hawthorne and the Uses of Primitivism." *ELH* 57 (1990): 901–37.

Bercovitch, Sacvan. *The American Jeremiad*. Madison: University of Wisconsin Press, 1978.

Bernstein, Susan Naomi. "Writing and *Little Women:* Alcott's Rhetoric of Subversion." *American Transcendental Quarterly* 7 (1993): 25–43.

Berthoff, Rowland. "Independence and Attachment, Virtue and Interest: From Republican Citizen to Free Enterpriser 1787–1837." In *Uprooted Americans: Essays to Honor Oscar Handlin.* Edited by Richard L. Bushman, Neil Harris, David Rothman, Barbara Miller Solomon, and Stephan Thernstrom. Boston: Little, Brown, 1979.

Bewley, Marius. *The Eccentric Design: Form in the Classic American Novel.* New York: Columbia University Press, 1959.

Birkhead, Edith. *The Tale of Terror: A Study of the Gothic Romance.* London: Constable, 1921.

Blair, Hugh. *Lectures on Rhetoric and Belles Lettres.* Philadelphia: Robert Aiken, 1784.

Blassingame, John. "Critical Essays on Sources." In *The Slave Community: Plantation Life in the Antebellum South.* 1972; revised and enlarged edition, New York: Oxford University Press, 1979.

Bloom, Harold. Introduction to *Edgar Allan Poe: Modern Critical Views.* Edited by Harold Bloom. New York: Chelsea House, 1985.

Bodziock, Joseph. "Richard Wright and Afro-American Gothic." In *Richard Wright: Myths and Realities.* Edited by C. James Trotman. New York: Garland, 1988.

Boynton, Percy H. *A History of American Literature.* 1919; reprint, New York: AMS Press, 1970.

Braude, Ann. *Radical Spirits: Spiritualism and Women's Rights in Nineteenth-Century America.* Boston: Beacon Press, 1989.

Braxton, Joanne M. "Harriet Jacobs' *Incidents in the Life of a Slave Girl:* The Redefinition of the Slave Narrative Genre." *Massachusetts Review* 27 (1986): 379–87.

The British Critic. "American Novels." London, Third Series II (1826): 53–78; 406–39.

Brodhead, Richard. *Hawthorne, Melville and the Novel.* Chicago: University of Chicago Press, 1976.

——. *The School of Hawthorne.* New York: Oxford University Press, 1986.

——. "Veiled Ladies: Toward a History of Antebellum Entertainment." *American Literary History* 1 (1989): 273–94.

Brown, Charles Brockden. "Editor's Address." *Literary Magazine* 1 (1803): 3–6.

——. "The Man at Home." *The Rhapsodist and Other Uncollected Writings.* Edited by Harry R. Warfel. New York: Scholar's Facsimiles and Reprints, 1943.

——. "Walstein's School." *The Rhapsodist and Other Uncollected Writings.* Edited by Harry R. Warfel. New York: Scholar's Facsimiles and Reprints, 1943.

——. *Wieland; or, the Transformation. An American Tale.* Vol. 1 of the Bicentennial Edition. Edited by Sydney J. Krause. Kent, Ohio: Kent State University Press, 1977.

———. *Arthur Mervyn; or, Memoirs of the Year 1793. First and Second Parts.* Vol. 3 of the Bicentennial Edition. Edited by Sydney J. Krause. Kent, Ohio: Kent State University Press, 1980.

———. *Ormond; or the Secret Witness.* Vol. 2 of the Bicentennial Edition. Edited by Sydney J. Krause. Kent, Ohio: Kent State University Press, 1982.

———. *Edgar Huntly; or, Memoirs of a Sleep-Walker.* Vol. 4 of the Bicentennial Edition. Edited by Sydney J. Krause and S. W. Reid. Kent, Ohio: Kent State University Press, 1984.

Brown, Gillian. *Domestic Individualism: Imagining Self in Nineteenth-Century America.* Berkeley: University of California Press, 1990.

Browne, Stephen. " 'Like Gory Spectres': Representing Evil in Theodore Weld's *American Slavery As It Is*." *The Quarterly Journal of Speech* 80 (1994): 277–92.

Buell, Lawrence. *New England Literary Culture: From Revolution Through Renaissance.* New York: Cambridge University Press, 1986.

Burnham, Michelle. "Loopholes of Resistance: Harriet Jacobs' Slave Narrative and the Critique of Agency in Foucault." *Arizona Quarterly* 49 (1993): 53–73.

Cairns, William. *British Criticisms of American Writings, 1815–33.* Madison: University of Wisconsin Studies in Language and Literature, No. 14, 1922.

Cameron, James. *A Time of Terror: A Survivor's Story.* Baltimore: Black Classics Press, 1994.

Cappello, Mary. " 'Looking about Me with All my Eyes': Censored Viewing, Carnival, and Louisa May Alcott's *Hospital Sketches*." *Arizona Quarterly* 50 (1994): 59–88.

Carby, Hazel. *Reconstructing Womanhood: The Emergence of the Afro-American Woman Novelist.* New York: Oxford University Press, 1987.

———. "The Canon: Civil War and Reconstruction." *Michigan Quarterly Review* 28 (1989): 35–43.

Carey, Mathew. *A Short Account of the Malignant Fever, lately prevalent in Philadelphia: with a statement of the proceedings that took place on the subject in different parts of the United States.* Philadelphia: Printed by the author, Nov. 14, 1793.

Carpenter, Lynette and Wendy K. Kolmar, eds. *Haunting the House of Fiction: Feminist Perspectives on Ghost Stories by American Women.* Knoxville: University of Tennessee Press, 1991.

Carroll, Noël. *The Philosophy of Horror, or Paradoxes of the Heart.* New York: Routledge, 1990.

Cash, W. J. *The Mind of the South.* 1941; reprint, New York: Vintage, 1991.

Castronovo, Russ. *Fathering the Nation: American Genealogies of Slavery and Freedom.* Berkeley: University of California Press, 1995.

Chase, Richard. *The American Novel and Its Tradition.* 1957; reprint, Baltimore: Johns Hopkins University Press, 1980.

Cheney, Ednah D. *Louisa May Alcott: Her Life, Letters and Journals.* Boston: Roberts Brothers, 1890.

Chesnutt, Charles. *The Conjure Woman*. Ann Arbor: University of Michigan Press, 1969.

Chevignard, Bernard. "St. John de Crèvecoeur in the Looking Glass: *Letters from an American Farmer* and the Making of a Man of Letters." *Early American Literature* 19 (1984): 173–90.

Cheyfitz, Eric. "The Irresistibleness of Great Literature: Reconstructing Hawthorne's Politics." *American Literary History* 6 (1994): 539–58.

Child, Lydia Maria. "Stand from Under!" *Massachusetts Daily Journal* 24 Aug. 1829; reprint, *The Liberator* 28 Jan. 1832: 16.

Christophersen, Bill. *The Apparition in the Glass: Charles Brockden Brown's American Gothic*. Athens: University of Georgia Press, 1993.

Clayton, Jay. *Romantic Vision and the Novel*. New York: Cambridge University Press, 1987.

Clemons, Walter. "The Ghosts of Sixty Million and More." *Newsweek* 110 (Sept. 28, 1987): 74–75.

Coad, Oral Sumner. "The Gothic Element in American Literature Before 1835." *Journal of English and Germanic Philology* 24 (1925): 72–93.

Cohen, Daniel. "Arthur Mervyn and His Elders: The Ambivalence of Youth in the Early Republic." *William and Mary Quarterly* 43 (1986): 362–80.

Cole, Phyllis. "Stowe, Jacobs, Wilson: White Plots and Black Counterplots." In *New Perspectives on Gender, Race, and Class in Society*. Edited by Audrey T. McCluskey. Bloomington: Indiana University Press, 1990.

Condie, Thomas and Richard Folwell. *History of the Pestilence, Commonly Called Yellow Fever, which almost desolated Philadelphia, in the months of August, September, and October, 1798*. Philadelphia: R. Folwell, 1799.

Conn, Peter. *Literature in America: An Illustrated History*. New York: Cambridge University Press, 1989.

Cooper, James Fenimore. *The Last of the Mohicans*. New York: New American Library, 1980.

Coultrap-McQuin, Susan. *Doing Literary Business: American Women Writers in the Nineteenth Century*. Chapel Hill: University of North Carolina Press, 1990.

Cowie, Alexander. *The Rise of the Novel*. New York: American Book Co., 1948.

Craven, Wayne. *Sculpture in America*. New York: Thomas Y. Crowell, 1968.

Crèvecoeur, J. Hector St. John de. *Voyage dans la Haute Pensylvanie et dans l'état de New-York*. 3 vols. Paris: Maradan, 1801.

———. *Sketches of Eighteenth Century America: More "Letters from an American Farmer"*. Edited by Henri L. Bourdin, Ralph H. Gabriel, and Stanley T. Williams. New Haven: Yale University Press, 1925.

———. *Letters from an American Farmer and Sketches of Eighteenth-Century America*. Edited by Albert E. Stone. New York: Penguin, 1986.

———. *More Letters from the American Farmer*. Edited by Dennis D. Moore. Athens: University of Georgia Press, 1995.

Crouch, Stanley. "Aunt Medea." *The New Republic* 197 (Oct. 19, 1987): 38–43.
Cunliffe, Marcus. "Crèvecoeur Revisited." *Journal of American Studies* 9 (1975): 129–44.
Curren, Erik. "Turning the Tables on the White Savage: The African American Appropriation of Gothic Horror." Paper presented at a conference on the American gothic, University of Montreal, Montreal, Canada, October 1994.
———. "Should Their Eyes Have Been Watching God?: Hurston's Use of Religious Experience and Gothic Horror." *African-American Review* 29 (1995): 17–25.
Daggett, Windsor. *A Down-East Yankee from the District of Maine*. Portland, Maine: A. J. Huston, 1920.
Dain, Norman. *Concepts of Insanity in the U.S., 1789–1865*. New Brunswick, N.J.: Rutgers University Press, 1964.
Dauber, Kenneth. "The Problem of Poe." *Georgia Review* 32 (1978): 645–657.
Davidson, Cathy. *Revolution and the Word: The Rise of the Novel in America*. New York: Oxford University Press, 1986.
Davis, Christina. "Interview with Toni Morrison." *Presence Africaine: Revue Culturelle du Monde Noir* 145 (1988): 141–50.
Davis, David Brion. *Homicide in American Fiction, 1798–1860*. Ithaca: Cornell University Press, 1957.
———. *The Problem of Slavery in the Age of Revolution, 1770–1823*. Ithaca: Cornell University Press, 1975.
Day, William Patrick. *In the Circles of Fear and Desire: A Study of Gothic Fantasy*. Chicago: University of Chicago Press, 1985.
Dayan, Joan. "Romance and Race." In *The Columbia History of the American Novel*. Edited by Emory Elliott. New York: Columbia University Press, 1991.
———. "Amorous Bondage: Poe, Ladies and Slaves." *American Literature* 66 (1994): 239–73.
———. *Haiti, History, and the Gods*. Berkeley: University of California Press, 1995.
DeLamotte, Eugenia. *Perils of the Night: A Feminist Study of Nineteenth-Century Gothic*. New York: Oxford University Press, 1990.
Derrida, Jacques. "The Law of Genre." Translated by Avital Ronell. *Glyph* 7 (1980): 55–81.
Deutsch, Albert. *The Mentally Ill in America: A History of their Care and Treatment from Colonial Times*. Garden City, N.Y.: Doubleday, Doran, 1937.
Dickinson, John. *Letters from a Farmer in Pennsylvania, to the Inhabitants of the British Colonies*. Philadelphia: David Hall and William Sellers, 1768.
Dickstein, Morris. "Popular Fiction and Critical Values: The Novel as a Challenge to Literary History." In *Reconstructing American Literary History*. Edited by Sacvan Bercovitch. Cambridge: Harvard University Press, 1986.
Dippie, Brian W. *The Vanishing American: White Attitudes and U.S. Indian Policy*. Middletown, Conn.: Wesleyan University Press, 1982.

Doherty, Thomas. "Harriet Jacobs' Narrative Strategies: *Incidents in the Life of a Slave Girl.*" *Southern Literary Journal* 19 (1986): 79–91.

Doody, Margaret Ann. "Deserts, Ruins and Troubled Waters: Female Dreams in Fiction and the Development of the Gothic Novel." *Genre* 10 (1977): 529–72.

Doriani, Beth Maclay. "Black Womanhood in Nineteenth-Century America: Subversion and Self-Construction in Two Women's Autobiographies." *American Quarterly* 43 (1991): 199–222.

Douglass, Frederick. *Narrative of the Life of Frederick Douglass, an American Slave.* Edited by Houston Baker. New York: Penguin, 1982.

———. *My Bondage and My Freedom.* Edited by William L. Andrews. Urbana: University of Illinois Press, 1987.

Drayton, John. "A Traveling Governor's View, 1802." In *South Carolina: The Grand Tour, 1780–1865.* Edited by Thomas D. Clark. Columbia: University of South Carolina Press, 1973.

Drinnon, Richard. *Facing West: The Metaphysics of Indian-Hating and Empire Building.* Minneapolis: University of Minnesota Press, 1980.

Dudden, Faye E. *Women in the American Theatre: Actresses and Audiences, 1790–1870.* New Haven: Yale University Press, 1994.

Dyer, Richard. "White." *Screen* 29 (1988): 44–64.

Elbert, Sarah. *A Hunger for Home: Louisa May Alcott's Place in American Culture.* Philadelphia: Temple University Press, 1984.

Elliott, Emory, ed. *The Columbia History of the American Novel.* New York: Columbia University Press, 1991.

Ellis, Joseph J. *After the Revolution: Profiles of Early American Culture.* New York: Norton, 1979.

Ellis, Kate Ferguson. *The Contested Castle: Gothic Novels and the Subversion of Domestic Ideology.* Urbana: University of Illinois Press, 1989.

Ellison, Ralph. *Invisible Man.* 1952; reprint, New York: Vintage, 1990.

Emerson's United States Magazine. "John Neal." 5 (1857): 49–58.

Engell, John. "Hawthorne and Two Types of Early American Romance." *South Atlantic Review* 57 (1992): 33–51.

Estes, Angela M. and Kathleen Margaret Lant. "Dismembering the Text: The Horror of Louisa May Alcott's *Little Women.*" *Children's Literature* 17 (1989): 98–123.

Fabré, Michel. "Black Cat and White Cat: Richard Wright's Debt to Edgar Allan Poe." *Poe Studies* 4 (1971): 17–19.

Feidelson, Charles. *Symbolism and American Literature.* Chicago: University of Chicago Press, 1953.

Ferguson, Moira. *Subject to Others: British Women Writers and Colonial Slavery, 1670–1834.* London: Routledge, 1992.

Ferguson, Robert A. "Yellow Fever and Charles Brockden Brown: The Context of the Emerging Novelist." *Early American Literature* 14 (1980): 293–305.

---. " 'We Hold These Truths': Strategies of Control in the Literature of the Founders." In *Reconstructing American Literary History*. Edited by Sacvan Bercovitch. Cambridge: Harvard University Press, 1986.

---. *The American Enlightenment, 1750–1820*. In *The Cambridge History of American Literature: Volume 1, 1590–1820*. Edited by Sacvan Bercovitch. New York: Cambridge University Press, 1994.

Fetterley, Judith. "Impersonating 'Little Women': The radicalism of Alcott's *Behind a Mask*." *Women's Studies* 10 (1983): 1–14.

Fiedler, Leslie. *Love and Death in the American Novel*. 1960; revised edition 1966; reprint, New York: Stein and Day, 1982.

Fiorelli, Edward A. "Literary Nationalism in the Works of John Neal (1793–1876)." Ph.D. dissertation, Fordham University, 1980.

Fishkin, Shelley Fisher. "Interrogating 'Whiteness,' Complicating 'Blackness': Remapping American Culture." In *Criticism and the Color Line: Desegregating American Literary Studies*. Edited by Henry B. Wonham. New Brunswick, N.J.: Rutgers University Press, 1996.

Fleenor, Juliann E. *The Female Gothic*. Montreal: Eden Press, 1983.

Fleischmann, Fritz. " 'A Likeness, Once Acknowledged': John Neal and the 'Ideosyncrasies' of Literary History." In *Myth and Enlightenment in American Literature*. Edited by Dieter Meindl and Friedrich W. Hurlacher. Erlangen: Universitatsbund Erlangen-Nurnberg, 1985.

Foley, Barbara. "History, Fiction, and the Ground Between: The Uses of the Documentary Mode in Black Literature." *PMLA* 95 (1980): 389–403.

---. *Telling the Truth: The Theory and Practice of Documentary Fiction*. Ithaca: Cornell University Press, 1986.

Foreman, P. Gabrielle. "The Spoken and the Silenced in *Incidents in the Life of a Slave Girl* and *Our Nig*." *Callaloo* 13 (1990): 313–24.

---. "Manifest in Signs: The Politics of Sex and Representation in *Incidents in the Life of a Slave Girl*." In *Harriet Jacobs and* Incidents in the Life of a Slave Girl. Edited by Deborah M. Garfield and Rafia Zafar. New York: Cambridge University Press, 1996.

Fortune, Stephen. *Merchants and Jews: The Struggle for British West Indian Commerce, 1650–1750*. Gainesville: University Presses of Florida, 1984.

Foster, Frances. " 'In Respect to Females': Differences in the Portrayals of Women by Male and Female Narrators." *Black American Literature Forum* 15 (1981): 66–70.

Foucault, Michel. *Madness and Civilization: A History of Insanity in the Age of Reason*. Translated by Richard Howard. New York: Vintage, 1973.

Fowler, Alastair. *Kinds of Literature: An Introduction to the Theory of Genres and Modes*. Cambridge: Harvard University Press, 1982.

Franchot, Jenny. "The Punishment of Esther: Frederick Douglass and the Construction of the Feminine." In *Frederick Douglass: New Literary and Historical*

Essays. Edited by Eric J. Sundquist. New York: Cambridge University Press, 1990.

Frank, Frederick S. *The First Gothics: A Critical Guide to the English Gothic Novel*. New York: Garland Publishers, 1987.

———. *Through the Pale Door: A Guide to and through the American Gothic*. New York: Greenwood Press, 1990.

Frankenberg, Ruth. *White Women, Race Matters: The Social Construction of Whiteness*. Minneapolis: University of Minnesota Press, 1993.

Fry, Gladys-Marie. *Night Riders in Black Folk History*. Knoxville: University of Tennessee Press, 1975.

Fuller, Robert C. *Mesmerism and the American Cure of Souls*. Philadelphia: University of Pennsylvania Press, 1982.

Garber, Frederick. "Meaning and Mode in Gothic Fiction." In *Studies in Eighteenth-Century Culture: Racism in the Eighteenth Century*. Edited by Harold E. Pagliaro. Cleveland: The Press of Case Western Reserve University, 1973.

Gardiner, William Howard. "Art. XII.—*The Spy, a Tale of the Neutral Ground*." *The North American Review* 15 (1822): 250–82.

Garfield, Deborah M. "Earwitness: Female Abolitionism, Sexuality, and *Incidents in the Life of a Slave Girl*." In *Harriet Jacobs and* Incidents in the Life of a Slave Girl. Edited by Deborah M. Garfield and Rafia Zafar. New York: Cambridge University Press, 1996.

Gates, Henry Louis, Jr. *The Signifying Monkey: A Theory of African-American Literary Criticism*. New York: Oxford University Press, 1988.

Gilbert, Sandra M. and Susan Gubar. *The Madwoman in the Attic: The Woman Writer and the Nineteenth-Century Literary Imagination*. New Haven: Yale University Press, 1979.

Gillman, Susan. *Dark Twins: Imposture and Identity in Mark Twain's America*. Chicago: University of Chicago Press, 1989.

Gilmore, Michael T. *American Romanticism and the Marketplace*. Chicago: University of Chicago Press, 1985.

———. *The Literature of the Revolutionary and Early National Periods*. In *The Cambridge History of American Literature: Volume 1, 1590–1820*. Edited by Sacvan Bercovitch. New York: Cambridge University Press, 1994.

Girard, René. *Violence and the Sacred*. Translated by Patrick Gregory. Baltimore: Johns Hopkins University Press, 1977.

Glasgow, Ellen. *A Certain Measure: An Interpretation of Prose Fiction*. New York: Harcourt, Brace, 1943.

Goddu, Teresa. "The Circulation of Women in *The House of the Seven Gables*." *Studies in the Novel* 23 (1991): 119–27.

Goldsby, Jacqueline. " 'I Disguised My Hand': Writing Versions of the Truth in Harriet Jacobs's *Incidents in the Life of a Slave Girl* and John Jacobs's 'A True Tale of Slavery.' " In *Harriet Jacobs and* Incidents in the Life of a Slave Girl. Edited

by Deborah M. Garfield and Rafia Zafar. New York: Cambridge University Press, 1996.
Grabo, Norman. "Historical Essay." *Arthur Mervyn; or, Memoirs of the Year 1793. First and Second Parts.* Vol. 3 of the Bicentennial Edition. Edited by Sydney J. Krause. Kent, Ohio: Kent State University Press, 1980.
———. *The Coincidental Art of Charles Brockden Brown.* Chapel Hill: University of North Carolina Press, 1981.
———. "Crèvecoeur's American: Beginning the World Anew." *William and Mary Quarterly* 48 (1991): 159–72.
Gray, Richard. *Writing the South: Ideas of an American Region.* New York: Cambridge University Press, 1986.
———. "Edgar Allan Poe and the Problem of Regionalism." In *The United States South: Regionalism and Identity.* Edited by Valeria Gennaro Lerda and Tjebbe Westendorp. Rome: Bulzoni Editore, 1991.
Green, Vivien. "Hiram Powers's *Greek Slave*: Emblem of Freedom." *The American Art Journal* 14 (1982): 31–39.
Griffin, Larry J. and Don H. Doyle, eds. *The South as an American Problem.* Athens: University of Georgia Press, 1995.
Griswold, Rufus Wilmot. *The Prose Writers of America.* Philadelphia: Carey and Hart, 1847.
Grixti, Joseph. *Terrors of Uncertainty: The Cultural Contexts of Horror Fiction.* New York: Routledge, 1989.
Gross, Louis. *Redefining the American Gothic: From* Wieland *to* The Day of the Dead. Ann Arbor: UMI Research Press, 1989.
Gross, Theodore L. *The Heroic Ideal in American Literature.* New York: The Free Press, 1971.
Grossman, Jay. " 'A' is for Abolition?: Race, Authorship, *The Scarlet Letter.*" *Textual Practice* 7 (1993): 13–30.
Grove, Gerald Robert. "John Neal: American Romantic." Ph.D. dissertation, University of Utah, 1974.
Haggerty, George E. *Gothic Fiction/Gothic Form.* University Park: Pennsylvania State University Press, 1989.
Hales, John. "The Landscape of Tragedy: Crèvecoeur's 'Susquehanna.' " *Early American Literature* 20 (1985): 39–63.
Halttunen, Karen. *Confidence Men and Painted Women: A Study of Middle Class Culture, 1830–1870.* New Haven: Yale University Press, 1982.
———. "The Domestic Drama of Louisa May Alcott." *Feminist Studies* 10 (1984): 233–54.
———. "Gothic Imagination and Social Reform: The Haunted House of Lyman Beecher, Henry Ward Beecher, and Harriet Beecher Stowe." In *New Essays on Uncle Tom's Cabin.* Edited by Eric Sundquist. New York: Cambridge University Press, 1986.

———. "Early American Murder Narratives: The Birth of Horror." *The Power of Culture: Critical Essays in American History*. Edited by Richard Wightman Fox and T. J. Jackson Lears. Chicago: University of Chicago Press, 1993.

———. "Humanitarianism and the Pornography of Pain in Anglo-American Culture." *American Historical Review* 100 (1995): 303–34.

Harris, Trudier. *Exorcising Blackness: Historical and Literary Lynching and Burning Rituals*. Bloomington: Indiana University Press, 1984.

Harrison, James. *Life and Letters of Edgar Allan Poe*. New York: Thomas R. Crowell, 1903.

Hart, Francis R. "Limits of the Gothic: The Scottish Example." In *Studies in Eighteenth-Century Culture: Racism in the Eighteenth Century*. Edited by Harold E. Pagliaro. Cleveland: The Press of Case Western Reserve University, 1973.

Hastings, William T. *Syllabus of American Literature*. 3rd edition. Chicago: University of Chicago Press, 1941.

Hawthorne, Nathaniel. *The Blithedale Romance and Fanshawe*. Vol. 3 of *The Centenary Edition of the Works of Nathaniel Hawthorne*. Edited by William Charvat, Roy Harvey Pearce, and Claude M. Simpson. Columbus: Ohio State University Press, 1964.

———. *The House of the Seven Gables*. Vol. 2 of *The Centenary Edition of the Works of Nathaniel Hawthorne*. Edited by William Charvat, Roy Harvey Pearce, and Claude M. Simpson. Columbus: Ohio State University Press, 1965.

———. *The Marble Faun: Or, the Romance of Monte Beni*. Vol. 4 of *The Centenary Edition of the Works of Nathaniel Hawthorne*. Edited by William Charvat, Roy Harvey Pearce, Claude M. Simpson, and Matthew J. Bruccoli. Columbus: Ohio State University Press, 1968.

———. *The American Notebooks*. Vol. 8 of *The Centenary Edition of the Works of Nathaniel Hawthorne*. Edited by Claude M. Simpson. Columbus: Ohio State University Press, 1972.

———. *Mosses from an Old Manse*. Vol. 10 of *The Centenary Edition of the Works of Nathaniel Hawthorne*. Edited by William Charvat, Roy Harvey Pearce, and Claude M. Simpson. Columbus: Ohio State University Press, 1974.

———. *The Letters, 1843–1853*. Vol. 16 of *The Centenary Edition of the Works of Nathaniel Hawthorne*. Edited by Thomas Woodson, L. Neal Smith, and Norman Holmes Pearson. Columbus: Ohio State University Press, 1985.

———. *The Letters, 1853–1856*. Vol. 17 of *The Centenary Edition of the Works of Nathaniel Hawthorne*. Edited by Thomas Woodson, James A. Rubino, L. Neal Smith, and Norman Holmes Pearson. Columbus: Ohio State University Press, 1987.

Hedges, William. "Benjamin Rush, Charles Brockden Brown, and the American Plague Year." *Early American Literature* 7 (1973): 295–311.

———. "Charles Brockden Brown and the Culture of Contradictions." *Early American Literature* 9 (1974): 107–42.

Hedin, Raymond. "Strategies of Form in the American Slave Narrative." In *The Art of the Slave Narrative: Original Essays in Criticism and Theory*. Edited by John Sekora and Darwin T. Turner. Macomb: Western Illinois University Press, 1982.

Hedrick, Joan. *Harriet Beecher Stowe: A Life*. New York: Oxford University Press, 1994.

Heller, Tamar. *Dead Secrets: Wilkie Collins and the Female Gothic*. New Haven: Yale University Press, 1992.

Heller, Terry. *The Delights of Terror: An Aesthetics of the Tale of Terror*. Urbana: University of Illinois Press, 1987.

Hemenway, Robert. "Gothic Sociology: Charles Chesnutt and the Gothic Mode." *Studies in the Literary Imagination* 7 (1974): 101–19.

Henderson, Andrea. " 'An Embarrassing Subject': Problems of Value and Identity in the Early Gothic Novel." In *At the Limits of Romanticism: Essays in Cultural, Feminist, and Materialist Criticism*. Edited by Mary A. Favret and Nicola J. Watson. Bloomington: Indiana University Press, 1994.

Hendler, Glenn. "The Limits of Sympathy: Louisa May Alcott and the Sentimental Novel." *American Literary History* 3 (1991): 685–706.

Herbert, T. Walter. *Dearest Beloved: The Hawthornes and the Making of the Middle-Class Family*. Berkeley: University of California Press, 1993.

Hills, Patricia. "Jacob Lawrence as Pictorial Griot: The 'Harriet Tubman' Series." *American Art* 7 (1993): 40–59.

Hofstadter, Richard. "The Paranoid Style in American Politics." In *The Fear of Conspiracy: Images of Un-American Subversion from the Revolution to the Present*. Edited by David Brion Davis. Ithaca: Cornell University Press, 1971.

Holliday, Carl. *A History of Southern Literature*. New York: Neale, 1906.

hooks, bell. "Representing Whiteness in the Black Imagination." In *Cultural Studies*. Edited by Lawrence Grossberg, Cary Nelson, and Paula A. Treichler. New York: Routledge, 1992.

Horsman, Reginald. *Race and Manifest Destiny: The Origins of American Racial Anglo-Saxonism*. Cambridge: Harvard University Press, 1981.

Hubbell, Jay. *The South in American Literature, 1607–1900*. Durham, N.C.: Duke University Press, 1954.

Hume, Robert D. "Gothic versus Romantic: A Revaluation of the Gothic Novel." *PMLA* 84 (1969): 282–90.

—— and Robert L. Platzner. " 'Gothic versus Romantic': A Rejoinder." *PMLA* 86 (1971): 266–74.

Hyman, Linda. "*The Greek Slave* by Hiram Powers: High Art as Popular Culture." *Art Journal* 35 (1976): 216–23.

Iannone, Carol. "Toni Morrison's Career." *Commentary* 84 (Dec. 1987): 59–63.

Jackson, Rosemary. *Fantasy: The Literature of Subversion*. London: Methuen, 1981.

Jacobs, Harriet A. *Incidents in the Life of a Slave Girl.* Edited by Jean Fagan Yellin. Cambridge: Harvard University Press, 1987.

Jefferson, Thomas. *Notes on the State of Virginia.* In *The Portable Thomas Jefferson.* Edited by Merrill D. Peterson. New York: Penguin, 1977.

Jehlen, Myra. "J. Hector St. John Crèvecoeur: A Monarcho-Anarchist in Revolutionary America." *American Quarterly* 31 (1979): 204–22.

———. *The Literature of Colonization.* In *The Cambridge History of American Literature: Volume 1, 1590–1820.* Edited by Sacvan Bercovitch. New York: Cambridge University Press, 1994.

Jones, Kathleen. "Moral Management and the Therapeutic Community." *Society for the Social History of Medicine* Bulletin No. 5 (1971): 6–10.

Jordan, Winthrop D. *White over Black: American Attitudes Toward the Negro, 1550–1812.* 1968; reprint, New York: Norton, 1977.

Justus, James H. "Arthur Mervyn, American." *American Literature* 42 (1970): 304–24.

Kahane, Claire. "The Gothic Mirror." In *(M)other Tongue: Essays in Psychoanalytic Interpretation.* Edited by Shirley Nelson Garner, Claire Kahane, and Madeleine Sprengnether. Ithaca: Cornell University Press, 1985.

Kaplan, Sidney. Introduction to *The Narrative of Arthur Gordon Pym* by Edgar Allan Poe. New York: Hill and Wang, 1960.

Kasson, Joy. *Marble Queens and Captives: Women in Nineteenth-Century American Sculpture.* New Haven: Yale University Press, 1990.

———. "Narratives of the Female Body: *The Greek Slave.*" In *The Culture of Sentiment: Race, Gender, and Sentimentality in Nineteenth-Century America.* Edited by Shirley Samuels. New York: Oxford University Press, 1992.

Keech, James M. "The Survival of the Gothic Response." *Studies in the Novel* 6 (1974): 130–44.

Kelley, Mary. *Private Woman, Public Stage: Literary Domesticity in Nineteenth-Century America.* New York: Oxford University Press, 1984.

Kerber, Linda K. *Federalists in Dissent: Imagery and Ideology in Jeffersonian America.* Ithaca: Cornell University Press, 1970.

———. "Republican Ideology and the Revolutionary Generation." *American Quarterly* 37 (1985): 474–95.

Kermode, Frank. *The Sense of an Ending: Studies in the Theory of Fiction.* New York: Oxford University Press, 1967.

Kerr, Howard. *Mediums, Spirit-Rappers, and Roaring Radicals: Spiritualism in American Literature, 1850–1900.* Urbana: University of Illinois Press, 1972.

———, John W. Crowley, and Charles L. Crow, eds. *The Haunted Dusk: American Supernatural Fiction, 1820–1920.* Athens: University of Georgia Press, 1983.

——— and Charles L. Crow, eds. *The Occult in America: New Historical Perspectives.* Urbana: University of Illinois Press, 1983.

Kessler-Harris, Alice. *Out to Work: A History of Wage-Earning Women in the United States.* New York: Oxford University Press, 1982.

Keyser, Elizabeth. *Whispers in the Dark: The Fiction of Louisa May Alcott*. Knoxville: University of Tennessee Press, 1993.

Kilgour, Maggie. *The Rise of the Gothic Novel*. London: Routledge, 1995.

Kirschke, Amy Helene. *Aaron Douglas: Art, Race and the Harlem Renaissance*. Jackson: University Press of Mississippi, 1995.

Kolodny, Annette. *The Lay of the Land: Metaphor as Experience and History in American Life and Letters*. Chapel Hill: University of North Carolina Press, 1975.

Kramnick, Isaac. "Republican Revisionism Revisited." *American Historical Review* 87 (1982): 629–64.

Kristeva, Julia. *Powers of Horror: An Essay on Abjection*. Translated by Leon S. Roudiez. New York: Columbia University Press, 1982.

Lang, Amy Schrager. "Class and Strategies of Sympathy." In *The Culture of Sentiment: Race, Gender, and Sentimentality in Nineteenth-Century America*. Edited by Shirley Samuels. New York: Oxford University Press, 1992.

Lang, Hans-Joachim, ed. "Critical Essays and Stories by John Neal." *Jahrbuch fur Amerikastudien* 7 (1962): 204–88.

——— and Benjamin Lease, eds. *The Genius of John Neal: Selections from His Writings*. Frankfurt: Peter Lang, 1978.

Lawrence, D. H. *Studies in Classic American Literature*. London: Mercury, 1965.

Lawson-Peebles, Robert. *Landscape and Written Expression in Revolutionary America*. New York: Cambridge University Press, 1988.

Lease, Benjamin. "Yankee Poetics: John Neal's Theory of Poetry and Fiction." *American Literature* 24 (1953): 505–19.

———. *That Wild Fellow John Neal and the American Literary Revolution*. Chicago: University of Chicago Press, 1972.

———. *Anglo-American Encounters: England and the Rise of American Literature*. New York: Cambridge University Press, 1981.

Levin, Harry. *The Power of Blackness: Hawthorne, Poe, Melville*. New York: Knopf, 1958.

Levine, Robert S. "Arthur Mervyn's Revolutions." *Studies in American Fiction* 12 (1984): 145–60.

Levy, Maurice. *Le Roman Gothique Anglais, 1764–1824*. Série A. Tome 9. Toulouse: Association des Publications de la Faculté des Lettres et Sciences Humaine, 1968.

Lewis, Matthew Gregory. *Journal of a West-India Proprietor*. London: John Murray, 1834.

Lewis, R. W. B. *The American Adam*. Chicago: University of Chicago Press, 1955.

The Liberator 22 (October 22, 1852).

Looby, Christopher. "Phonetics and Politics: Franklin's Alphabet as a Political Design." *Eighteenth-Century Studies* 18 (1984): 1–34.

———. *Voicing America: Language, Literary Form, and the Origins of the United States*. Chicago: University of Chicago Press, 1996.

Loshe, Lillie Deming. *The Early American Novel 1789–1830*. 1907; reprint, New York: Frederick Ungar, 1958.
Lott, Eric. *Love and Theft: Blackface Minstrelsy and the American Working Class*. New York: Oxford University Press, 1993.
Lowell, James Russell. *A Fable for Critics*. In *The Poetical Works of James Russell Lowell*. Edited by Marjorie R. Kaufman. Cambridge Edition, revised. Boston: Houghton Mifflin, 1978.
MacAndrew, Elizabeth. *The Gothic Tradition in Fiction*. New York: Columbia University Press, 1979.
Maddox, Lucy. *Removals: Nineteenth-Century American Literature and the Politics of Indian Affairs*. New York: Oxford University Press, 1991.
Malin, Irving. *New American Gothic*. Carbondale: Southern Illinois University Press, 1962.
Martin, Harold C. "The Colloquial Tradition in the Novel: John Neal." *New England Quarterly* 32 (1959): 455–75.
Marx, Leo. *The Machine in the Garden: Technology and the Pastoral Ideal in America*. New York: Oxford University Press, 1964.
Massé, Michelle A. *In the Name of Love: Women, Masochism, and the Gothic*. Ithaca: Cornell University Press, 1992.
Matthiessen, F. O. *American Renaissance: Art and Expression in the Age of Emerson and Whitman*. London: Oxford University Press, 1941.
———. "Edgar Allan Poe." In *Literary History of the United States*. Edited by Robert Spiller. New York: Macmillan, 1948.
Mayer, Brantz. *Tah-Gah-Jute or Logan and Captain Michael Cresap*. Baltimore: John Murphy, 1851.
McCoy, Drew. *The Elusive Republic: Political Economy in Jeffersonian America*. New York: Norton, 1982.
McDowell, Deborah E. "In the First Place: Making Frederick Douglass and the Afro-American Narrative Tradition." In *Critical Essays on Frederick Douglass*. Edited by William L. Andrews. Boston: G. K. Hall, 1991.
McKenney, Thomas L. *Memoirs, Official and Personal*. Lincoln: University of Nebraska Press, 1973.
McMillen, Neil R. *Dark Journey: Black Mississippians in the Age of Jim Crow*. Urbana: University of Illinois Press, 1989.
McQuade, Donald, ed. *The Harper American Literature*. Vol. 1. New York: Harper and Row, 1987.
McWhiney, H. Grady and Francis B. Simkins. "The Ghostly Legend of the Ku-Klux Klan." In *Mother Wit from the Laughing Barrel: Readings in the Interpretation of Afro-American Folklore*. Edited by Alan Dundes. New York: Garland Publishing, 1981.
McWilliams, John. "The Rationale for 'The American Romance.'" *Boundary 2* 17 (1990): 71–82.

Melville, Herman. "Hawthorne and His Mosses." In *The Piazza Tales and Other Prose Pieces 1839–1860*. Edited by Harrison Hayford et al. Evanston, Ill.: Northwestern University Press, 1987.

Merish, Lori. "Sentimental Consumption: Harriet Beecher Stowe and the Aesthetics of Middle-Class Ownership." *American Literary History* 8 (1996): 1–33.

Michaels, Walter Benn. "Romance and Real Estate." In *The American Renaissance Reconsidered*. Edited by Walter Benn Michaels and Donald E. Pease. Baltimore: Johns Hopkins University Press, 1985.

Miller, John C. *The Alien and Sedition Acts*. Boston: Little, Brown, 1952.

Mills, Bruce. "Lydia Maria Child and the Endings to Harriet Jacobs's *Incidents in the Life of a Slave Girl*." *American Literature* 64 (1992): 255–72.

Mims, Edwin and Bruce R. Payne. *Southern Prose and Poetry for Schools*. New York: Charles Scribner and Sons, 1910.

Mitchell, Isaac. *The Asylum; or, Alonzo and Melissa*. Poughkeepsie, N.Y.: J. Nelson, 1811.

Mitchell, Julia Post. *St. Jean De Crèvecoeur*. New York: Columbia University Press, 1916.

Modleski, Tania. *Loving with a Vengeance: Mass-Produced Fantasies for Women*. Hamden, Conn.: Archon Books, 1982.

Moers, Ellen. *Literary Women*. Garden City, N.Y.: Doubleday, 1976.

Mogen, David. "Frontier Myth and American Gothic." *Genre* 14 (1981): 329–46.

———, Scott P. Sanders, and Joanne B. Karpinski, eds. *Frontier Gothic: Terror and Wonder at the Frontier in American Literature*. London: Associated University Presses, 1993.

Mohr, James C. "Calculated Disillusionment: Crèvecoeur's *Letters* Reconsidered." *South Atlantic Quarterly* 69 (1970): 354–63.

Moore, R. Laurence. *In Search of White Crows: Spiritualism, Parapsychology, and American Culture*. New York: Oxford University Press, 1977.

Morgan, Edmund S. *American Slavery, American Freedom: The Ordeal of Colonial Virginia*. New York: Norton, 1975.

———. *Inventing the People: The Rise of Popular Sovereignty in England and America*. New York: Norton, 1988.

Morrell, Benjamin. *A Narrative of Four Voyages*. 1832; reprint, Upper Saddle River, N.J.: The Gregg Press, 1970.

Morris, David B. "Gothic Sublimity." *New Literary History* 16 (1985): 299–320.

Morrison, Toni. *Beloved*. New York: Knopf, 1987.

———. "Five Years of Terror." *U.S. News and World Report* 103 (Oct. 19, 1987): 75.

———. "Unspeakable Things Unspoken: The Afro-American Presence in American Literature." *Michigan Quarterly Review* 28 (1989):1–34.

———. *Playing in the Dark: Whiteness and the Literary Imagination*. Cambridge: Harvard University Press, 1992.

Morton, Samuel George. *Crania Americana; or, A Comparative View of the Skulls of Various Aboriginal Nations of North and South America. To Which is Prefixed an Essay on the Varieties of the Human Species.* Philadelphia: J. Dobson, 1839.

———. *Crania AEgyptiaca; or, Observations on Egyptian Ethnography, Derived from Anatomy, History and the Monuments.* Philadelphia: J. Penington, 1844.

Moses, Montrose J. *The Literature of the South.* New York: Thomas Crowell and Co., 1910.

Mussell, Kay. *Women's Gothic and Romantic Fiction: A Reference Guide.* Westport, Conn.: Greenwood Press, 1981.

Napier, Elizabeth R. *The Failure of Gothic: Problems of Disjunction in an Eighteenth-Century Literary Form.* Oxford: Clarendon Press, 1987.

Neal, John. *Logan, a Family History.* 2 vols. Philadelphia: H. C. Carey and I. Lea, 1822.

———. *Errata, or the Works of Will Adams.* 2 vols. New York, 1823.

———. *Randolph, A Novel.* 2 vols. New York, 1823.

———. *Seventy-Six.* 2 vols. Baltimore: Joseph Robinson, 1823.

———. "Unpublished Preface to the North-American Stories." In *Rachel Dyer: A North American Story.* Portland, Maine: Shirley and Hyde, 1828; facsimile, with introduction by John D. Seelye, Gainesville, Fla.: Scholars' Facsimiles and Reprints, 1964.

———. "Otter-Bag, the Oneida Chief." *The Token* (1829): 221–84.

———. *Wandering Recollections of a Somewhat Busy Life.* Boston: Roberts Brothers, 1869.

———. *American Writers: A Series of Papers Contributed to* Blackwood's Magazine *(1824–1825) by John Neal.* Edited by Fred Lewis Pattee. Durham, N.C.: Duke University Press, 1937.

Nelson, Dana. *The Word in Black and White: Reading "Race" in American Literature 1638–1867.* New York: Oxford University Press, 1992.

New England Galaxy. "American Literature." Vol. 5, No. 260 (Oct. 4, 1822).

Newbury, Michael. "Eaten Alive: Slavery and Celebrity in Antebellum America." *ELH* 61 (1994): 159–87.

Niemtzow, Annette. "The Problematic of Self in Autobiography: The Example of the Slave Narrative." In *The Art of the Slave Narrative: Original Essays in Criticism and Theory.* Edited by John Sekora and Darwin T. Turner. Macomb: Western Illinois University, 1982.

Nudelman, Franny. "Harriet Jacobs and the Sentimental Politics of Female Suffering." *English Literary History* 59 (1992): 939–64.

Nye, Russel B. "Michel-Guillaume St. John de Crèvecoeur: *Letters from an American Farmer.*" In *Landmarks of American Writing.* Edited by Hennig Cohen. New York: Basic Books, 1969.

O'Brien, Michael. *The Idea of the American South, 1920–41.* Baltimore: Johns Hopkins University Press, 1979.

Orestano, Francesca. "The Old World and the New in the National Landscapes of John Neal." In *Views of American Landscapes*. Edited by Robert Lawson-Peebles and Mick Gidley. New York: Cambridge University Press, 1989.

Paine, Thomas. *Common Sense*. Edited by Isaac Kramnick. New York: Penguin, 1986.

Parker, Bettye J. "Complexity: Toni Morrison's Women—An Interview Essay." *Sturdy Black Bridges: Visions of Black Women in Literature*. Edited by Roseann P. Bell, Bettye J. Parker, and Beverly Guy-Sheftall. Garden City, N.Y.: Anchor Books, 1979.

Parrington, Vernon. *Main Currents in American Thought*. 3 vols. New York: Harcourt, Brace and World, 1927–30.

Pattee, Fred Lewis. *The First Century of American Literature, 1770–1870*. New York: Appleton-Century, 1935.

———. Introduction to *American Writers: A Series of Papers Contributed to Blackwood's Magazine (1824–1825) by John Neal*. Edited by Fred Lewis Pattee. Durham, N.C.: Duke University Press, 1937.

Patterson, Mark R. *Authority, Autonomy, and Representation in American Literature, 1776–1865*. Princeton: Princeton University Press, 1988.

Paulson, Ronald. "Gothic Fiction and the French Revolution." *ELH* 48 (1981): 532–54.

Pearce, Roy Harvey. *Savagism and Civilization: A Study of the Indian and the American Mind*. 1953; revised edition, Baltimore: Johns Hopkins University Press, 1965.

Pernick, Martin S. "Politics, Parties and Pestilence: Epidemic Yellow Fever in Philadelphia and the Rise of the First Party System." In *Sickness and Health in America: Readings in the History of Medicine and Public Health*. Edited by Judith Walzer Leavitt and Ronald L. Numbers. Madison: University of Wisconsin Press, 1978.

Peterson, Carla. "Capitalism, Black (Under)Development, and the Production of the African-American Novel in the 1850s." *American Literary History* 4 (1992): 559–83.

Petter, Henri. *The Early American Novel*. Columbus: Ohio State University Press, 1971.

Pfister, Joel. *The Production of Personal Life: Class, Gender and the Psychological in Hawthorne's Fiction*. Stanford: Stanford University Press, 1991.

Philbrick, Nathaniel. "The Nantucket Sequence in Crèvecoeur's *Letters from an American Farmer*." *New England Quarterly* 64 (1991): 414–32.

Philbrick, Thomas. *St. John de Crèvecoeur*. New York: Twayne Publishers, 1970.

———. "Crèvecoeur as New Yorker." *Early American Literature* 11 (1976): 22–30.

———. "The American Revolution as a Literary Event." In *The Columbia Literary History of the United States*. Edited by Emory Elliott. New York: Columbia University Press, 1988.

Pickett, LaSalle Corbell. *Across My Path: Memories of People I Have Known.* New York: Brentano's, 1916.

Pinkerton, John. *A Dissertation on the Origin and Progress of the Scythians or Goths.* London: G. Nicol, 1787.

Plotkin, Norman A. "Saint-John De Crèvecoeur Rediscovered: Critic or Panegyrist?" *French Historical Studies* 3 (1964): 390–404.

Plumstead, A. W. "Hector St. John de Crèvecoeur." In *American Literature, 1764–1789: The Revolutionary Years.* Edited by Everett Emerson. Madison: University of Wisconsin Press, 1977.

Pocock, J. G. A. *The Machiavellian Moment: Florentine Political Thought and the Atlantic Republican Tradition.* Princeton: Princeton University Press, 1975.

Poe, Edgar Allan. *Marginalia.* Charlottesville: University Press of Virginia, 1981.

——. *The Narrative of Arthur Gordon Pym.* In *The Collected Writings of Edgar Allan Poe. Volume 1, The Imaginary Voyages.* Edited by Burton R. Pollin. Boston: Twayne Publishers, 1981.

Poirier, Richard. *A World Elsewhere: The Place of Style in American Literature.* New York: Oxford University Press, 1966.

The Port Folio. Philadelphia. Fourth Series. Vol. 16 (July–December, 1823): 152–57.

Powell, J. H. *Bring Out Your Dead: The Great Plague of Yellow Fever in Philadelphia in 1793.* Philadelphia: University of Pennsylvania Press, 1949.

Praz, Mario. *The Romantic Agony.* Translated by Angus Davidson. London: Oxford University Press, 1933.

Prucha, Francis Paul. *American Indian Policy in the Formative Years: The Indian Trade and Intercourse Acts, 1780–1834.* Cambridge: Harvard University Press, 1962.

Punter, David. *The Literature of Terror: A History of Gothic Fictions from 1765 to the Present Day.* London: Longmans, 1980.

Putz, Manfred. "Dramatic Elements and the Problem of Literary Mediation in the Works of Hector St. John de Crèvecoeur." *REAL: The Yearbook of Research in English and American Literature* 3 (1985): 111–30.

Quinn, Arthur Hobson. *American Fiction: An Historical and Critical Survey.* New York: Appleton-Century, 1936.

——, ed. *The Literature of the American People.* New York: Appleton-Century-Crofts, 1951.

Railo, Eino. *The Haunted Castle: A Study of the Elements of English Romanticism.* New York: E. P. Dutton, 1927.

Rapping, Elayne Antler. "Theory and Experience in Crèvecoeur's America." *American Quarterly* 19 (1967): 707–18.

Regis, Pamela. *Describing Early America: Bartram, Jefferson, Crèvecoeur, and the Rhetoric of Natural History.* DeKalb: Northern Illinois University Press, 1992.

Restuccia, Frances L. "Female Gothic Writing: 'Under Cover to Alice.'" *Genre* 19 (1986): 245–66.

Reynolds, David. *Beneath the American Renaissance: The Subversive Imagination in the Age of Emerson and Melville*. 1988. Cambridge: Harvard University Press, 1989.

Rice, Grantland S. "Crèvecoeur and the Politics of Authorship in Republican America." *Early American Literature* 28 (1993): 91–119.

Richards, Irving T. "The Life and Works of John Neal." 4 vols. Ph.D. dissertation, Harvard University, 1928.

Richardson, James D., ed. *A Compilation of the Messages and Papers of the Presidents*. Vol. 3. 1897; reprint, New York: Bureau of National Literature, 1925?.

Ringe, Donald. *American Gothic: Imagination and Reason in Nineteenth-Century Fiction*. Lexington: University Press of Kentucky, 1982.

Roach, Joseph. *Cities of the Dead: Circum-Atlantic Performance*. New York: Columbia University Press, 1996.

Roberts, Diane. *The Myth of Aunt Jemima: Representations of Race and Region*. New York: Routledge, 1994.

Robinson, David M. "Community and Utopia in Crèvecoeur's *Sketches*." *American Literature* 62 (1990): 17–31.

Roediger, David. *The Wages of Whiteness: Race and the Making of the American Working Class*. London: Verso, 1991.

Rogin, Michael Paul. *Fathers and Children: Andrew Jackson and the Subjugation of the American Indian*. New York: Knopf, 1975.

Rollins, Richard. "Words as Social Control: Noah Webster and the Creation of the American Dictionary." *American Quarterly* 28 (1976): 415–30.

Rosen, George. "Political Order and Human Health in Jeffersonian Thought." *Bulletin of the History of Medicine* 26 (1952): 32–44.

Rosenthal, Bernard. "Poe, Slavery, and *The Southern Literary Messenger*: A Reexamination." *Poe Studies* 7 (1974): 29–38.

Rowe, John Carlos. "Poe, Antebellum Slavery, and Modern Criticism." In *Poe's Pym: Critical Explorations*. Edited by Richard Kopley. Durham, N.C.: Duke University Press, 1992.

Rubin, Joseph Jay. "John Neal's Poetics as an Influence on Whitman and Poe." *New England Quarterly* 14 (1941): 359–62.

Rubin, Louis D., Jr. *The Edge of the Swamp: A Study in the Literature and Society of the Old South*. Baton Rouge: University of Louisiana Press, 1989.

Rucker, Mary E. "Crèvecoeur's *Letters* and Enlightenment Doctrine." *Early American Literature* 13 (1978): 193–212.

Rush, Benjamin. *Medical Inquiries and Observations Upon the Diseases of the Mind*. Philadelphia: Kimber and Richardson, 1812.

Rushdy, Ashraf H. A. "Reading Black, White, and Gray in 1968: The Origins of the Contemporary Narrativity of Slavery." In *Criticism and the Color Line:*

Desegregating American Literary Studies. Edited by Henry B. Wonham. New Brunswick, N.J.: Rutgers University Press, 1996.

Russo, James. "The Chameleon of Convenient Vice: A Study of the Narrative of *Arthur Mervyn.*" *Studies in the Novel* 11 (1979): 381–405.

Saar, Doreen Alvarez. "Crèvecoeur's 'Thoughts on Slavery': *Letters from an American Farmer* and Whig Rhetoric." *Early American Literature* 22 (1987): 192–203.

St. Armand, Barton Levi. "Veiled Ladies: Dickinson, Bettina, and Transcendental Mediumship." *Studies in the American Renaissance* (1987): 1–51.

Samuels, Shirley. "Plague and Politics in 1793: *Arthur Mervyn.*" *Criticism* 27 (1985): 225–46.

——. "Infidelity and Contagion: The Rhetoric of Revolution." *Early American Literature* 22 (1987): 183–91.

Sanchez-Eppler, Karen. *Touching Liberty: Abolition, Feminism, and the Politics of the Body.* Berkeley: University of California Press, 1993.

Sandiford, Keith. "Gothic Intertextual Constructions in *Linden Hills.*" In *Gloria Naylor: Critical Perspectives Past and Present.* Edited by Henry Louis Gates, Jr. and Kwame Anthony Appiah. New York: Amistad Press, 1993.

Sands, R. C. "Domestic Literature." *The Atlantic Magazine* 1 (1824): 130–39.

Satz, Ronald N. *American Indian Policy in the Jacksonian Era.* Lincoln: University of Nebraska Press, 1975.

Sayre, Robert F. *Thoreau and the American Indians.* Princeton: Princeton University Press, 1977.

Sears, Donald A. *John Neal.* Boston: Twayne Publishers, 1978.

Sedgwick, Eve. "The Character in the Veil: Imagery of the Surface in the Gothic Novel." *PMLA* 96 (1981): 255–70.

——. *The Coherence of Gothic Conventions.* 1980. New York: Methuen, 1986.

Sekora, John. "Black Message/White Envelope: Genre, Authenticity, and Authority in the Antebellum Slave Narrative." *Callaloo* 10 (1987): 482–515.

Seltzer, Mark. "Saying Makes it So: Language and Event in Brown's *Wieland.*" *Early American Literature* 13 (1978): 81–91.

Seydow, John J. "The Sound of Passing Music: John Neal's Battle for American Literary Independence." *Costerus* 7 (1973): 153–82.

Sheehan, Bernard W. *Seeds of Extinction: Jeffersonian Philanthropy and the American Indian.* Chapel Hill: University of North Carolina Press, 1973.

Showalter, Elaine. *Sister's Choice: Tradition and Change in American Women's Writing.* Oxford: Clarendon Press, 1991.

Simms, William Gilmore. *Views and Reviews in American Literature, History and Fiction: First Series.* Cambridge: The Belknap Press of Harvard University Press, 1962.

Simpson, David. *The Politics of American English, 1776–1850.* New York: Oxford University Press, 1986.

Sisney, Mary F. "The Power and Horror of Whiteness: Wright and Ellison Respond to Poe." *College Language Association* 29 (1985): 82–90.

Slotkin, Richard. *Regeneration Through Violence: The Mythology of the American Frontier, 1600–1860*. Middletown, Conn.: Wesleyan University Press, 1973.

Smith, James Morton. *Freedom's Fetters: The Alien and Sedition Laws and American Civil Liberties*. Ithaca: Cornell University Press, 1956.

Smith, Samuel Stanhope. *An Essay on the Causes of the Variety of Complexion and Figure in the Human Species*. Philadelphia: Robert Aiken, 1787.

[Smith, Sydney]. "Art. III. *Statistical Annals of the United States of America*. By Adam Seybert." *The Edinburgh Review* 33 (1820): 69–80.

Smith, Valerie. *Self-Discovery and Authority in African-American Narrative*. Cambridge: Harvard University Press, 1987.

Smith-Rosenberg, Carroll. *Disorderly Conduct: Visions of Gender in Victorian America*. New York: Oxford University Press, 1985.

———. "Domesticating 'Virtue': Coquettes and Revolutionaries in Young America." In *Literature and the Body: Essays on Populations and Persons*. Edited by Elaine Scarry. Baltimore: Johns Hopkins University Press, 1988.

Smith-Wright, Geraldine. "In Spite of the Klan: Ghosts in the Fiction of Black Women Writers." In *Haunting the House of Fiction: Feminist Perspectives on Ghost Stories by American Women*. Edited by Lynette Carpenter and Wendy K. Kolmar. Knoxville: University of Tennessee Press, 1991.

The Southern Literary Messenger Vol. 3, No. 1 (January 1837).

The Southern Literary Messenger Vol. 16, No. 3 (March, 1850).

Spangler, George. "C. B. Brown's *Arthur Mervyn*: A Portrait of the Young American Artist." *American Literature* 52 (1981): 578–92.

Spencer, Benjamin T. *The Quest for Nationality: An American Literary Campaign*. Syracuse, N.Y.: Syracuse University Press, 1957.

Spiller, Robert et al., eds. *Literary History of the United States*. New York: Macmillan, 1948.

Spillers, Hortense J. "Changing the Letter: The Yokes, the Jokes of Discourse, or, Mrs. Stowe, Mr. Reed." In *Slavery and the Literary Imagination*. Edited by Deborah E. McDowell and Arnold Rampersad. Baltimore: Johns Hopkins University Press, 1989.

Stanton, William. *The Great United States Exploring Expedition of 1838–42*. Berkeley: University of California Press, 1975.

Stepan, Nancy. *The Idea of Race in Science: Great Britain 1800–1960*. Hamden, Conn.: Archon Books, 1982.

Stern, Madeleine. Introduction to *Behind a Mask: The Unknown Thrillers of Louisa May Alcott*. Edited by Madeleine Stern. Mattituck, N.Y.: Aeonian Press, 1979.

———. *Critical Essays on Louisa May Alcott*. Boston: G. K. Hall, 1984.

———. "Louisa May Alcott's Self-Criticism." *Studies in the American Renaissance* (1985): 333–82.

Stone, Albert E. Introduction to *Letters from an American Farmer* by Hector St. John de Crèvecoeur. Edited by Albert E. Stone. New York: Penguin, 1986.

Stowe, Harriet Beecher. *Uncle Tom's Cabin or Life Among the Lowly*. Edited by Ann Douglas. New York: Penguin, 1986.

———. *The Key to Uncle Tom's Cabin*. Salem, N.H.: Ayer, 1987.

———. *Dred: A Tale of the Great Dismal Swamp*. Edited by Judie Newman. Halifax, England: Ryburn, 1992.

Summers, Montague. *The Gothic Quest: A History of the Gothic Novel*. London: The Fortune Press, 1938.

Sundquist, Eric. *To Wake the Nations: Race in the Making of American Literature*. Cambridge: The Belknap Press of Harvard University Press, 1993.

———. *The Literature of Expansion and Race*. In *The Cambridge History of American Literature: Volume 2, 1820–1865*. New York: Cambridge University Press, 1995.

Symmes, John Cleves. *Symzonia, A Voyage of Discovery, by Adam Seaborn*. Gainesville, Fla.: Scholars' Facsimiles and Reprints, 1965.

Takaki, Ronald T. *Iron Cages: Race and Culture in Ninteenth-Century America*. New York: Knopf, 1979.

Tatar, Maria M. *Spellbound: Studies on Mesmerism and Literature*. Princeton: Princeton University Press, 1978.

Tate, Allen. "Our Cousin Mr. Poe." In *Poe: A Collection of Critical Essays*. Edited by Robert Regan. Englewood Cliffs, N.J.: Prentice-Hall, 1967.

Tate, Claudia. *Domestic Allegories of Political Desire: The Black Heroine's Text at the Turn of the Century*. New York: Oxford University Press, 1992.

Thompson, G. R., ed. *The Gothic Imagination: Essays in Dark Romanticism*. Pullman: Washington State University Press, 1974.

———. "Edgar Allan Poe and the Writers of the Old South." In *Columbia Literary History of the United States*. Edited by Emory Elliott. New York: Columbia University Press, 1988.

Tise, Larry. *Proslavery: A History of the Defense of Slavery in America, 1701–1840*. Athens: University of Georgia Press, 1987.

Titus, Mary. " 'This Poisonous System': Social Ills, Bodily Ills, and *Incidents in the Life of a Slave Girl*." In *Harriet Jacobs and* Incidents in the Life of a Slave Girl. Edited by Deborah M. Garfield and Rafia Zafar. New York: Cambridge University Press, 1996.

Tompkins, Jane. *Sensational Designs: The Cultural Work of American Fiction: 1790–1860*. New York: Oxford University Press, 1985.

———. " 'Indians': Textualism, Morality, and the Problem of History." In *"Race," Writing, and Difference*. Edited by Henry Louis Gates, Jr. Chicago: University of Chicago Press, 1986.

Tragle, Henry Irving. *The Southampton Slave Revolt of 1831: A Compilation of Source Material*. Amherst: University of Massachusetts Press, 1971.

Tropp, Martin. *Images of Fear: How Horror Stories Helped Shape Modern Culture, 1818–1918.* Jefferson, N.C.: McFarland, 1990.

Tuke, Samuel. *Description of the Retreat, An Institution near York, for Insane Persons of the Society of Friends: Containing an Account of its Origin and Progress, the Modes of Treatment, and a Statement of Cases.* Philadelphia: Isaac Pierce, 1813.

Tyler, Moses Coit. *The Literary History of the American Revolution. Vol. 2, 1776–1783.* 1897; reprint, New York: Barnes and Noble, 1941.

Varma, Devendra P. *The Gothic Flame.* 1957. New York: Russell and Russell, 1966.

Wald, Priscilla. *Constituting Americans: Cultural Anxiety and Narrative Form.* Durham, N.C.: Duke University Press, 1995.

Walker, Alice. *In Search of Our Mother's Gardens.* San Diego: Harcourt Brace Jovanovich, 1983.

Walpole, Horace. *The Castle of Otranto.* Edited by W. S. Lewis. Oxford: Oxford University Press, 1982.

Walter, Krista. "Surviving in the Garret: Harriet Jacobs and the Critique of Sentiment." *American Transcendental Quarterly* 8 (1994): 189–210.

Walters, Ronald G. "The Erotic South: Civilization and Sexuality in American Abolitionism." *American Quarterly* 25 (1973): 176–201.

———. *The Antislavery Appeal: American Abolitionism After 1830.* Baltimore: Johns Hopkins University Press, 1976.

Warner, Anne Bradford. "Carnival Laughter: Resistance in *Incidents.*" In *Harriet Jacobs and* Incidents in the Life of a Slave Girl. Edited by Deborah M. Garfield and Rafia Zafar. New York: Cambridge University Press, 1996.

———. "No *Key* to Cassy: Jacobs Rewrites Stowe." Paper presented at the Nineteenth-Century American Women Writers in the Twenty-First Century Conference, Hartford, Connecticut, May 30–June 2, 1996.

Warner, Michael. *The Letters of the Republic: Publication and the Public Sphere in Eighteenth-Century America.* Cambridge: Harvard University Press, 1990.

Washington, George. *The Washington Papers.* Edited by Saul K. Padover. New York: Harper and Brothers, 1955.

Watts, Steven. *The Republic Reborn: War and the Making of Liberal America, 1790–1820.* Baltimore: Johns Hopkins University Press, 1987.

———. *The Romance of Real Life: Charles Brockden Brown and the Origins of American Culture.* Baltimore: Johns Hopkins University Press, 1994.

Webster, Noah, compiler. *A Collection of Papers on the Subject of Bilious Fevers, Prevalent in the United States for a few years past.* New York: Hopkins, Webb, 1796.

Weld, Theodore. *American Slavery as It Is; Testimony of a Thousand Witnesses.* 1839. New York: Arno Press, 1968.

Wheat, Ellen Harkins. *Jacob Lawrence: The* Frederick Douglass *and* Harriet Tubman *Series of 1938–40.* Hampton, Va.: Hampton University Museum, 1991.

Wideman, John Edgar. *Fever: Twelve Stories.* New York: Henry Holt, 1989.

Williams, Anne. *Art of Darkness: A Poetics of Gothic*. Chicago: The University of Chicago Press, 1995.
Williams, William Carlos. *In the American Grain*. 1925. New York: New Directions, 1956.
Wilt, Judith. *Ghosts of the Gothic: Austen, Eliot, and Lawrence*. Princeton: Princeton University Press, 1980.
Winston, Robert P. " 'Strange Order of Things!': The Journey to Chaos in *Letters from an American Farmer*." *Early American Literature* 19 (1984/5): 249–67.
Winter, Kari J. *Subjects of Slavery, Agents of Change: Women and Power in Gothic Novels and Slave Narratives, 1790–1865*. Athens: University of Georgia Press, 1992.
Witherington, Paul. "Benevolence and the 'Utmost Stretch': Charles Brockden Brown's Narrative Dilemma." *Criticism* 14 (1972): 175–91.
Wolstenholme, Susan. *Gothic (Re)Visions: Writing Women as Readers*. Albany: State University of New York Press, 1993.
Wood, Gordon S. *The Creation of the American Republic, 1776–1787*. New York: Norton, 1969.
Woodward, C. Vann. *The Burden of Southern History*. Baton Rouge: Louisiana State University Press, 1960.
Wright, Richard. *Native Son*. New York: Harper and Row, 1940.
———. *Black Boy*. New York: Perennial Library, 1966.
Wrobel, Arthur. *Pseudo-Science and Society in Nineteenth-Century America*. Lexington: University Press of Kentucky, 1987.
Yellin, Jean Fagan. "Written By Herself: Harriet Jacobs's Slave Narrative." *American Literature* 53 (1981): 479–86.
———. "Text and Context of Harriet Jacobs' *Incidents in the Life of a Slave Girl: Written by Herself*." *The Slave's Narrative*. Edited by Charles T. Davis and Henry Louis Gates, Jr. New York: Oxford University Press, 1985.
———. Introduction to *Incidents in the Life of a Slave Girl* by Harriet Jacobs. Edited by Jean Fagan Yellin. Cambridge: Harvard University Press, 1987.
Young, Samuel. *Tom Hanson, the Avenger*. Pittsburgh: J. W. Cook, 1847.
Ziff, Larzer. *Writing in the New Nation: Prose, Print, and Politics in the Early United States*. New Haven: Yale University Press, 1991.

Index

Abject, 10, 13–14, 19–21, 26, 41, 42, 53, 63, 94–96, 155–56

Adams, John, 164*n*3

African-American gothic, 12, 131–32, 187*n*16; haunting back in, 12, 132, 143, 147, 151–52, 155, 158; as revision of American gothic, 12, 74, 132, 140, 153; *see also* Douglass, Jacobs, Lawrence, Morrison, Wright

Alcott, Louisa May, 8, 11, 117–30; "Behind a Mask," 122–25; and commercial capital, 117–19, 129; and cultural capital, 117, 130; "How I Went Out to Service," 120–22; "La Jeune," 123; *Little Women*, 117–20, 129; as market manipulator, 96, 105, 117–19, 121–22, 129–30; *A Modern Mephistopheles*, 118; *Moods*, 118, 183*n*22; "The Skeleton in the Closet," 118; and slavery, 121–22, 128, 130; "V.V.: or, Plots and Counterplots," 125–29; *Work*, 184*n*26

American literary canon: gendered models of, 95–96; gothic's disruption of, 8, 10, 30, 60, 132; gothic's marginalization in, 6–7, 11, 26, 28–29, 53–54, 70, 72, 76–78; Indian's exclusion from, 70, 72; lack of history in, 9, 54–55, 132; racial hauntings in, 7–8, 13, 74–76, 93, 156; *see also* Gothic and literary nationalism; critical assessments of *Letters from an American Farmer*, Neal, and Poe

American Revolution, 24, 31, 69

Index

Andrews, William, 150, 186*n*9
Appleby, Joyce, 168*n*2, 171*n*15
Arch, Stephen Carl, 167*n*17
Arthur Mervyn, 31–51, 53; and commercial corruption, 31–32, 34, 36–39, 41, 44–47, 49–51; commercial self in, 34–36, 38, 40, 42–44; diseased discourse in, 32, 35–36, 38–41, 43, 45–51; narrative and credit in, 35–36, 38–40, 45–49, 51; and national health, 11, 31–34, 40–41, 49, 51; republican citizen in, 34, 38, 39–41, 45; self-evident discourse in, 32, 39–40, 45–49; and slave economy, 34, 37, 43–45, 49, 50; textual history of, 32; yellow fever in, 11, 31, 33–34, 37–38, 44–45, 49

Bailyn, Bernard, 166*n*13, 168*n*2
Bain, Robert, 177*n*23
Banta, Martha, 163*n*11, 165*n*9
Barnard, A. M., 117, 119
Barnett, Louise, 173*n*5
Barthes, Roland, 165*n*6
Baym, Nina, 6, 9
Beaver, Harold, 78
Beckford, William, 133
Bell, Michael Davitt, 172*n*18
Bentley, Nancy, 179*n*6
Bernstein, Susan Naomi, 119, 184*n*24
Berthoff, Rowland, 164*n*2
Bertram, John, 22, 23
Bewley, Marius, 29, 165*n*9
Birkhead, Edith, 4
Blackness, 7–9, 73–76, 79, 80–81, 84–86, 89–92, 147, 176*n*6, 181*n*12
Blair, Hugh, 164*n*4
Blassingame, John, 140
The Blithedale Romance, 11, 105–13, 115–16; and literary marketplace, 112–13; and market self, 106–8; and slavery, 107, 110, 130; and stable self, 108–9; and veiled lady, 105–11; Zenobia's tale in, 109–12, 116
Bloom, Harold, 77, 78
Bodziock, Joseph, 9, 185*n*4
Boynton, Percy, 27–28
Braude, Ann, 180*n*5
Braxton, Joanne, 189*n*23, 190*n*29
Brodhead, Richard, 114–16, 182*n*16, 183*n*20
Brown, Charles Brockden, 55, 62, 72, 95; critical reputation, 6, 51; *Edgar Huntly*, 4, 32, 51, 52, 59, 173*n*22; *Ormond*, 32, 170*n*12; retreat from gothic, 32, 51; *Wieland*, 32, 51, 172*n*22
Brown, Gillian, 181*n*12
Buell, Lawrence, 9, 182*n*15

Cameron, James, 187*n*14
Cappello, Mary, 184*n*24
Cash, W. J., 79, 178*n*5
Castronovo, Russ, 163*n*13
Chase, Richard, 6, 28–29
Chesnutt, Charles, 74, 153
Cheyfitz, Eric, 179*n*6
Child, Lydia Maria, 133, 137, 145, 146
Christophersen, Bill, 34, 169*n*7
Clayton, Jay, 162*n*4
Coad, Oral Sumner, 175*n*13
Cohen, Daniel, 168*n*6
Conn, Peter, 29
Cooper, J. California, 153
Cooper, James Fenimore, 53; *The Spy*, 54, 55
Coultrap-McQuin, Susan, 180*n*2
Cowie, Alexander, 177*n*23
Cowley, Malcolm, 6
Craven, Wayne, 181*n*8
Crèvecoeur, J. Hector St. John de: crafted persona in *Letters*, 15–16, 28; *More Letters from an American Farm-*

er, 30; *Sketches of Eighteenth Century America*, 27, 29–30, 167*n*19; *Voyage dans la Haute Pensylvanie*, 27; *see also Letters from an American Farmer*
Crouch, Stanley, 187*n*15
Cultural capital, 96, 97, 114, 115, 117, 130
Cultural contradiction, 10, 25, 29; Indian massacre and removal as, 3, 11, 53, 62, 69; market as, 3, 11, 31; revolution as, 3, 11; slavery as, 3, 10, 11, 13, 18, 19, 22, 26, 30, 49, 132
Cunliffe, Marcus, 27, 30

Davidson, Cathy, 9, 170*n*13, 171*n*14
Davis, David Brion, 37, 166*n*13
Dayan, Joan, 85, 86, 178*n*4, 179*n*8, 185*nn*4, 7
Dehon, Theodore, 55
DeLamotte, Eugenia, 59, 95, 162*n*2
Derrida, Jacques, 5
Dewey, Orville, 100
Dickinson, John, 164*n*2
Dickstein, Morris, 162*n*6
Dippie, Brian, 173*n*4, 176*n*15
Douglas, Aaron, 191*n*1
Douglass, Frederick, 136, 145, 153, 186*n*10; *Narrative*, 137–39
Drayton, John, 83
Drinnon, Richard, 176*n*16
Dudden, Faye, 181*n*9

Elbert, Sarah, 119, 184*n*25
Ellis, Joseph, 170*n*11
Ellison, Ralph: *Invisible Man*, 153–54
Emerson, Ralph Waldo, 72, 77
Enlightenment narrative, 4, 8, 10, 11, 13, 23, 30, 32, 39–41, 46, 49, 51, 53

Feidelson, Charles, 78
Female gothic, 11–12, 94–96, 147, 189*n*24; *see also* Alcott, Hawthorne

Ferguson, Moira, 178*n*2
Ferguson, Robert, 15, 164*n*3
Fetterley, Judith, 183–84*n*24
Fiedler, Leslie, 6, 9, 75, 95–96, 161*n*2
Fields, James, 114
Fishkin, Shelley Fisher, 178*n*3
Fleischmann, Fritz, 177*n*23
Foreman, P. Gabrielle, 188*nn*18, 19
Fortune, Stephen, 172*n*19
Foucault, Michel, 25
Fowler, Alastair, 162*n*5
Frank, Frederick, 9
Franklin, Benjamin, 27
Freneau, Philip, 56
Frontier, 17, 25, 57, 60, 62
Fruitlands, 118, 120
Fry, Gladys-Marie, 187*n*14

Garber, Frederick, 162*n*5
Gardiner, William Howard, 54, 55–56
Garfield, Deborah, 150
Gilmore, Michael, 170*n*11, 183*n*19
Girard, René, 64
Glasgow, Ellen, 80
Godwin, William, 3, 53, 133
Goldsby, Jacqueline, 188*n*18
Gothic: British, 3–4, 9, 53–56, 67, 73, 95, 106, 133; as conservative mode, 2, 10, 20–21, 24, 50–51, 57, 60, 132, 134–37, 144; conventions of, 3–5, 8, 53, 59, 73, 87, 136–39, 145, 147, 148; and dematerialization of history, 132, 134–37, 138, 142–44, 148–50; as escapist, 2; as historical mode, 2, 9–10, 12, 30, 73, 131–34, 139–40, 143, 145, 153–55, 158; and literary nationalism, 11, 53–60, 70–72; as market mode, 36, 96, 106–8; as national form, 76, 80, 93, 146, 150–51, 158–59; as pejorative, 5, 187*n*15; as psychological mode, 9; as regional form, 3–4, 75–76, 80, 82,

93, 158; versus romantic, 5–7; *see also* African-American, Female, and Southern gothic
Grabo, Norman, 29, 41, 167*nn*18, 19, 168*n*3, 171*nn*14, 17, 18
Gray, Richard, 76, 178*n*5
The Greek Slave, 98–102
Green, Vivien, 180*n*7
Grey, Zane, 1
Grimké, Angelina, 136
Grimké, Sarah, 135
Griswold, Rufus Wilmot, 71, 177*n*22
Gross, Louis, 161*n*2
Grossman, Jay, 179*n*6

Haggerty, George, 59
Hales, John, 167*n*19
Halttunen, Karen, 9–10, 102, 181*n*10, 186–87*n*12, 189*n*22
Harris, Trudier, 184*n*2
Hart, Francis, 162*n*5
Hastings, William, 27
Hawthorne, Nathaniel, 7, 11, 71, 75, 77, 119, 130; *The House of the Seven Gables*, 105, 115; and literary marketplace, 96, 105, 113–17, 130, 182*nn*17, 18; *The Marble Faun*, 54, 116; *Fanshawe*, 114; *The Scarlet Letter*, 114–15; late phase, 116; *see also The Blithedale Romance*
Hawthorne, Sophia, 114
Hedges, William, 171*n*18
Hedin, Raymond, 188*n*19
Hemenway, Robert, 74, 185*n*4
Henderson, Andrea, 36, 106, 133
Hendler, Glenn, 180*n*2
Herbert, T. Walter, 183*n*19
Hills, Patricia, 191*n*1
Hofstadter, Richard, 24
Holliday, Carl, 179*n*7
Hopkins, Pauline, 153

Horsman, Reginald, 84
Hume, Robert, 4, 162*n*7
Hyman, Linda, 180*n*7

Iannone, Carol, 187*n*15
Incidents in the Life of a Slave Girl, 12, 137, 144–52, 154; and fictional conventions, 140–41, 144–45, 148; North in, 150–51; repetition in, 146, 150, 190*n*27; revision of gothic in, 147–52; as revision of *Uncle Tom's Cabin*, 141, 149–50; and sentimental, 141, 147–48, 188*n*19
Indian, 25, 61; abject presence of, 53, 63–64, 70, 72; civilization and removal, 53, 55, 60, 66–70; demonized, 56–57, 62–63; as gothic material, 55–56, 58–60; and national identity, 55–57, 63–70
Irving, Washington, 52, 134
Ives, Chauncey, 97, 100, 102, 103

Jackson, Andrew, 56, 57
Jacobs, Harriet, 12, 132, 153, 154; relation to Stowe, 141; *see also Incidents in the Life of a Slave Girl*
James, Henry, 54
Jefferson, Thomas, 15, 60–61, 176*n*20
Jehlen, Myra, 166*n*17
Justus, James, 168*n*6

Kaplan, Sidney, 81–82, 91
Kasson, Joy, 100, 180*n*7, 181*n*8
Keech, James, 162*n*7
Kessler-Harris, Alice, 97
Keyser, Elizabeth, 184*n*24
Kirschke, Amy, 191*n*1
Kolodny, Annette, 167*n*18
Ku Klux Klan, 1, 2, 184*n*14
Kristeva, Julia, 19, 20

Lang, Amy Schrager, 180*n*2

Lawrence, Jacob, 156; *Harriet Tubman Series*, 156–59
Lawson-Peebles, Robert, 165*n*9
Lease, Benjamin, 71, 175*n*13
Letters from an American Farmer, 11, 13–30, 53, 132; critical assessments of, 26–30; Enlightenment fable in, 8, 13, 27–28, 30; frontier in, 17, 25; gothic discourse in, 13–14, 16, 18–26, 28–30; mythic discourse in, 15–19, 21–24, 26–30; pastoral in, 10–11, 19–20, 21; and plain style, 14–16, 19; revolution in, 24–25; slavery in, 18–26, 28–30, 165*n*9; South in, 17–18, 20, 21, 23; textual history of, 163–64*n*1; and yeoman identity, 14, 17
Levin, Harry, 7, 75, 78, 81
Levine, Robert, 171*n*16
Lewis, Matthew Gregory, 3, 73, 74, 95, 133, 178*n*1
Logan, 55, 57, 59, 60–70, 177*n*21; civilizing the Indian in, 66–70; demonizing the Indian in, 62–63; historical referent of, 60–61; and massacre, 11, 53, 61, 63–65, 67, 68–70; and narrative form, 61–64, 66; and national identity, 63–70; sacrificial crisis in, 64–69
Lord Dunmore's War, 60
Loshe, Lillie Deming, 62, 68, 70
Lott, Eric, 86
Lowell, James Russell, 62, 177*n*22

Maddox, Lucy, 72, 176*n*15
Malin, Irving, 161*n*2
Market, 3, 11, 31; as context for gothic, 36; depicted as gothic, 11, 34–36, 42–43, 106–11, 119–20; and domestic ideology, 94, 97–98, 105, 118–30; literary, 96, 113–18, 129–30; and slavery, 32, 34, 37, 43–45, 49–50, 90, 96, 98–102, 107–8, 110, 121–22, 127, 130; women's manipulation of, 96, 105, 111–13, 117–19, 122–30
Marx, Leo, 28
Matthiessen, F. O., 77, 78
Mayer, Brantz, 57
McKenney, Thomas, 56
McMillen, Neil, 184*n*2
McWilliams, John, 168*n*8
Melodrama, 6
Melville, Herman, 7, 75, 77, 133
Merish, Lori, 180*n*2
Mesmerism, 97–98, 100, 106–7, 111, 124, 127–28
Michaels, Walter Benn, 116, 181*n*12
Mills, Bruce, 190*n*30
Mims, Edwin, 80
Minstrel show, 86
Mitchell, Isaac, 4
Mitchell, John, 85
Mitchell, Julia Post, 166*n*14
Model artist shows, 97, 102
Moers, Ellen, 94
Mogen, David, 57, 174*n*7
Mohr, James, 166*n*17
Monogenism, 83–85, 90
Moore, Dennis, 30, 164*n*1
Morgan, Edmund, 164*n*2, 185*n*3
Morrell, Benjamin, 86
Morrison, Toni, 140, 153, 159, 178*n*3; *Beloved*, 154–5, 187*n*15; *Playing in the Dark*, 8, 13, 74–75, 91, 93, 155–56; "Unspeakable Things Unspoken," 72, 74, 155–56
Morton, Samuel George, 84
Moses, Montrose, 79
Mozier, Joseph, 100, 102, 104

Napier, Elizabeth, 5
The Narrative of Arthur Gordon Pym, 81–93; blackness and whiteness in,

81, 84–88, 89, 90–93; and national discourse of race, 80, 82–84, 93; as proslavery allegory, 81–82; racial convertibility in, 84–89; racial hauntings in, 88, 92–93; scientific discourse in, 87–88; and South Sea Exploring Expedition, 83

National narrative, 15, 21, 29; as gothic, 32, 49, 53; gothic's coalescing of, 2, 10–11, 57, 60, 70, 158–59; gothic's disruption of, 10–11, 13–14, 20, 23, 26, 30, 40, 49, 51, 53, 60, 63, 66, 68–70, 158–59

Naylor, Gloria, 153

Neal, John, 8; appropriation of Indian by, 55, 57–60, 62–63, 70–71; biographical information, 173*n*1; critical assessments of, 11, 53, 62, 70–72; *Errata*, 59; and indigenous style, 52–53, 58–59, 66; literary nationalism and, 52–55, 57–60, 70–72; literary output, 174*n*9; literature of the blood, 11, 53, 58, 59, 70; "Otter-Bag," 58–59; *Randolph*, 54, 174*n*11, 177*n*21; *see also* Logan

Nelson, Dana, 174*n*6, 179*nn*6, 8

Newbury, Michael, 122, 181*n*12

Niemtzow, Annette, 188*n*19

North, 17, 20, 21, 45, 75, 137, 150–51, 159

Nott, Josiah C., 84

Nudelman, Franny, 185*n*8

Nye, Russel, 166*n*15, 167*n*17

O'Brien, Michael, 178*n*5

Paine, Thomas, 15
Parlor theatricals, 102, 105
Parrington, Vernon, 27, 78
Pattee, Fred Lewis, 55, 70, 71, 177*n*23
Patterson, Mark, 172*n*18
Paulson, Ronald, 133

Payne, Bruce, 80
Pearce, Roy Harvey, 55, 61, 173*n*4, 176*n*15
Pernick, Martin, 33
Peterson, Carla, 186*n*9, 189*n*23
Petry, Ann, 153
Pfister, Joel, 180*n*2, 181*n*11
Philbrick, Nathaniel, 167*n*18
Philbrick, Thomas, 30, 165*n*9, 166*n*12, 167*n*19
Pickering, Charles, 84
Pickett, LaSalle Corbell, 117
Pinkerton, John, 83
Platzner, Robert, 4
Plotkin, Norman, 27
Pocock, J. G. A., 168*n*2
Poe, Edgar Allan, 3, 24, 51, 62, 72, 131, 177*n*22, 179*n*6, 184*n*1; critical assessments of, 11, 75–81, 93; and race, 11, 75–82; as southern writer, 75–82; *see also The Narrative of Arthur Gordon Pym*
Poirier, Richard, 9
Polygenism, 84–85, 90
Post, Amy, 152
Powers, Hiram: *The Greek Slave*, 98–100, 102, 180–81*n*7
Punter, David, 161*n*2, 163*n*10, 180*n*3
Putz, Manfred, 29, 167*n*19

Quinn, Arthur Hobson, 28

Radcliffe, Anne, 3, 95
Rapping, Elayne Antler, 17, 166*n*12
Regis, Pamela, 165*n*9
Removal Act of 1830, 58, 176–77*n*20
Republicanism, classical, 32; commercial, 32, 39, 41–42
Reynolds, David, 6–7, 162*n*6, 177*n*24, 183*n*24
Reynolds, Jeremiah, 83

Rice, Grantland, 27, 164*n*5, 166*nn*11, 14
Richardson, James, 57
Ringe, Donald, 161*n*2
Roach, Joseph, 100, 180–81*n*7
Roberts, Diane, 189*n*22
Robinson, David, 29, 167*n*19
Rogin, Michael Paul, 176*nn*15, 17
Romance, 3, 6, 9, 28–29, 62, 95, 115–16, 136, 140, 141, 156; and race, 7–8, 74–76, 80
Rosenthal, Bernard, 179*n*6
Rowe, John Carlos, 78, 81
Rowson, Susanna, 95
Rubin, Louis, 79, 80
Rush, Benjamin, 33, 173*n*4
Rushdy, Ashraf H. A., 188*n*17
Russo, James, 170*n*13

Saar, Doreen Alvarez, 165*n*8
Samuels, Shirley, 168*n*5
Sands, R. C., 56
Satz, Ronald, 177*n*20
Savagism, 55
Sayre, Robert, 173*n*4
Sears, Donald, 65, 71
Sedgwick, Eve, 4, 59, 106, 162*n*6
Sedition Act, 50
Seltzer, Mark, 172*n*18
Sentimental, 57, 141, 147–48, 152, 188*n*19; refusal of, 126–28; relationship to gothic, 11–12, 38, 95–96, 111, 119–20, 129; veiling of marketplace by, 49, 51, 96, 100, 105, 109–10, 112–13, 116–17, 119–25, 129
Sheehan, Bernard, 173*n*4
Simms, William Gilmore, 72
Simpson, David, 14
Slave narrative, 8; as factual fiction, 136–37, 140, 144–45, 148, 186*n*9; *see also* Frederick Douglass, *Incidents in the Life of a Slave Girl*

Slavery, 3, 10, 11, 12, 16, 18, 28–29, 53, 74–75, 80, 82, 84, 88, 132, 141, 154; as abject presence, 13, 21–24, 26, 30, 49, 156–59; as commercial activity, 32, 34, 37, 43–45, 49–50, 90, 96, 98, 100–1, 107–8, 110, 121–22, 128, 130; as context for gothic, 73–74, 133–34, 143, 145; as gothic spectacle, 19–23, 76, 133–39, 142–43, 147–50, 152; white responses to, 20–21, 134–35, 137–38, 144, 146, 151, 185*n*8
Slotkin, Richard, 64, 176*n*15
Smith, Samuel Stanhope, 83
Smith, Sydney, 52
Smith, Valerie, 190*nn*25, 29
Smith-Rosenberg, Carroll, 180*n*4
South, 20, 21, 23, 44, 45, 84, 135, 151, 158, 159; as nation's "other," 3–4, 17–18, 76, 78, 178*n*5; and race, 75–82, 93
Southern gothic, 3–4, 11, 75–76, 80–82, 93, 159; *see also* Edgar Allan Poe
Southern Literary Messenger, 77, 80, 82
Southern Renaissance, 3, 80
Spangler, George, 172*n*18
Spencer, Benjamin, 53, 173*n*3
Spiller, Robert, 28, 78
Spillers, Hortense, 187*n*13
Stepan, Nancy, 8, 168*n*4
Stone, Albert, 28–29, 164*n*1, 166*n*15
Stowe, Harriet Beecher, 135–6, 146, 150; *The Key to Uncle Tom's Cabin*, 141–42; *Uncle Tom's Cabin*, 140–44, 147, 149
Summers, Montague, 180*n*3
Sumner, Charles, 136
Sundquist, Eric, 135, 166*n*13, 185*n*6
Symmes, John Cleves, 83; *Symzonia*, 89–91

Takaki, Ronald, 176*n*15

Tate, Allen, 79, 80
Tate, Claudia, 188*n*19
Thompson, G. R., 79
Thoreau, Henry David, 77
Ticknor, William, 113–15
Tise, Larry, 82
Titus, Mary, 190*n*26
Tompkins, Jane, 41, 170*n*13, 171*n*14, 178*n*25, 182*n*16
Tubman, Harriet, 156–58
Turner, Nat, 133–34
Twain, Mark, 71
Tyler, Moses Coit, 27

Undine, 100, 102, 104
Undine Receiving Her Soul, 100, 102–3
U.S. Exploring Expedition, 84

Veiled lady, 97–105; as commodity, 97–98, 105–6, 109–10, 116, 122–24, 127, 129, 130; as slave, 98–102, 107–8, 110, 128; as "true woman," 97–98, 100, 102, 105, 109–10, 122–24, 127–29
"The Virginian Slave," 100, 101

Wald, Priscilla, 163*n*13, 176*n*15
Walker, Alice, 139
Walpole, Horace, 3
Walters, Ronald, 178*n*5, 186*n*12

Warner, Anne Bradford, 189*n*21
Warner, Michael, 170*n*11
Washington, George, 27
Watts, Steven, 168*n*2, 169*n*6, 172*n*21
Webster, Noah, 14
Weld, Theodore, 133, 186*n*11; *American Slavery as It Is*, 134, 145, 184*n*2, 185*n*8
Wheat, Ellen Harkins, 190*n*1
Whiteness, 75, 76, 81, 84–93, 178*n*3
Whitman, Walt, 71, 77
Whittier, John Greenleaf, 175*n*13
Wideman, John Edgar, 31, 167*n*1
Williams, Anne, 162*n*5, 162–63*n*7
Williams, William Carlos, 77, 80
Wilson, August, 153
Winston, Robert, 28–29, 167*n*17
Winter, Kari, 73, 133, 189*n*19
Witherington, Paul, 171*n*18
Wollstonecraft, Mary, 133
Wood, Gordon, 168*n*2
Woodward, C. Vann, 178*n*5
Wright, Richard, 3, 153, 184*n*1; *Black Boy*, 1–2; *Native Son*, 12, 131–32

Yellin, Jean Fagan, 141, 188*n*18
Young, Samuel, 56

Ziff, Larzer, 167*n*18, 172*n*18

CPSIA information can be obtained
at www.ICGtesting.com
Printed in the USA
LVHW05s2341080818
586375LV00015B/974/P

9 780231 108171